Skills for Business and Management

Study Skills

Academic Success
Academic Writing Skills for International Students
The Business Student's Phrase Book
Cite Them Right (11th edn)
Critical Thinking and Persuasive Writing for
    Postgraduates
Critical Thinking Skills (3rd edn)
Dissertations and Project Reports
Doing Projects and Reports in Engineering
The Employability Journal
Essentials of Essay Writing
The Exam Skills Handbook (2nd edn)
Get Sorted
Great Ways to Learn Anatomy and Physiology
    (2nd edn)
How to Begin Studying English Literature
    (4th edn)
How to Use Your Reading in Your Essays (3rd edn)
How to Write Better Essays (4th edn)
How to Write Your Undergraduate Dissertation
    (3rd edn)
Improve Your Grammar (2nd edn)
The Mature Student's Guide to Writing (3rd edn)
The Mature Student's Handbook
Mindfulness for Students
The Macmillan Student Planner
The Personal Tutor's Handbook
Presentation Skills for Students (3rd edn)
The Principles of Writing in Psychology
Professional Writing (4th edn)
Simplify your Study
Skills for Success (3rd edn)
Stand Out from the Crowd
The Student Phrase Book (2nd edn)
The Student's Guide to Writing (3rd edn)
Study Skills Connected
The Study Skills Handbook (5th edn)
Study Skills for International Postgraduates
Studying in English
Studying History (4th edn)
Studying Law (4th edn)
Studying Physics
The Study Success Journal
Success in Academic Writing (2nd edn)
Smart Thinking
Teaching Study Skills and Supporting Learning
The Undergraduate Research Handbook (2nd edn)
The Work-Based Learning Student Handbook
    (2nd edn)
Writing for Biomedical Sciences Students
Writing for Engineers (4th edn)
Writing History Essays (2nd edn)
Writing for Law
Writing for Nursing and Midwifery Students
    (3rd edn)
Write it Right (2nd edn)
Writing for Science Students
Writing Skills for Education Students
You2Uni: Decide, Prepare, Apply

Pocket Study Skills

14 Days to Exam Success (2nd edn)
Analyzing a Case Study
Blogs, Wikis, Podcasts and More
Brilliant Writing Tips for Students
Completing Your PhD
Doing Research (2nd edn)
Getting Critical (2nd edn)
How to Analyze Data
Managing Stress
Planning Your Dissertation (2nd edn)
Planning Your Essay (3rd edn)
Planning Your PhD
Posters and Presentations
Reading and Making Notes (2nd edn)
Referencing and Understanding Plagiarism
    (2nd edn)
Reflective Writing (2nd edn)
Report Writing (2nd edn)
Science Study Skills
Studying with Dyslexia (2nd edn)
Success in Group Work
Successful Applications
Time Management
Using Feedback to Boost Your Grades
Where's Your Argument?
Where's Your Evidence?
Writing for University (2nd edn)

Research Skills

Authoring a PhD
The Foundations of Research (3rd edn)
Getting to Grips with Doctoral Research
Getting Published
The Good Supervisor (2nd edn)
The Lean PhD
PhD by Published Work
The PhD Viva
The PhD Writing Handbook
Planning Your Postgraduate Research
The Postgraduate's Guide to Research Ethics
The Postgraduate Research Handbook (2nd edn)
The Professional Doctorate
Structuring Your Research Thesis

Career Skills

Excel at Graduate Interviews
Graduate CVs and Covering Letters
Graduate Entrepreneurship
How to Succeed at Assessment Centres
Social Media for Your Student and Graduate Job
    Search
The Graduate Career Guidebook (2nd edn)
Work Experience, Placements and Internships

For a complete listing of all our titles in this area please visit
www.macmillanihe.com/study-skills

Skills for Business and Management

Martin Sedgley

First published 2020 by
RED GLOBE PRESS

Red Globe Press in the UK is an imprint of Macmillan Education Limited, registered in England, company number 01755588, of 4 Crinan Street, London, N1 9XW.

Red Globe Press® is a registered trademark in the United States, the United Kingdom, Europe and other countries.

ISBN 978-1-137-60335-7 paperback

This book is printed on paper suitable for recycling and made from fully managed and sustained forest sources. Logging, pulping and manufacturing processes are expected to conform to the environmental regulations of the country of origin.

A catalogue record for this book is available from the British Library.

A catalog record for this book is available from the Library of Congress.

To my wife, Kathie.
Always there for me, always believing.

Contents

PART V Personal Development Planning

Acknowledgements

I would like to thank my two editors at Red Globe Press, Helen Caunce and Rosie Maher, for their patient, yet rigorous guidance on how to translate my higher education experience into a practical textbook for business and management students. This was vital to keeping me on the right track throughout.

Academic colleagues provided the inspiration for many of the resources in the book. Over the last 12 years at Bradford Faculty of Management and Law, it has been a great privilege to work closely with such caring, dedicated lecturers, too numerous to mention. Special thanks to friends who have shared my passion for learning development and made important contributions to the book: Ellie Clement, Librarian, and Hermione Berry, Careers Advisor, for their invaluable guidance on academic research and employability skills respectively; Amy Allhouse, Academic Skills Advisor, who shared the vision for building a unique Effective Learning Service (ELS); Colin Neville, writer and founder of ELS, who has been a consistently affirming mentor throughout this long journey.

Most of all though, of course, I want to thank the thousands of business and management students from all over the world that I have had the honour to work with. They provided the raw materials for this book, but, much more importantly, they have enriched my life beyond description.

The Distinctive Learning Journey on a Business and Management Degree

At the heart of your business and management degree, there are five essential skills for success. This first chapter presents an overview of the book showing how the chapters are structured around these five skills:

Box 1.1   Five essential skills for success in business and management studies

Time management	Academic reading	Academic writing	Group working
INDEPENDENT LEARNING			

Independent learning underpins all university programmes, presenting any student with the challenge of spending a significant proportion of time studying away from class, and with limited direction from tutors. While this more self-reliant form of study has been sweepingly adopted by UK universities, it is likely to confront you with a different educational landscape to the one you have been used to before. Business and management studies programmes, in particular, are deliberately designed in this way to foster students' resourcefulness – a crucial requirement for your future success in the dynamic workplaces of the modern corporate world.

An employability skill that is closely related to independent learning and correspondingly vital to meeting the demands of the business world is **time management**. With so much time left to your own devices on management degrees, you must develop a rigorous self-discipline and learn techniques to organise your studies efficiently. Again, this will be invaluable once you enter the fast-paced working environment.

Similarly, effective **team-working** is a crucial skill for those entering the corporate world. There are likely to be several assessed group projects on each year of your business degree, and successful students also take every opportunity to work together outside class in less formal study groups. Whilst these can be challenging experiences at times, learning to work effectively with others on business projects is vital training for your future employability.

The other two skills indicated in Box 1.1 as essential to business and management programme study are **academic reading and writing**. Not surprisingly, these are the major factors in determining your academic performance at university and are paramount to academic success. Business and management degree assessments have specific reading and writing requirements, particularly in terms of research, referencing and critical analysis. These skills are covered in depth over several chapters of this textbook so that you come to understand and directly meet your management tutors' academic expectations.

Before we move on to a more detailed explanation of each chapter's coverage of the essential skills for success, try this quiz to find out how much you already know about what university study involves:

ACTIVITY 1.1

How will this programme differ from your previous education?

1 How much time will you spend in class on a typical business degree compared with your previous education?

   A. Half as much   B. Twice as much   C. The same   D. A third as much

2 What is the appropriate ratio of independent learning to classroom study?

   A. 1:2   B. 3:1   C. 2:1   D. 1:3

3 What is likely to be the biggest demand on your time for successful study on business and management programmes?

   A. Group work with others   B. Academic writing

   C. Socialising   D. Academic reading

4 Which type of external support will best help you adapt to university study?

   A. Personal tutor   B. Peer support

   C. Subject teacher   D. Learning support, e.g. library, academic skills, language unit

5 Which personal attribute will best enable academic achievement?

   A. Self-management   B. Motivation to study

   C. Reflecting on your learning   D. Self-confidence

6 What is the most common cause of low grades in management students' coursework?

   A. Poor referencing   B. English language

   C. Not answering the question   D. Confused structure

7 What is the most important skill for high marks in coursework?

   A. Referencing   B. Critical analysis

   C. English fluency   D. Essay structure

8 What do we mean by critical analysis in management studies?

   A. Applying academic theory to business practice

   B. Describing an academic theory or a business situation

   C. Finding weakness in academic arguments

   D. Comparing and contrasting different authors' views on the same subject

Compare your answers against those shown at the end of this chapter.

Like any other major life transition, the university learning journey is essentially an emotional process. Whilst each student's experience will be unique, you may well experience a confusing variety of feelings at first. Typical challenges for many students finding their way into this new learning community can include: feeling different; not belonging; being 'a small fish in a big pond'. At the same time, of course, you will naturally be excited about embarking on this whole new stage of life: a chance to make new friends from other backgrounds, try different activities, and lay the foundation for your career.

As we can see from these students' comments, this new adventure invokes quite mixed responses:

Actually ... to some extent ... I'm confident. How much I can clear this target, I don't know ... but as long as I keep trying very hard, concentrate on studies ... yes, I'm confident ... to get a degree.

(Hiro, MBA)

There are some questions that I don't know anything about ... I'm clueless ... everyone in my family thinks I'm the smartest because of my previous educational results. But I don't know ... I don't think it counts for much here!

(Mary, BSc Accounting and Finance)

I'm not afraid. If I were afraid I wouldn't be here ... No, just normal. Maybe sometimes I just feel upset if I don't understand ... but over the whole year, I will make my self-belief very strong ... to take me through that.

(Victoria, MSc International Business Management)

Many students will find the tumult of new experiences quite disorientating, for a while at least. You are bound to need some time to settle into this new life. During this transition phase, whether it be weeks or even months, remember that you must

Pause for Thought

So how are you feeling about your own situation? Take your attention inwards for a few moments. Ask yourself how you really feel right now about being a university student. Jot down your instinctive responses in the space below:

already be a successful student to have reached university in the first place. That has taken hard work, dedication and intelligence – all vital capabilities for maintaining your success in this new learning environment. Remember, too, that your tutors and other support services are all there to help you succeed. They understand the challenges that thousands of business and management students have faced before, and can enable you to overcome those.

However, you also need to quickly reach a functional level of understanding of the higher education (HE) learning environment generally, and how to effectively study unfamiliar business subjects in particular. You need a refocussed set of skills to plan your studies and pass the assessments that you face in each semester. As you then see your personal and academic skills improving, so too will your overall self-confidence rise accordingly.

To help you make that transition, the rest of this chapter presents an overview of the **Five Essential Skills for Success**. Each section includes a key to where you can then find more detailed guidance throughout the book on how to develop that skill.

Independent learning

You will have seen in Box 1.1 that independent learning is depicted as the foundation to the other four key skills for success. Business and management taught programmes at both undergraduate (UG) and postgraduate (PG) level are particularly characterised by independent learning – typically requiring only 10–15 hours of class attendance per week. For the rest of the time, you are working mostly without direct tutor guidance, predominantly reliant on yourself and to some extent other students.

There are some subjects that you actually have no clue about, and then the lecturer comes and has this assumption that everybody in class knows about the subject. Then he just rattles on, so either I'm very stupid ... or I'm very stupid [laughing].

(Esther, MSc Sustainable Operations Management)

The education system here is totally different. I was always being spoon-fed before, but here you have to do everything on your own ... maybe I'm feeling that burden is on me.

(Ali, BSc Financial Planning)

The challenge of independent learning can create an anxious, confusing experience for many students, especially in their first few months. Ironically, this may well be because of the new and strangely undisciplined freedom that you encounter as more independent adults at university. You have to make the shift to more autonomous learning, and this demands greater resourcefulness than you may have typically needed before. As a management student, this is all part of the employability skills development that is inherent to a degree programme designed to prepare you for the business world – whether that be in the corporate workplace or as an entrepreneur.

Box 1.2   Independent learning map

HE CHALLENGES	CORE SKILLS	CHAPTERS
Anxiety or confusion	Self-efficacy	2
Disorganised group work	Project management	10
Interpersonal conflicts	Communication	11
Procrastination	Time management	3
Minimal tutor guidance	Academic reading Referencing Academic writing Reflective writing	4 & 5 7 6 & 8 9

In addition to the range of personal and academic skills required for success at university, there is no escaping the crucial importance of developing the quality of self-discipline. It is clear that independent learning is inextricably linked to time management, which is as much about your attitude as it is about your abilities. So this is the next of the Five Essential Skills for Success:

Time management

The apparently liberating experience of becoming an independent adult at university can create unconscious work avoidance mechanisms. In other words, without someone regularly telling you what to do, it is sometimes too easy to put off important tasks until the last minute. Such procrastination results in disorganised academic reading, which can lead in turn to 'all-nighter' assignment writing – the 'too little, too late' syndrome. This is both stressful and unproductive.

Effective time management is therefore crucial for well-being and academic performance. Success-oriented students soon realise that they need a systematic process to:

- Organise their study appropriately across all subjects.
- Allow flexibility to focus on key tasks or difficulties within certain subjects when necessary.
- Break tasks and projects down into manageable 'chunks'.
- Achieve high productivity within dedicated blocks of time.
- Balance study, social and personal needs healthily.

Developing these key self-management skills will not only realise immediate improvements in your studies, but they will also significantly enhance your employ-ability in the graduate marketplace. Practising and refining productive time manage-ment techniques will make you that much more capable of coping with the high pressure of achieving targets, managing multiple projects and meeting deadlines that all characterise the modern corporate world. This second essential skill is another example of how business and management programmes prepare you for this world not only from the business knowledge that you learn but also through the soft skills that you develop in the process.

There are masses of online resources prescribing the 'best' techniques for effective time management. Many of these could be useful, but for such a subjective issue, you will need to find the system that works best for you. As most people eventually discover, you must engage in a process of trial and error over several weeks or months to become consistently well organised. A wide choice of potential strategies to achieve this capability is therefore presented in the chapters shown in Box 1.3.

Box 1.3   Time management map

HE CHALLENGES	CORE SKILLS	RELEVANT CHAPTERS
Variety of tasks/activities	Organising and scheduling	3
Procrastination/ distractions	Values-based prioritising	3 & 10
Reading volume/ complexity	Research	4 & 5

The biggest 'consumer' of your time is likely to be academic reading. This is the next area of university study covered in the Five Essential Skills for Success:

Academic reading

Reading is a skill we all learned as small children. So it can be easy to assume that any kind of reading is second nature to us now, and that this should present no significant challenges by the time we reach university.

However, educational research tells a different story: Academic reading may actually be the biggest problem of all for degree-level study (Ryan 2010; Strauss and Mooney 2011). Why do you think this is?

Pause for Thought

What do you think are the main reasons cited by students for finding academic reading so difficult? Write your immediate thoughts below:

Management academics demand that their students read 'widely but also deeply'. This high volume of reading can soon become overwhelming as students try to prepare for classes, learn the module materials and research for assignments – all across multiple subjects. Most of these business subjects are highly discursive – the topics involve ongoing debates fuelled by evolving research from many different studies. Their findings are published in management journals, business reports and government documents, requiring you to extend your reading well beyond the course textbooks. This pressure can be compounded by minimal direction from tutors on how to prioritise the most relevant texts from their long reading lists.

In addition to being highly selective in finding the 'right' texts in the first place, you need to carefully target which sections of those texts you actually concentrate on. A process of smarter academic reading helps you develop the capability to quickly sift through each source to find the 'nuggets of gold' that you actually need for an assignment. This can save you vast amounts of wasted time and effort in both reading and writing for management degree programmes.

A key proposition of this book is that you read and write *in parallel*. As well as saving time, this also means that you learn as much from the process of writing as you do from reading. In other words, you do not need to read lots of texts, and

Box 1.4   Academic reading map

HE CHALLENGES	CORE SKILLS	CHAPTERS
Volume of potential sources	Selective research	4
Volume of text in each source	Targeted, smarter reading	5
Competing module demands	Time management	3

amass pages of notes, *before* you actually start writing a draft essay. Once you have established a rough structure for your assignment from the core reading material, you feed in ideas and data from other texts as you go along. As you begin to master the process of effective academic research, this naturally leads to academic writing, which is therefore covered next in the Five Essential Skills for Success:

Academic writing

Business and management modules are assessed almost entirely by written assignments and exams. Four chapters of this book are therefore devoted to academic writing. These offer several examples of high-grade student texts, including a complete essay, from a selection of business and management subjects at both undergraduate and postgraduate level. These are complemented by further exercises for you to practise and develop this skill. You can then check your own examples against model paragraphs in the Activity Answers.

The pathway to success in business and management studies lies in **critical thinking**. This is the foremost requirement for achieving high assignment and exam grades on these degree programmes. This means that you must learn how to:

- **Develop your arguments by integrating ideas and information from multiple academic sources in the field of management literature.**
- **Evaluate the meaning and value of those data in the context of the topic that you are researching.**
- **Demonstrate your understanding of that topic by relating those concepts directly to your assignment or exam question in every paragraph of your writing.**

A major characteristic of this critical style of writing in management assignments and exams is **objectivity**. As you can see from the three points above, tutors expect you to put aside your existing opinions as you conduct research into a topic. You need to examine the range of other authors' ideas as neutrally as possible so that you can build a reasoned, impartial argument encompassing different sides of the relevant, current debate around that subject. As these theoretical debates are continuously evolving in most of the business topics you will be studying, the foremost purpose of your academic writing is to explicitly show the tutor your understanding of these complex, ongoing discussions.

Whilst this objective, theoretical and discursive style of writing is predominant in management degree assessments, a minority of your essays will require a more *subjective* approach. This personalised style of writing, usually termed self-reflection, involves writing about your own experiences as a business student, e.g. a report on an industrial placement, albeit still in an analytical way. A summary of the key characteristics of self-reflective writing include:

- Using first person, e.g. 'This experience showed *me* that ...'; '*I* found that ...'; 'As a group, *we* didn't seem to ...'
- Exploring *how* experiences affected you, i.e. emotionally as well as practically.
- Not just describing what happened, or what you did, but, more importantly, *analysing why* you acted or reacted in these ways.

Box 1.5 Academic writing map

HE CHALLENGES	CORE SKILLS	CHAPTERS
Academic writing style – finding the 'right level'	Sentence/paragraph construction	6
Integrating sourced ideas and information	Referencing	7
Developing a convincing academic argument	Critical analysis	8
Learning constructively from 'good and bad' experiences	Self-reflection	9

Whilst some university coursework will be assessed individually, a proportion of your assignments will be required as group work submissions. This presents an altogether different challenge: How do you work collaboratively with a group of other students who may well have quite different ideas and capacities for effective academic writing?

This thorny issue is considered as the last of the Five Essential Skills for Success below.

Group working

Your fellow students will play a significant role in your university experience. On the positive side, there is so much to discover from others' backgrounds, cultures, personal aptitudes and academic subject knowledge. Some of this peer-assisted learning will be formalised: your university tutors will often set group work projects in which you may be required to work together, sometimes to produce graded reports or presentations. They know that employers are looking for graduates who can show that they have developed positive, collaborative, interpersonal skills. These soft skills are seen as paramount to your capacity to work effectively in teams on business projects in the workplace. So, it is likely that a majority of your business and management module assessments will involve an element of group work.

You can also set up your own, informal peer groups to help each other by sharing reading tasks, discussing ideas and exploring essay plans. There is no doubt that this **peer support** will strongly complement your individual academic study. Each of you will have different strengths to contribute, in terms of both subject knowledge and personal skills. When all of these attributes are combined together across a group, the total outcome of that collaboration can be even greater than the apparent sum of your individual contributions. This is referred to as **synergy**.

However, whilst synergy is the ideal aim of group work, students do often find the reality to be rather different (Elliott and Robinson 2012; Kimmel and Volet 2012). Working with a diverse group of people can produce some unexpected **interpersonal challenges**. Competing aims, personality clashes and contrasting values are just some of the potential barriers to effective communication in teams, especially on assessed projects.

As this is such an important and challenging employability issue, two chapters of this book are devoted to helping you manage your group working experiences effectively. These chapters include self-assessment quizzes to identify what kind of team player you are and practical communication strategies for the group to harness everyone's participation synergistically. They are followed by a further chapter on making presentations – the typical format for delivering your group work reports on business and management topics:

Box 1.6 Group work map

HE CHALLENGES	CORE SKILLS	CHAPTERS
Differences of cultural and personal values	Empathic communication	10 & 11
Unequal contributions	Organised planning	10
	Conflict management	11
Making group presentations	Public speaking	12

How to best use this book

You may well have hoped to just read sections of this book, and somehow absorb all the important points deeply enough to transform your approach to studying. However, that *passive* form of reading – that you might use for browsing a website or social media – has been proven to be most ineffective for academic study (Ryan 2005). Instead, each chapter of the book is based around regular exercises that encourage your *active reading*, which is imperative for a genuine learning process. This dynamic form of study involves:

- **Pause for Thought** boxes, which encourage you to stop and reflect on how the presented ideas relate to your own experience.
- **Activities** that give you the chance to gain a meaningful understanding of those ideas by trying them out in practice.

In addition to the answers you write in the book exercises, it is recommended that you also start a **reflective writing journal** to consolidate your learning. You can capture deeper insights by using this separate journal to record your feelings, thoughts, concerns, anxieties and breakthroughs. Self-reflection is recognised by business schools as an important employability skill involved in processes such as Continuous Professional Development (CPD) that are inherent to career progression in the modern workplace. Examples of typical modules that focus on personal development in this way include: Employability and Enterprise Skills; Student Self-development; Personal Development Planning. Chapter 9 explains more about how to use a reflective journal to support your learning throughout a management degree.

Activity Answers

Activity 1.1

Q.1:   Answers A or D

This depends, of course, on how much time you spent in class in your previous education. But the emphasis on independent learning at university is likely to mean that you will have significantly less classroom-based teaching than before.

Q.2:   Answer B or perhaps C

Business and management students may only spend around 12 hours per week in lectures and tutorials. Yet tutors can expect them to engage in around three times that many hours of learning away from class, mostly on academic reading. So if you chose Answer B, you are likely to be closest to the reality of management degree study at many universities.

Q.3:   Answer D

Working with other students in groups, and writing your management essays, will certainly involve a lot of your time. But, how well you do those tasks will depend on how much research you have carried out, and how well you have understood that academic reading.

Tutors in most of your business subjects will expect you to 'read widely and deeply'. There are so many potential texts for each subject, and the volume of this research can easily become overwhelming. Learning how to manage this reading selectively is explained in Chapter 5.

Q.4:   'All of the above'

The real point of this question is to highlight the range of support services that are likely to be available to you at your university. You will find different types of support helpful at different times. Help-seeking is regarded as a positive learning strategy in higher education. Although so much reliance is laid on independent learning, this does not mean you are on your own. Module leaders, personal tutors, support services and other students can all offer useful guidance in different ways that will contribute to your personal development.

Q.5:   'All of the above'

Which of the factors is the most important for successful study is debatable, of course. We can easily recognise that any of the personal qualities mentioned in this question are critical to ongoing success. How you manage your work–life balance, reflect on your achievements, improve from your setbacks, and maintain your belief in your capabilities (self-efficacy) … all of these are vital factors for getting the most from your university experience. Just as importantly, they are all crucial to effective performance in the corporate world for which business and management degrees are preparing you.

Q.6:   Answer C

Management tutors will typically set quite specific questions, i.e. with a narrow focus on a particular topic. They expect you to address that focus directly and consistently throughout your assignment. If you diverge from this, perhaps to try and show your wider knowledge of the general business context, they will not find the depth of investigation required at degree level and are likely to mark you down accordingly.

Q.7:   Answer B

Critical analysis can be a quantum leap in many university students' way of thinking about academic subjects. Yet this is perhaps the most important skill that must be developed for achieving high grades in business studies assignments. The answer to Q. 8 below gives an initial idea of what management tutors mean by critical thinking.

Q.8:   Definitely Answer D, probably A, and possibly C

Tutors across the range of business and management subject areas differ to some extent in what they mean by critical analysis. In the relatively practical field of Accounting, for example, they may have rather different expectations from those in the more theoretically discursive area of Human Resource Management. However, recent UK business school research did identify some common themes to what their lecturers are looking for in terms of critical analysis:

Answer D

Much of your academic research should involve reading widely and thoughtfully enough for you to understand the similarities and differences between different authors' views on a business topic. You need to show your understanding of the ongoing debates evident in many management subjects.

Answer A

Management tutors expect you to further demonstrate your understanding of theoretical ideas by showing how these explain what has been happening in certain business situations and perhaps how to develop strategies to improve those.

Answer C

Some authors argue that critical thinking is at least partly about finding the weaknesses in academic arguments (Cottrell 2017). However, great care needs to be taken to not do this subjectively, i.e. simply from your own opinion. Limitations emerge more credibly from the application of the two critical processes in A and D above. So you may best concentrate on mastering those first.

See Chapter 8 for much more explanation on this challenging process of critical analysis.

Self-management

Believe in Yourself

To be yourself in a world that is constantly trying to make you something else is the greatest accomplishment.

Ralph Waldo Emerson

You have embarked on the long journey of a business and management degree at university, where so much is different to what you have known before. This is a transformational stage of your life, and it is natural to initially feel excited about the adventure ahead of you. Higher education is a new learning environment with many opportunities to develop personally and socially, as well as academically.

This major life change brings challenges too, of course. Unfamiliar subjects, masses of strangers and a large campus complex full of distracting activities all demand your attention and energy. It is easy to lose sight of yourself in this alien world, feeling perhaps for the first time that you are 'a small fish in a big pond'. A natural response to these external pressures of university can be to search for a sense of belonging by directing all your efforts outwardly, striving to somehow fit in.

However, in the above quote, Emerson urges us to stay true to ourselves at such times. It is (only) from **within yourself**, he seems to be saying, that you will find the capabilities to overcome these tests of character. You have proven yourself to be a successful student in reaching university in the first place, and it is the **positive attributes that you already possess** which will provide the foundation for your future success. The focus of this chapter is therefore to help you:

- **Pinpoint your unique set of personal capabilities** that can become the bedrock of your success throughout university.
- **Monitor your varying levels of self-efficacy** – the extent to which you believe you can be successful – and learn how to maintain this self-belief more consistently.
- **Recognise typical emotional challenges** of the learning journey on a business and management degree, and learn simple, effective strategies to manage these difficulties.
- **Sustain your motivation** through a reflective journal that keeps your experiences in a realistic perspective. Learn expressive writing techniques that enable you to reframe negative emotions and harness positive insights.
- Establish a consistent practice of **self-supportive strategies** and techniques that enables your success.
- Identify which **university support services** can also support that success.

Identifying your unique set of personal capabilities

Everyone has a constellation of personal strengths. The trick is for you to pinpoint your own so that you can keep raising your sights to these stellar qualities. They have already enabled you to reach the higher level of university education, and they will certainly continue to enable your success here. The exercise below helps you to recognise these strengths, using the technique of 'clustering' (Rico 2000). This gathers ideas visually as a creative method to start the self-reflective writing process.

Clustering is a simple concept. First, you write a single theme in the centre of a large piece of paper. Then, *immediately and instinctively*, you write anything that comes to mind about that central topic. Clustering is a 'free writing' exercise, in which you do not limit yourself. The key principle is to allow the creative, right hemisphere of the brain to express ideas and the connections between them in an unrestricted, intuitive way. You allow yourself to write *without regard to any rules* that might apply in much of the rest of your academic writing.

This process is devised to help you deliberately bypass your logical, critical mind. Clustering puts that left hemisphere of the brain to rest for a few minutes. So, throughout the process, if you stop writing for a few seconds because your critical self has started arguing against a positive idea, just remember to simply *keep writing*: 'The goal of freewriting is in the process, not the product' (Elbow 1998: 13).

An example is shown in Box 2.1 so you can see how clustering works:

Box 2.1   An example of clustering

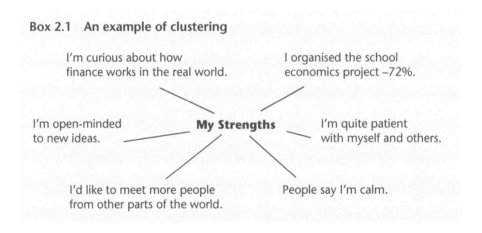

Create your personal cluster now, in Activity 2.1. Remember to go with the flow of your own ideas when you try this for yourself. The only 'rule' is to focus on the positive. Apart from that, there are no limits to the ideas you bring to this exercise.

ACTIVITY 2.1

Clustering my strengths as a business and management student

1   Take a separate piece of blank paper – as large as possible, preferably A3 – to allow plenty of space to express your ideas freely.

- Write in the centre of your paper, 'My strengths as a business and management student'.
- Pause for a few moments before starting to write. Close your eyes, and take three deep, slow breaths. Allow your mind to come inwards, away from thoughts of the outside world. Feel your body sitting on the chair, moving gently with your breathing.
- Remind yourself that this is a time to acknowledge the **positive attributes that have already helped you reach where you are now**. Trust a part of yourself to know what those qualities and capabilities are.
- Open your eyes. Stay centred, with your attention still mainly inside yourself. Take up your pen and, *without really thinking*, write your ideas automatically, expansively and continuously in strands emerging from that central theme.
- Do not censor any thoughts that come to mind – write down immediately, without challenge, any positive factors that you sense have helped you on your educational journey so far.
- Keep going. Do not stop until you have covered *a lot* of the paper with your qualities, skills, capabilities and knowledge.

2   Once you feel that you have reached a natural conclusion to the clustering process, take some time to look over your writing so you can absorb those affirming personal truths. How would you describe the overall, positive feeling from reviewing this picture of yourself? This may be a phrase or just a single word. Write that here:

3   Take a few moments to really absorb that feeling – breathe it in, slowly and deeply. You can 'anchor' that by repeating the word or phrase to yourself as you continue to breathe in the positive feeling. If you then repeat this **breathing/anchoring** connection in stressful situations, you will find this can trigger that positive feeling to help you act effectively at those times.

4   Some other questions you could ask yourself at this time are:
- What surprises have emerged for you from the clustering process?
- Which of your strengths will be especially important for you as a business and management student over the next few weeks?
- How can you use these to best effect this week?

You can write your answers to these questions and others in a self-reflective journal. See below for more explanation of how to keep track of your challenges, insights *and* progress.

The importance of reflection in life, work and study

Why reflect at all?

It is not sufficient simply to have an experience in order to learn. Without reflecting upon this experience, it may quickly be forgotten, or its learning potential lost. It is from the feelings and thoughts emerging from this reflection that generalisations or concepts can be generated.

(Gibbs 1988: 9)

Life tends to move us along at a fast pace throughout the day. As a university student, there are so many activities to potentially occupy you – from classroom study to independent reading to browsing the Internet and social media. It is so easy to be taken over by all these external demands on your time. They can assume a momentum all of their own, which results in you 'bouncing' from one thing to the next without really taking stock of these ongoing experiences.

In his above statement, Gibbs observes that this passive way of living means you may not learn much of value from any of those experiences. He advocates the need to stop and reflect: to take time out from the continuous carousel of daily life and look back over each significant event. This allows you the opportunity to consciously re-experience the emotions this evoked in you, and to think about what this experience has meant for you. Then, he argues, you can draw some conclusions from that experience about how to respond more consciously next time you encounter a similar situation.

Continuous professional development (CPD)

In the management context, reflective thinking underpins the CPD process that has become a mandatory requirement for many business executives. Membership of most professional associations, e.g. Chartered Institute of Personnel and Development (CIPD) and Chartered Management Institute (CMI), is dependent nowadays on maintaining an ongoing, reflective portfolio of your training, experience and work-based learning.

The employability-related modules on your business degree may well provide the first opportunities for you to start practising a skill that is essential for your later career development. The work placements and internships that are becoming an integral element of most business and management degrees also provide fertile ground for reflective writing projects, which may well be the main form of assessment for such work-based programmes.

You will find a lot more guidance to developing this skill in Chapter 9, which is devoted entirely to reflective writing. As an introduction to this process, the following section explains more about starting this practice with a reflective journal.

Why keep a reflective journal?

The section above has emphasised that reflective writing is a common form of assessment on business and management programmes. Yet, many students find it quite difficult at first to write fluently and deeply about their thoughts and feelings, and may often struggle at these kinds of reflective projects. The key to developing this skill, like many others, is regular practice.

Keeping a journal is a practical way of doing this, and one that offers further, surprising benefits too. The process of writing in itself can often reveal personal insights that you had not consciously recognised before. As Moon (2006: 33) observes, 'I write in order to learn something I didn't know before I wrote it.'

Reflective writing in a journal enables deeper insights into your true feelings about a situation. The emotional impact of any experience can otherwise become stuck in the unconscious, which inhibits understanding and prevents positive action. The writing itself expresses the thoughts so that you can see them more clearly and reach an often surprising realisation of the best way to respond *for you.*

The individual nature of reflection

It is salutary to recognise that whilst 20 students in a tutorial all seem to be receiving the same experience, the way in which you *interpret* that experience may be distinctly different from all those other students. Some would say this means that you create a different world to anyone else – at least in your own mind. Your self-reflective journal provides a medium for you to explore and better understand that uniquely personal world.

There are several benefits to this self-reflective process:

- This allows you important, rare opportunities – away from social media and other contemporary pressures – to express yourself privately in an uncensored way.
- You can be unconditionally honest with yourself, and that reveals a true reflection of your thoughts and feelings at any given time.
- This is best used as a continuous, regular process, which can become a reliable, reassuring touchstone in times of difficulty (Brockbank and McGill 2006 in Bassot 2016: 18).

How to use your journal

First of all, find a blank-page notebook with an attractive cover – one that you easily imagine wanting to open to write in (and read back) regularly. A4 or even A5 size will provide plenty of space for writing freely. You can choose lined or unlined pages, whichever you prefer. Some creative journals come with inspirational quotes, which may also encourage your self-reflection.

You may decide to develop an electronic journal because you do all your other writing on a computer or mobile device. The choice is yours, of course. However, do be aware that an intrinsic beauty of journaling is to escape from your habitual way of thinking and doing. Many people find that the act of creating a special, personal notebook in itself makes the process of self-reflection that much more productive and enjoyable.

There can be a tendency to focus on **negative experiences** in journal writing. Students encounter some difficult situations during the long process of a university degree, and these are certainly a valuable source of self-reflection. You can use the journal to recognise how you currently react to such challenges and to explore how to manage similar experiences constructively in the future. This important aspect of learning through adversity is introduced in the section below entitled, 'Managing the challenging times at university', and explored in further depth in Chapters 10 and 11.

However, as a natural balance, **positive experiences** must also play their part in your personal development. You can build on your self-portrait of strengths from the clustering exercise in Activity 2.1 by consciously recognising your achievements throughout the academic year. Taking time to acknowledge these positive experiences *immediately* in your journal will accomplish the following outcomes:

- The journal captures each **positive experience** while the thoughts and feelings are fresh in your mind. This becomes an *authentic* record of what has gone well for you, and why.
- This maintains a **realistically balanced view** of what you have enjoyed as well as what you find more challenging.
- You can read back through this over time to remind yourself of the **overall progress** you are making, at least in certain important areas.

Do not think of your journal as a daily routine. Whether the experiences you write about have been positive or negative, these are likely to have been triggered by some kind of significant event. The best times to write in your journal could therefore be when you notice yourself reacting strongly to particular life events that could be anything from the thrill of your first ascent of the university climbing wall to a personality clash in a group project meeting. Dynamic situations such as these can invoke physical sensations, racing thoughts and powerful feelings. It is these experiences that are likely to be most worth writing about in your journal.

One approach to reflective writing is shown in Box 2.2 to provide a structure for you to write meaningfully about these kinds of rewarding or challenging situations:

Box 2.2   A structured reflection on a life event

1   What happened?
2   How did I react (feel, think, behave ...)?
3   What's good about that?
4   What might I like to have done differently?
5   How can I best think and act in similar, future situations?

Overcoming 'writer's block'

In common with many (successful) authors, you may find that the hardest part of writing is simply *getting started*. Researchers in reflective writing commonly agree that the best way to overcome this block is to begin by writing whatever is in your mind (Cameron 1995; Bolton and Delderfield 2010; Bassot 2016). This does not have to serve any purpose in itself, other than expressing your immediate thoughts and feelings, hence the term, 'free writing'. You do not need to show this to anyone else, or even keep it yourself – it is just a first step in developing your confidence to express your ideas fluently and creatively. The process is summarised in Box 2.3.

Box 2.3   The free-writing approach

- Set yourself a fixed target; some authors suggest three pages while others recommend six minutes.
- Keep writing until you reach your target and then stop.
- Write whatever comes into your mind.
- Do not analyse your writing critically; just keep going without needing to make sense of what is emerging.
- Do not concern yourself with punctuation or spelling; the only requirement is to let the writing flow.
- Write honestly without censoring anything. You do not even have to re-read this yourself if you do not want to, let alone show it to anyone else.

ACTIVITY 2.2

Trying out reflective writing

Choose one of the two approaches suggested in Boxes 2.2 and 2.3 to write reflectively about an interesting situation that you experienced recently. It does not have to be directly related to your university studies, although it could be. Select something that happened which evoked a noticeable reaction in you, especially if you recognise those feelings have not yet been resolved.

Take some quiet time by yourself now to write about that, following one of the two methods shown above. If you do not yet have a journal, just do that on a blank sheet of paper.

Self-efficacy

Countless inspirational leaders across time have emphasised that it is not your personal capabilities that define your potential, but rather *what you believe those capabilities to be*. This belief in your capacity for success has been called self-efficacy. Albert Bandura, the psychologist who coined the term, defines self-efficacy as the 'belief in one's capabilities to organize and execute the course of action required to produce given attainments' (1997: 3). In other words, self-efficacy is about how strongly *you believe* you can be successful.

A fundamental proposition of this book is that self-efficacy is vital for resourcefully managing the challenges of academic life. Take a few moments now to be honest with yourself about your current level of self-efficacy:

Pause for Thought

How confident do you feel about your capability to succeed on your business or management degree? Instinctively rate your self-efficacy for the core skills below:

I feel:	very confident ...								... not confident at all
	10	9	8	7	6	5	4	3	2	1
Group working									
Searching for texts									
Academic reading									
Time management									
Academic writing									
Referencing									
Presenting									
Overall									

Note some of the main reasons for the various points where you have placed yourself on the self-efficacy scale:

This simple self-assessment may help you decide which chapters of this book to prioritise. Every student will feel more confident in certain skills than others. Wherever you have placed yourself on the self-efficacy scales, you will most certainly not be alone. Undertaking a university degree is an **emotional learning journey** for any student, which naturally engenders some fear as well as excitement. Whether you have progressed from a local school or you have recently arrived from another country, your self-efficacy is likely to fluctuate throughout that learning journey as you meet the various challenges of independent learning at university.

Box 2.4 shows a generalised picture of the emotional challenges and rewards potentially experienced by students during an academic year:

Box 2.4   Model of the affective learning journey

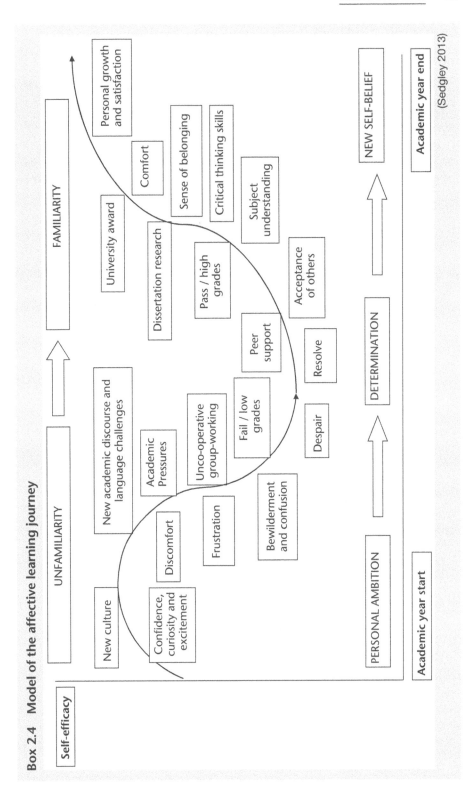

(Sedgley 2013)

Managing the challenging times at university

Initial self-confidence

New students may well enter HE with high levels of existing self-efficacy founded on hard work and successful achievements from their previous educational culture. This positive self-belief is often then enhanced by the early excitement of undertaking a university degree.

At some stage, however, the new educational expectations, combined with mounting academic pressures, can erode that initial self-efficacy. The emotional experience of the downward section of the curve can be summarised as follows:

Unfamiliar learning environment

I hope I can contribute more in class or understand more, but not so far. I'm not following that very well, so that is a problem … speaking, inefficient reading, the whole thing really.

(Michael, BSc International Marketing)

Basically I'm not comfortable, I'm not feeling at all confident. I have work experience and I was a very bright student before, but still somewhere I'm not feeling that great about myself. At the moment, if you asked me how successful I am going to be, I would be like … I'm scared, I don't know where I will be.

(Maryam, MBA)

Disappointing grades

The decline along the transition curve is deepened by any early assessment grades that fall short of the students' own expectations. During Semester 1, they may receive some lower pass marks in the 40–59 per cent range, or perhaps even fail grades.

Cumulative negativity

As the academic year advances into the second semester, and all Semester 1 marks are finally confirmed, students may report a variety of emotional states, including confusion, frustration, anger or depression.

Deteriorating self-efficacy does not only characterise new HE learning journeys for first-year students and post-graduates. This can occur at later stages of an undergraduate degree, as these too involve transition into a more demanding level of study. Some students can therefore encounter similar challenges as they move through their second or even final year.

Emotional challenges

No two students are the same, of course. So although your academic learning journey might follow the U-curve pattern suggested in Box 2.4, this could be flatter or perhaps fluctuate more than suggested by the model. The important point really is that the model identifies typical emotional changes that may well occur along any student's learning journey. This shows that the causes of diminishing self-belief are not individual weaknesses as such. In fact, they are mainly **extrinsic issues**, i.e. unfamiliar aspects of the new HE learning environment, and consequently disappointing academic performances.

Few students are likely to escape these challenges altogether. You may well be a hard-working, intelligent student, and you could naturally think that is enough to ensure reasonable academic success. However, until you become skilled at adapting your earlier study patterns to HE academic requirements, you may well continue to struggle.

The downward curve in Box 2.4 clearly shows that if you experience any of these negative emotional states, they are quite 'normal' reactions to the challenges of your new learning environment. You do not need to be frightened by these early warning signals. If you were to ignore or even deliberately repress such feelings, they could lead to escalating levels of stress. However, you can recognise them instead as calls to positive action. The good news is that many students come to realise that these emotional challenges hold the keys to release their latent capabilities to transform early disappointments into emergent successes, as explained in the following sections.

Developing success strategies

Students' potential for success can depend to a large extent on their own resourceful-ness, i.e. the collection of physical, mental and emotional attributes that keeps them focussed and moving towards the goal with a powerful self-belief. The points below indicate some positive developments that students do typically achieve as they take responsibility for proactively managing their emotional learning journeys through university as depicted earlier in Box 2.4.

Expanding subject knowledge

Part of your motivation as a management student will be to learn more about how the business world works. Any management degree covers a wide range of subjects, some of which are bound to be unfamiliar to you. Your tutors will open your eyes to the fascinating, myriad ways that business is conducted across the world. Your confidence in yourself as a management student will grow in proportion to your increasing ability to understand these quite complex business concepts.

Assessment successes

As Bandura (1997) asserts, there is nothing quite like personal success to truly establish self-belief. Your self-efficacy naturally develops as you become a high-performing student. Ultimately, this self-belief is likely to become firmly established as your grades consistently improve overall.

Peer support

It takes time for people to become comfortable working with one another. As the academic year unfolds, you will find others like-minded enough to want to help you, and for you to help them. You will discover that you each have complementary personal strengths and subject knowledge so that you can supplement each other's learning. 'Teaching' someone else is a great way to consolidate your own learning and boost your self-efficacy.

Growing familiarity

All in all, you will naturally feel more confident as you become more sure of the tutors' academic expectations across the business and management curriculum. You may actually sense this more keenly because of the contrast with how confused you had felt earlier in the programme. This can involve a profound change in self-belief. Once you know the 'rules of the game', anything becomes possible.

Pause for Thought

Return to Box 2.4 now, and mark where you feel yourself to be at the moment on the Affective Learning Journey Curve.

If you have marked your present level of self-efficacy somewhere along the downward part of the curve, do not worry. The majority of students experience a resurgence of positive growth over time:

The life here makes me confident. I don't know why exactly, but probably I have contact with different kinds of people, and learn more knowledge. That makes me see things from different sides. I feel very happy that I can learn such different perspectives, like critical thinking. For me it's a very good experience. If I review my whole life, I think this year is a very colourful period.

(Dagmara, BSc Financial Planning)

I didn't have a student life before, but the feeling that I have now is like really, really nice. I started enjoying my life, and I'm kind of feeling bad that I have to go back!

(Sebastian, MSc International Business Management)

Ambition and determination

These two personal qualities are depicted in the Emotional Learning Curve (Box 2.4) as the 'bedrock' running beneath your sense of self throughout the year. It is essential that you identify why you are here at university studying this particular programme. If you do not have a clear goal, it will be so much harder for you to sustain your motivation over the full period of your degree studies. Ultimately, *you* are the true source of your self-efficacy. You are the one who has the answers that you need to enjoy your learning journey and succeed at university. This realisation depends on asking yourself the right questions:

1 *What* will success look like for me as a business and management student?
2 *Why* do I really want to experience that success?
3 *How* do I need to change my approach to study to achieve that success?

It's quite likely that you do not yet know the answer(s) to question 3 – that's why you are reading this book, of course. Perhaps the most important question for you right now is number 2 – which is all about your motivation. If you are to truly commit to a new way of thinking and acting – in your studies, for example – *you have to really want that change in your life.*

However, as indicated in question 1, before you can decide why you want to enact a change in yourself, you have to identify *quite precisely* what that change will be:

Pause for Thought

Sit quietly, perhaps close your eyes, take two deeper breaths, and just allow an instinctive sense to come into your mind of an achievable change *that you truly believe you want* for yourself as a student. Write that below:

After you have identified the specific change above, close your eyes again, and ask yourself, *'Why is this so important for me?'* Once you are sure of your genuine motivation to experience this success in your studies, write that reason below:

Resourcefulness is about learning to depend on yourself even when others may not acknowledge your qualities and capabilities. Many of us worry about seeking others' approval, when that is an unreliable benchmark at best. It is certainly fair to say that you, like anyone else, will benefit most of all by valuing yourself. Yet this is not necessarily what we have been taught to do. The rest of this chapter suggests some further ideas that you can apply in your life on a regular basis to support and strengthen your self-efficacy.

Self-acceptance

One small step you can take each day is to stop and appreciate what you have achieved, or at least tried hard to achieve. It can be easy to get caught up in a pattern of constant activity. As you finish one task, you may well already be looking ahead to 'what next?' This continuous thinking ahead does not allow us times to catch our breath and admire the view from where we have already reached. You need to somehow recognise how each of your apparently small achievements actually is leading you towards the top of the mountain.

When you do take the opportunity to turn around and look back over your journey even from just the last few hours, you may well be amazed at how much ground you have covered. This is about remembering to appreciate just how far you have already come, and it applies just as much to a learning journey as a mountaineering expedition.

Here are a few simple techniques that you can practise to establish genuine self-appreciation:

ACTIVITY 2.3

Clearing your day

This exercise can contribute to peaceful sleep and a clear mind for the next day. When you are settled for the night, allow yourself to reflect backwards over your day to when you were in bed that morning. Briefly, 'skim' back in your mind through each of the main events and activities in reverse order to when you first woke up that morning. Clearing your day can have two major benefits:

* You recognise just how much you experience in any one day. If you notice any particular achievements, allow yourself some self-congratulation (see next exercise) while you continue to scan back through the day's timeline. Overall, you can simply observe the range of activities, thoughts and feelings that occupy your time, perhaps realising how much is different compared to your life before university.
* This process also seems to clear your mind of unresolved issues or feelings associated with any negative experiences from the day. Decide that you can let these go. If necessary, recognise that you may need to resolve some of them the following day, but in the meantime, there is nothing more you can do. The best thing for you now is rest.

ACTIVITY 2.4

Loving your day

Again, before going to sleep, and perhaps after doing the above exercise, you can recognise three especially positive aspects from your day:

1 What is one thing that happened to you, for which you are *grateful*?

2 What is one thing that you have *enjoyed* about today?

3 What is one thing that you have *achieved*?

You could write these down in your journal so that you can later reflect back over your cumulative positive experiences.

While much of this chapter has concentrated on how you can help yourself, personal transformation will be accelerated by you proactively seeking help. Fortunately, plenty of support is available at university to enable students to develop and maintain high levels of self-efficacy:

University support services

Here are some typical student challenges and the corresponding departments that can help with those:

I'm stuck before I've even got started – I don't know how to find the right textbooks or articles to read for my modules.

(Yilun, BSc Accounting and Finance)

I can't get going on my course-work because I don't know how to do research or referencing … there's just too many sources to choose from in the library.

(Olivia, MSc Management)

These are quite normal student worries at the early stages of degree study. Consult your **librarians**, who are experts in how to find the right types of sources for your assignments. Some universities have subject librarians, so also enquire if there is anyone specialising in business and management.

The librarians will be happy to lead you through the process of searching the library's electronic resources so that you will be able to do that yourself next time. It is satisfying for them to see students becoming confident in using the library's full range of resources.

I'm struggling in my studies, e.g. understanding journal articles; trying to write in an academic style; understanding what the tutors mean by critical analysis.

(Agata, BSc Marketing)

I feel like I'm losing control of my time. I can't seem to manage the volume of reading. I can't focus for more than a few minutes before I get distracted.

(Will, BSc Business and Management)

You have two major options for these types of study management issues:

The learning support department: This may be based centrally, or even within your faculty. Your university learning support department(s) may go by a different name, e.g. Academic Skills Advice, Effective Learning Service, but all these staff teams are experts in academic skills. More importantly, they love to help students and will have advised countless students before you with the same problems.

Provision varies across universities, according to available resources, but some will offer some form of confidential one-on-one guidance with an advisor to discuss difficulties with your studies, perhaps even being able to focus on specific coursework. Also, look out for promotions on the website or university emails for workshops that they will regularly run on academic skills development and others such as time management.

Your personal tutor: Their role is to build a supportive relationship with you over your time at university. They are academics, so they will also be able to provide guidance on how to become a successful student. Business and management tutors can also help with advice on employability skills such as time management. Most universities will expect tutors to meet with their personal tutees on a regular basis – at least once a semester.

I seem to be a slower reader than my friends. I can't take notes quickly, and I make a lot of mistakes when I write down my ideas.

(Lerato, MSc HRM)

The university disability unit: A surprising proportion of students experience barriers to reading and writing. These are not necessarily any indication of intelligence capabilities, but rather derive from conditions such as dyslexia, which are becoming increasingly well recognised and easy to diagnose. If you have any concerns in this respect, ask for an assessment. This could then lead to tailored support in the form of extra time in exams, a 'study buddy' to take notes in lectures or additional guidance from subject tutors.

I'm getting stressed by an overload of different business subjects that I haven't studied before, and I'm feeling anxious … can't sleep.

(Cheng, BSc International Business Management)

These are natural feelings that are common to many students at some points on their learning journey. They are signals from your mind–body system to ask for help. In addition to the above suggestions, you can also seek support from the **university counselling service** to share your stress and explore its causes. This can help to normalise that experience so that you can find your way forward more positively.

A university chaplain: There will be a representative from your faith to share your challenges confidentially and in the spiritual context that brings you comfort.

I've lost my appetite, I get headaches and always seem to be tired. I feel depressed.

(Ikra, BSc Accounting and Finance)

Any of these symptoms may well be attributable to stress or could indicate other issues that are important for you to have checked out at the **university health centre**. As a student, regardless of country of origin, you will have access to that GP practice and NHS provision during your time at university. If you have concerns about your physical or mental health, do not hesitate to seek support.

I'm lonely because I haven't made many friends. I don't really feel like I belong here, and I'm bored.

(Geoff, MSc Marketing and Management)

Student union (or guild):   Making friends on campus is not as easy as the virtual environment of social media. It may seem to you that other students have cosy groups that they immediately gravitate to outside classes. One easy way to find new friends is through a common interest. The union will have a club or society for any activity that you already love, or you would like to try for the first time. Whether it is rock-climbing, philosophy or international food, go along to the union office or check out their website for notifications of the next meeting or event. A shared passion cuts straight through any awkward interpersonal barriers.

The student guild is also an important source of impartial advice about any difficulties that you might meet with university regulations. If you find yourself in a situation where you want to appeal or complain about a decision that affects your progression on your course, a union advisor will be able to direct you in the best course of action. They can also represent you at any disciplinary meetings with university staff.

> *I hear a lot about the competitive nature of the graduate employment market for business graduates. I'm not sure how to best promote myself to future employers.*

(Grace, BSc Business Economics)

Students need to develop a distinctive portfolio of study and work experience right through their degree in order to distinguish themselves from the large number of graduates each year. All universities recognise the importance of this vocational context and have invested considerable resources in supporting their students' employability.

You will find that the **careers service** has a wealth of resources, including guidance on writing applications, performing at assessment centres and succeeding at interviews. It is recommended that you develop a relationship with a careers counsellor so that they can advise you over time on how to best build your personal portfolio. That could include: vetting your CV; suggesting graduate opportunities; arranging internships or work placements; running mock interviews.

Chapter summary

- Keep a journal to track the highs and lows so that you remember just how far you have already progressed.
- There may be more 'down' than 'up' for a while. Remember the typical 'U-shaped curve' of most students' university experience that generally leads to ultimate success and that the learning journey will be an emotional one.
- Do all that you can to safeguard your self-efficacy – that is crucial to academic progress, and your well-being throughout life.
- Recognise your strengths, and focus on these much more than any perceived 'weaknesses'.
- Seeking help is also a strength in itself – make full use of relevant university support services at key points of your learning journey.

Effective Time Management

This chapter enables you to develop a personalised set of extrinsic and intrinsic time management techniques. The extrinsic approach is covered in the first half of the chapter, which presents a choice of rational methods for organising your time around targets, schedules and a structured way of working. These are fundamental, external requirements of business managers in the workplace, where you are expected to demonstrate measurable standards of efficiency. However, these are not enough in themselves to sustain an effective self-management practice in the long term. The second half of the chapter therefore explores intrinsic factors – the personal, unconscious tendencies such as procrastination – that can often sabotage the best of conscious intentions. This presents transformative techniques to help you overcome such barriers.

A balanced combination of extrinsic and intrinsic time management skills will help you to maintain motivation, organise your life efficiently and achieve a sense of accomplishment each day. You can practise these throughout your business and management degree so that they will have become integral to your way of working by the time you enter the corporate world. This chapter will show you how to:

- **Evaluate your current level of time management** with a simple self-assessment questionnaire that helps identify the most important aspects for improvement.
- **Establish a regular, extrinsic practice** for organising your time and prioritising your activities that helps you to proactively control each day.
- **Identify the unconscious, intrinsic blocks** that have frustrated your past attempts at consistent, productive time management:

  o Gauge your tendencies for unrealistic self-expectation such as perfectionism, and learn how to moderate this 'inner critic'.
  o Recognise the common, internal causes of procrastination, and learn how to move beyond this classic problem of study avoidance.

- **Sustain your motivation** by exploring a radical way of re-examining your life values to ensure that your daily activities are congruently aligned to these, and therefore realistically sustainable.

ACTIVITY 3.1

How well do you currently manage your time?

Try this self-assessment quiz to identify the important areas for improvement:

Score yourself on the following questions: 3 for 'always', 2 for 'regularly', 1 for 'occasionally', 0 for 'never'. Total your score at the end of the questionnaire.

☐ I prioritise things in order of importance, not urgency or preference.

☐ I accomplish what needs to be done during the day.

☐ I start thinking about tasks and assignments well ahead of the deadlines.

☐ I prepare a 'To-do' list.

☐ I build additional contingency time into my schedule to cope with the unexpected.

☐ I am happy to share tasks with others.

☐ I am able to meet deadlines without rushing at the last minute.

☐ I estimate accurately how long a task will take me.

☐ I remain focused on high-priority tasks and do not get distracted.

☐ I plan my available time across the range of tasks I need to address.

☐ I integrate relaxation and social time into my weekly schedule.

☐ I record fixed commitments in a weekly schedule.

☐ I do the most important tasks during my most energetic periods of the day.

☐ When travelling or waiting for an appointment, I use the time to study.

☐ I assess my activities in relation to my goals.

☐ I quickly discontinue any wasteful or unprofitable activities.

☐ I judge myself by accomplishment of tasks rather than by 'busy-ness'.

☐ I decide what needs to be done and am not controlled by events or what other people want me to do.

☐ I have a clear idea of what I want to accomplish this year.

☐ I know where to find the resources that I need.

☐ I turn up on time for commitments.

☐ **Total score**

YOUR SCORE

55–65 points: You are an excellent manager of your own time. Some of the tips throughout the book may help you further refine your skills.

45–54 points: Generally, you are a good time manager, and you can choose from the suggestions in this chapter to develop techniques that will complement your existing skills.

35–44 points: You manage your time fairly well, but sometimes feel overwhelmed. Read the advice that follows and apply the relevant ideas for you.

25–34 points: You can take steps to manage your time more effectively. Study this chapter carefully for relevant ideas to manage your daily and weekly activities efficiently. You may also wish to access further guidance through university support systems.

Fewer than 25 points: Try out all the ideas in this chapter to find how to take charge of your life. You will also benefit from university support departments such as your personal tutor, study or employability skills providers.

(Inspired by Neville 2007)

Time management trainers mostly agree on the need for a formalised structure to maintain focus on the important tasks in our complex lives. This involves schedules based around commitments, priorities and other life needs (High Speed Training 2016; University of Kent 2018). The section below identifies some common techniques for these rational processes of time management:

A project management approach

Before drilling down to weekly and daily planning, consider the bigger picture of a whole term – around three to four months long. Academic years for undergraduate programmes typically involve two of these terms (hence the use of 'semester' at some universities). Postgraduate management programmes usually run over three terms, with the final one devoted to a dissertation project.

Box 3.1 below shows a typical range of subjects for a management student in a single semester at university. As indicated in the left-hand column, this could involve up to six modules, with perhaps as many as nine different assessments in those 12–16 weeks of study. This presents a steep, intensive learning curve for any student, and it is easy to become quickly overwhelmed. In the face of such a daunting prospect, it is vital to focus on your key priorities. Box 3.1 illustrates a way of **mapping out your assignment research and exam revision** well in advance of submission deadlines.

There is no exact formula for how much time to spend on the different tasks of an assessed piece of work. However, many students do fall into the trap of not starting that process soon enough. You can see that the staggered project timings for each subject assessment have been allocated *by working backwards from the deadline*. So you must identify these deadlines (indicated by the **X** symbols) well ahead to allow enough time for study across all of the conflicting subject priorities.

Box 3.1   Project managing your semester study tasks

WEEKS / TASK	3–4	5–6	7–8	9–10	11–12	13–15	NOTES
Info systems report			Research	Writing	Edit **X**		100% assignment
Economics essay			Research	Writing	Edit **X**		100% essay
Marketing case study		Group meetings	Research	Creation **X**			30% group project
Marketing plan						Read Write Edit **X**	70% individual assignment
Employability presentation	Group meetings	Research	Creation **X**				30% group report
Employability essay				Research	Writing	Edit **X**	70% individual essay
Accounting analysis			Research	Writing	Edit **X**		50% group report
Accounting exam						Revise **X**	50%
Ops Mgt exam						Revision **X**	100%

N.B. A rough guide has been applied of around three weeks for combined research and writing, and up to one week for final editing. The first two weeks of the term have been excluded from this planner. This is likely to be the minimum time that you will need just to get used to preparing for lectures and tutorials, concentrating on how to learn from those classes and just generally orientating yourself to the new learning environment.

The notes column reminds you of the relative importance of each of the assignments. The suggestion here is to spend proportionally more time on those that carry greater grade weightings. Otherwise, it could be easy, for example, to expend a disproportionate amount of time on the 30 per cent Marketing group project to the potential detriment of your individual performance in the heavier weighted assignment in that subject.

Overall, you can see that a term-long planner customised to your particular assessment deadlines enables you to concentrate on the right assignments at the right time. As the semester progresses, more deadlines will come into play, and you will need to be working on several different assessments during the later weeks. If we look at weeks 9–10 in the above example, it emerges that you should be working on four assignments over that period.

This means that you need to plan each of the weeks in more detail so that you can allocate time according to the urgency and importance of overlapping assignments that require attention during that week. This leads us logically to the next steps of developing schedules for each week and then each day. These are explored in the next section.

Weekly and daily scheduling

There are, of course, plenty of apps and Internet sources for this type of scheduling tool. Many of these are designed for business executives, e.g. Mindtools.com, which can be interesting for management students to explore. There are other sites specialising in academic time management tools, e.g. Learnhigher.ac.uk, and it is likely that your own university will also provide these types of planners, perhaps customised to your academic year timetables. You can find the version that feels most accessible for you to create your personal timetable. To get you started on this process, Activity 3.2 below illustrates how you can create your own time planner with a simple table in an Excel file.

Blocking off essential commitments

This first stage identifies the times of 'non-negotiable' activities that have to be booked in for any given week:

ACTIVITY 3.2

Scheduling weekly commitments

Using the blank template in Box 3.2, fill in the slots for your next available full week. Make sure that you include the following:

(a) All lectures and tutorials

(b) Cooking and meal times

(c) Exercise sessions

(d) Social activities

Box 3.2   A blank template for creating your weekly/daily schedule

	MON	TUE	WED	THU	FRI	SAT	SUN
7.00							
8.00							
9.00							
10.00							
11.00							
12.00							
13.00							
14.00							
15.00							
16.00							
17.00							
18.00							
19.00							
20.00							
21.00							

One fundamental principle of effective time management is the need for a healthy work–life balance. As a student, this means that you allocate appropriate time to a combination of study tasks, leisure/social activities and rest/relaxation. Planning for essential activities therefore ideally includes three healthy meals a day, plenty of time for your favourite forms of physical exercise and social time with friends, as well as regular 'me time'. All of these are vital for maintaining that crucial work–life balance.

Once you have allocated all these activities into your blank time planner, you are likely to experience quite a wake-up call. As you will see, the week already looks quite full. Clearly, your remaining study time has to be organised carefully to then fit in enough independent learning around the essential activities.

Scheduling regular independent learning sessions

The second stage of weekly/daily planning ensures enough time is 'ring-fenced' for important study tasks outside classes. Your university is likely to advocate a ratio of

at least two hours of independent learning for every hour spent in scheduled classes if you want to achieve high academic performance (Birkbeck, University of London 2019). On that basis, if your timetable involves 10 hours of lectures and seminars each week, you would need a further 20 hours of study in your own time, amounting to around 30 hours of academic work each week.

On a business and management degree, that figure is likely to be a minimum requirement. You will need to work out the corresponding level of study required for your programme, depending on the timetabled hours per week and your faculty's academic expectations of students' study commitments. These are often stated in student handbooks or perhaps explained by staff during your inductions. As an example, here are some guidelines published by the University of Bradford (2017) in their programme handbook for business and management students:

- 10 credits of assessed study require around 100 hours of work (covering lectures, assessment, tutorials, reading, group working …).
- Each semester of a degree involves a total of 60 credits across a number of modules. Total study time therefore requires 6 × 100 = 600 hours.
- In a 12-week semester, this would involve 600 ÷ 12 = *50 hours of total study time per week.*

Perhaps this represents an upper limit for academic work each week, as that equates to a ratio of around three hours of independent learning to each hour of class attendance. If we take an average of the two examples above, this suggests that a reasonable expectation of commitment for a business and management student will be **around 40 hours of total study each week**. An example of how these 40 hours might be distributed throughout a week is shown below. This has been based on week 9 from the Box 3.1 Semester Planner shown earlier.

There are, of course, countless permutations of how you might allocate independent study tasks to available time slots in any given week. Priority should be given to the assessment tasks and their grade weightings identified in the semester plan for that week. In the case illustrated in Box 3.1 earlier, these are:

- Information Systems (IS) research (100 per cent)
- Economics writing (100 per cent)
- Employability research (70 per cent)
- Accounts group work writing (50 per cent)

Box 3.3   A sample weekly plan

DAY / TIME	MON	TUE	WED	THU	FRI	SAT	SUN
7.30	Breakfast/ travel		Breakfast/ travel		Breakfast/ travel		
9.00	Acc lecture	Breakfast/ travel	Employ workshop	Breakfast	IS lecture	Breakfast	
10.00	Acc tutorial	Mkting lecture		Econ writing	IS research		
11.00	Acc group work		Employ research		IS tutorial		Brunch
12.00	Ops Mgt lecture	Lunch			Lunch	Lunch	
13.00	Lunch	Study skills	Lunch	Lunch			
14.00	Ops Mgt tutorial	IS research	Hockey match (& travel)	Econ lecture	IS research	Football match (& travel)	Employ research
15.00	Acc writing			Econ tutorial	Personal tutor		Econ writing
16.00		Mkting tutorial		IS pre-read	IS research		Econ writing
17.00	Gym	IS research	Econ pre-reading	Football training			Dinner
18.00	Dinner	Dinner	Dinner	Dinner	Dinner	Social	
19.00	Acc writing		Econ writing				Acc writing
20.00	Mkting pre-read				Plan next week		Monday pre-read

The above example illustrates the idea of trying out different options on different days, including:

- Working on assessment tasks in the same day as that module's classes. Some students benefit from this kind of intensified approach of concentrating each day on a particular subject. Other students prefer a variety of topics to maintain study motivation each day.
- More time has been allocated overall to the higher-weighted module assessments.
- One slot has been given to **pre-reading** for each of the following day's classes.
- Contingency breaks of at least one hour have been built into each day. This is to provide **'downtime'** for activities such as social media, although these need to be moderated as they are the kind of distractions that will otherwise consume too much of your time.
- Evening work has been scheduled at different times on different days. This is very much a matter of personal choice. Some students like to work later, or even during the night, so you may prefer to adjust those times.
- Thursday evening has been left free altogether when the morning has been allocated for study instead. The early part of the day can be a **creative time** for some students, so this may be worth trying.
- Saturday has been kept entirely for leisure. It can be healthy to have a **full day off** to refresh your mind and body. Sunday morning has time for a lie-in to consolidate that. Again, these are just suggestions to try and must be balanced by sufficient study time.
- Part-time work has not been included in this sample. If you have a casual job in retail, for example, you will need to adapt the schedule accordingly. This will need to come mostly from your leisure time as it is important that you do not compromise the minimum study requirements indicated above. Assuming you are a full-time student, your university expects you to **prioritise study commitments** ahead of other demands on your time.

Try out these ideas and invent more variations of your own. You may need to experiment with different approaches for several weeks before you find your optimal combination of activities and timings. Do not be discouraged by those that do not produce positive results – we all experience these time management 'failures'. You can turn such stumbling blocks into stepping stones to reach the system that will ultimately produce the best results for you.

You can put some of those principles into practice now by trying Activity 3.3.

ACTIVITY 3.3

Creating your own semester time planner

1   Go back to Box 3.1, and create your version of that semester schedule. Insert the deadlines for all your coursework, then plan backwards from those to block off weeks of reading, discussion, writing and editing activities for each assignment.
2   Taking the first available week within the schedule that you have created, follow the example in Box 3.3 to allocate activities to time slots. Remember to do that in two stages, firstly for *essential activities*, followed by sessions for *independent learning*.

Summary: extrinsic time management

The chapter so far has covered planning and scheduling. This has concentrated on how to organise the relevant time periods within the university year, i.e. the days in each week, set in the context of each term. Some key points that have emerged are:

- To achieve high academic performance, you need to adopt **a minimum 2:1 ratio of independent learning to class study.** In other words, spend at least twice as much time studying outside class as you do in lectures and tutorials.
- At the same time, you are aiming for **a healthy, productive work–life balance (WLB).** So build in regular relaxation time for activities that you enjoy and that promote your physical and mental well-being.
- Successful time management evolves from *ongoing trial and error.* Do not be frustrated by setbacks. This is part of the process of finding **the personalised system that works most effectively for you.**
- You therefore need to have **contingency plans each day.** Allow some free time that is not scheduled for anything specific.
- Be aware of how easily distractions can soak up too much of your time. Successful students advocate **switching off social media** altogether while studying.
- **Reward yourself** after completion of important study tasks to maintain motivation over time.
- Ultimately, you cannot escape the reality that effective time management requires a **consistent self-discipline.**

All that we have discussed so far could be termed the *rational* side of time management. This proposes that planning, scheduling, prioritising and organising should be strong predictors of personal success. The concepts discussed above are not actually that difficult to understand, yet many students still struggle to manage their time effectively.

So what is the problem?

Pause for Thought

Reflecting on your existing experience of time management, write your instinctive thoughts below. Why do you think students seem to find such difficulties with this crucial skill?

The human condition is such that we do not act purely from logic. There is the powerful, emotive side to our nature that seems to drive our behaviour. Sometimes, this can manifest in ways that are counter-productive to our best intentions. In terms of time management, these can result in unhelpful thoughts and actions that present significant intrinsic barriers to success. Two such major 'self-saboteurs' are: *perfectionism* and *procrastination*.

Managing perfectionism

You may have thought of perfectionism as a productive trait for a student, and that it should be a good thing to continuously strive for the highest level of academic performance. This ideal of being the best may well reflect the prevailing messages from tutors at university as well as the wider media in society. We seem to be constantly exhorted to do more, achieve more, be more:

> *Living your life as a perfectionist, however, will inevitably deny you peace of mind – because even if you achieve an exceptional result, the chances are that you'll still not be satisfied, as you'll find additional reasons for thinking the result was not good enough. That's the destructive nature of perfectionism ... nothing is ever good enough.*

(Neville 2007: 14)

ACTIVITY 3.4

Am I (too much of) a perfectionist?

You may already have a sense of whether a tendency towards perfectionism is one of your personal traits and the extent to which that may be a positive or negative feature in your life. Here are some typical characteristics of perfectionists. Tick those that apply strongly to you:

- ☐ If I do nine things 'right' and one thing wrong, I focus on the latter.
- ☐ I deflect praise or compliments.
- ☐ I regularly compare myself negatively with others.
- ☐ I get involved in details and lose sight of the 'bigger picture'.
- ☐ When I pay attention to my feelings, I am aware of a sense of dissatisfaction.
- ☐ Activities take a lot longer than I anticipated.
- ☐ Other people do not have the same standards as me.
- ☐ I am disappointed by assessment grades below first-class/distinction level.
- ☐ I like to work on projects on my own.

This is not a comprehensive checklist to assess perfectionism, of course, as each of us is uniquely placed somewhere along a spectrum from highly self-demanding to very laid back. If you have ticked more than half the boxes above, however, the drive for self-improvement may be more of an undermining factor than a positive one in your university studies. You could try the following exercise in your own time as a way of revealing the reasons for that and exploring how to reframe perfectionist tendencies into a healthier, balanced approach.

Activity 3.5 involves identifying a relevant, positive affirmation for the situation you are facing, e.g. for *perfectionism* you could counter this with, *'I am good enough'*. Use a writing pad to express your feelings about this statement. Do not use an electronic device, as you need to write freely and perhaps destroy your notes afterwards.

ACTIVITY 3.5

'11 × 22' technique for changing unhelpful ways of thinking

1 Write the positive affirmation. Then, beneath that, write *any* thoughts or feelings that arise, whatever they are, completely uncensored. Write everything that comes to mind however trivial, awful or fantastic.

2 Once there is a gap in your thoughts, rewrite the affirmation, and write freely again whatever comes to mind. Do this for a total of 22 times. It will help to number each time you write the affirmation, so you keep track. Store the sheets of paper somewhere private and secure.

3 Repeat this process each day for 11 days. If you miss a day, you have to start from Day 1 again! You must keep going each day as you are **digging out the roots of your negative belief**.

4 After you have finished the whole process, quickly skim read back through your notes. You are looking for the statements that have an especially emotional charge for you. Do not overthink this. Simply highlight the negative points that really make an impact on you, and then continue looking for the next significant statement.

5 Once you have been through all the notes, go back to those highlighted, negative expressions. These provide you with the raw material for the most important step of this process: **Reframing. Take each negative statement and turn that directly into an affirmation**. Use the 4 Ps approach for creating these:

   (a) *Positive* – the affirmation expresses how you want to be.

   (b) *Personal* – this is about only *you*, not anyone else.

   (c) *Present* – write the affirmation as if it is happening *now*, i.e. in the present tense.

   (d) *Proactive* – this encourages you to take realistic *action*.

   For example, if one of your highlighted statements had been, *'I don't even understand enough Economics to pass the assignment'*, then you could reframe that as: *'I enjoy learning to understand new subjects'*.

6 Once you have created your set of new affirmations, then you can safely destroy the 11 × 22s notes, e.g. safely burning those, so that no-one else can read them, and as a symbolic release of old, negative beliefs.

7 You can then **concentrate on enacting your new affirmations**. Put the list somewhere you will easily see them. Remind yourself of at least one of these each day, so that you consciously apply them regularly in your life, until they become a habitual way of thinking and acting.

The 11 × 22 technique can be used more widely, of course, to help you express, recognise and release any unhelpful, limited belief. You can apply this to any situation where you recognise that you might somehow be 'sabotaging' your own potential success.

Overcoming procrastination

Collins English Dictionary (2018) defines procrastination simply as to '… defer (an action) until a later time'. This derives from the original Latin form literally meaning to postpone until tomorrow.

Procrastination confounds even the best-laid plans. Although you may have organised your schedule according to the time planners illustrated earlier in this chapter, you can still find that you just do not apply these in practice. Each day can seem to slip away without achieving anything worthwhile. The resulting dissatisfaction erodes self-efficacy and motivation – the two intrinsic factors that are fundamental to a successful university experience.

So what can you do to outmanoeuvre this time management saboteur?

Top tips for overcoming procrastination

'A journey of a thousand miles begins with a single step.'

(Laozi 604–531 BCE)

Start with an easy task

At the start of any academic assignment, you can feel as if you have been given a mountain to climb. At this stage, if you keep looking at that massive rock face rising up in front of you, fear of failure can stop you before you even get started. Procrastination has taken hold. Instead of looking so far upwards, you only need to aim for the first, visible landmark just a little way ahead. At the start of assignment research, for example, this could be a simple objective of finding the relevant chapter in your core textbook for that topic and identifying from the contents page and chapter introduction which sections of that chapter are really worth skim reading.

Break the project down into a series of manageable tasks

Use the planning tools illustrated above to realistically allocate definite tasks into short blocks of time. 'Micro-scheduling' assignment reading and writing in this way means that any one task seems readily achievable. In this way, you develop momentum, and that will carry you naturally from one task to the next.

Even 15 minutes of skim reading to simply highlight potentially useful sentences and paragraphs for later, detailed study may well carry you through that one chapter.

Keep your momentum going

In the early stages of your learning journey, you do not have to take the hardest path. Students can sometimes convince themselves that academic research, by its very nature, must be especially complex. Actually, there is always another way to the top of the mountain. For example, if you find yourself trying to read a particularly dense journal article, it may well be fine to dismiss that and look for an easier one to understand on that same topic. Risky as this may sound, there will be plenty of alternative texts to choose from, and at least some of them written in more accessible language. Remember that time is your most precious resource.

Focus only on the next specific task

Big expeditions can invoke anxiety if we keep thinking ahead to the ultimate goal. Once you are on the move, simply concentrate on the next, obvious steps immediately ahead of you. This could be to carefully re-read the first highlighted section of text and paraphrase those ideas into some draft writing in your essay template.

Set yourself a short time limit for each scheduled activity

The time planner shown earlier suggests dividing your day into one-hour slots. For your independent learning sessions within that schedule, it is suggested that you study for around 45 minutes, and then take a short break. You can do some physical exercise, have something to eat, talk to friends; a work–life balance within each day is important for maintaining concentration, energy and enjoyment.

Reward your progress

Stop from time to time to acknowledge what you have already achieved. Sometimes, it is only by looking back to where we started that we realise how far we have travelled. For your assignments, this could be the number of references from different sources, word count, a completed section of the essay or simply the satisfying sense of understanding a new subject in depth.

Remember to keep your study active rather than passive

Keep relating theoretical ideas to real-life situations, case studies, your own experience or your existing knowledge from previous study. The more you can make sense of new ideas by connecting to your current understanding, the more likely you are to continue studying with *curiosity* – the fuel of motivation.

Eliminate distractions from the times you have blocked off for study

You should have scheduled regular downtime into your time management planner. This helps to protect your independent learning sessions in the knowledge that you have time to engage with other displacement activities later. Switch off your electronic media, block off calls or put a note on your study room door. If other students are still distracting you, go somewhere else where others are concentrating and working.

Concentrate on one task at a time

This should be to the exclusion of all other thoughts, knowing (from all the above) that the task in hand is time-limited and manageable. Afterwards, reward yourself with a refreshing break of your own choosing.

Overcoming procrastination will kick-start your motivation. As you then gather momentum, you need to ensure that you keep on the right track towards what you really want to achieve, and all that energy is not going to waste! So how can you transform this positive potential into sustainable success while you are studying at university?

Self-motivation

Self-discipline and motivation coexist in a 'virtuous circle'. Each is fuelled by the other. Motivation comes from believing you are working towards something meaningful in your life. Yet some students have not really reflected on what it is that they really want from university and life beyond that.

Hicks and Hicks (2004) describe the Place Mat Process, which is a simple, yet powerful technique that encourages you to distinguish between what you can actually do today and what you really want to achieve longer term. The rather unusual name for this technique derives from the inspiration that Esther Hicks had while she happened to be in a restaurant. She jotted this down on the table mat to ensure that she did not forget the idea.

Box 3.4 gives an illustration of a Place Mat adapted to university study.

Aligning your daily time management to longer-term aspirations

Box 3.4   Example of a Place Mat

Things I am doing today...	Things I would like Life to bring...
• *Enjoying HR classes*	Clear understanding of complex ideas.
• *Skim reading Econ Ch.1*	60+ % essays.
• *Assigning group tasks*	Positive group members.
• *Deep reading case study*	Deepening curiosity.
• *Re-energising -swimming*	Vibrant health and loads of energy.
• *Sharing meal and DVD with friends*	Long-lasting friendships.
	London internship.
	Growing confidence.
	Graduate trainee scheme.

On the right-hand side of the Place Mat, the student has clustered the important experiences or core values they really want from life in the foreseeable future. On the other side, they commit each day to a shortlist of achievable tasks.

Try this for yourself in Activity 3.6.

Creating your personal Place Mat

Using a sheet of A4 card, take some time to devise your own template. Here are a few important points to follow:

- Draw a vertical line down a landscape format page, one-third of the way across from the left. This asymmetrical format recognises that it is your values and aspirations on the right-hand side that represent a larger power in your life.
- The left-hand column in Box 3.4 is headed, '*... I am doing ...*' This encourages you to start with verbs in the present (continuous) tense, e.g. '*researching* and *writing up*'. This reminds you of your *definite intention* to complete these tasks during the same day.
- Most people devise ever-increasing 'to-do' lists that soon become overwhelming and therefore counter-productive. It is stressful and de-motivational to see a list of outstanding jobs at the end of each day. So the point of this part of the Place Mat is to only write **a shortlist of activities that you know you can achieve that day**.
- The right-hand heading uses the language, '*... Life to bring ...*' This acknowledges that there is a greater, creative power at work in our lives. We can trust that will enable us to start to believe we can experience what we are seeking. All you need to do is accomplish the tasks on the left-hand side each day and allow the rest to follow naturally.
- In the main section of the right-hand side, you write what you best understand you would like those experiences to be. Cluster these instinctively and boldly as they represent the **core values that you realise will bring greater fulfilment in your life**, long-term.

Applying the Place Mat in your daily life

1 At the beginning of each day, in the left-hand column, write *a shortlist* of actions that are realistically achievable for you. Write these in pencil so that you can erase them the following day, ready for a new list. *Your aim is to be able to tick all those as completed by the end of the day.* It is recommended to keep this list of daily tasks to six or seven at the most, depending on the scale of the tasks.

2 As you work through the day, tick off each of the tasks as you accomplish them. Monitor how realistic your task-setting has actually been, and adjust your targets accordingly. This is crucial because your self-belief is bolstered by a solid sense of accomplishment from seeing a list of fulfilled tasks (see 'To-Do lists' in the next section below).

3 At the end of the day, set aside a few minutes of quiet time to **reflect on your achievements**. Enjoy the sense of satisfaction from knowing that you have accomplished what you set out to do.

4 Once you have fully recognised your day's achievements, look across at the values on the right-hand side. Slowly and carefully, *remind yourself why these are so important to you* – how they enhance your life. Each time that you engage in this

exercise of deliberately **focussing on your life values**, you are embedding these more firmly into your consciousness.

5 Affirm, too, that the tasks you have undertaken today are leading you steadily towards those objectives. In this way, you also gradually embed into your unconscious mind the links between the left- and right-hand sides of the Place Mat. Each time you do this, you remind yourself that it is your personal values that are most important in driving your daily actions.

Developing achievable 'to-do' lists

Some days, human nature being what it is, you will not manage to tick off all the points in your left-hand column. This is a useful opportunity for constructive self-reflection. There are essentially two ways that you can view this situation:

(a) *'I haven't done enough today. I should have done more.'*
(b) *'I wasn't realistic in setting out achievable objectives today.'*

Either of these statements captures a major challenge for most of us in the process of trying to manage our busy, complex lives effectively: We have too much going on, and not enough time in which to do it all. So we have to prioritise, and we have to do that *realistically.*

Pause for Thought

Write in your journal your thoughts about (a) and (b) above. Take the opportunity through your intuitive writing to reveal some insights about:

- How you put pressure on yourself.
- How you feel about that.
- How constructive or not that may be.
- How you might set your tasks in a more self-supportive way.

This brings us to *the* fundamental principle of effective time and stress management:

Realism

Positive self-belief is developed and maintained through the *satisfaction of consistent achievement.* If you reach the end of each day feeling dissatisfied with yourself, this undermines your self-efficacy. The next day, it then becomes a little harder to maintain that.

The Place Mat process recognises that it is better to set small targets each day and see how you get on with those. If these prove easy to achieve, then you can expand on them. That is motivational in itself – to realise you can stretch yourself a little further the next day.

Summary: intrinsic time management

- Time management is as much emotive as it is logical.
- Unconscious resistance to success can manifest in self-defeating behaviours such as perfectionism and procrastination.
- Bringing these hidden drivers into conscious view can enable you to reframe them into positive motivators.
- Break big projects down into smaller, manageable tasks.
- Affirm your progress regularly and genuinely.
- Sustain your motivation by focussing on what is really important for you, i.e. your long-term aspirations and your life values.
- Realism will sustain your momentum.

Academic Research

Searching for Relevant Texts

A primary purpose of business and management studies is to broaden and deepen students' understanding of business practice by directing their study into the theoretical views of management researchers. A full chapter is therefore devoted here to establishing a clear framework for selecting the best sources of data and ideas for your assignments. A set of activities guide you through that framework so that its application becomes second nature to you. These exercises will help you to:

- Establish a process for conducting your research that will **save time** by finding the data that are directly relevant to your management assignments and tutorials.
- **Develop confidence** in your independent learning capabilities through a growing understanding of how to find especially useful information quickly and easily.
- Identify your explicit reading purpose for each assignment through careful **question analysis**.
- Accelerate your selection of the relevant texts that directly address your reading purpose through **skim reading**.
- Become comfortable with **accessing the physical and electronic library resources** that are important for business and management research.

The challenges of independent research

The distinctive feature of higher education is the emphasis placed on *independent learning* (see Chapter 1). This process of unsupervised study outside timetabled classes primarily involves academic reading. University students can be shocked to discover that this occupies much more of their time than assignment writing, group work and extra-curricular activities.

> *For the first two or three weeks, I was really willing to spend time on reading – two or three hours in a night, four or six on a week-end day. But recently I feel that I've just run out of energy for reading.*

> (Angelo, BSc Strategic Marketing)

It is not just the *volume* of reading that proves so demanding. Students need to read deeply as well as widely so that they can understand complex issues, and integrate these ideas intelligently into their essays.

> *I couldn't deal with the reading in terms of speed. I need to understand all the learning content, otherwise I don't know what I'm going to write.*

> (Shabina, MSc HRM)

Take the opportunity below to reflect on how these students' experiences of reading might relate to your own past and current studies.

Pause for Thought

How do you believe university academic reading differs from your past education? Tick the boxes that match the type of reading required in your previous educational institutions:

☐ Most of my reading was for examination revision.
☐ My teachers told me mostly what to read.
☐ I usually studied only one textbook per subject.
☐ I spent more time studying in class than reading on my own.

Looking ahead, jot down your responses to the following questions:

In what ways do you believe academic reading is different in your new learning environment?

What are your personal challenges with this different way of studying?

Your reflections above will depend, of course, on the type of educational culture in which you previously studied. You may be attending university in your home country, having completed secondary school with an examination-based system or from a vocational college with more portfolio-based learning. Whatever your past study experience, it is likely that academic reading at university will differ in some significant way(s) from your previous education. In Box 4.1, you will find some major differences cited by a group of international management students after a few weeks in their new learning environment at a UK business school.

Box 4.1   Students' typical research challenges

- Tutors' varying expectations of student reading across the range of disparate business subjects.
- Not knowing how to select the most relevant texts without direction from tutors.
- Uncertainty about how to research library electronic databases.

These three points are clearly about finding your *own* way to the 'right' research sources, i.e. without directive tutor guidance. This reality of independent learning is more demanding for all new students, regardless of previous educational background. Any student can struggle to know where to start their reading and how to then develop that into a research trail that leads logically onto other, relevant texts.

I don't have problems writing, in fact, I love to write. For me, the main problem is to read selectively – five, ten sources, where are you going to start?

(Andrew, MBA)

Time management issues

Most module leaders will expect you to study many of the included texts on their reading list. Whilst this is often extensive, tutors also tend to reward students who have studied texts that they found themselves beyond that reading list.

With the advent of databases of electronic information sources, however, the problem can be knowing when to *stop* this process – to decide when you have done enough research. Beyond a certain point, the law of diminishing returns comes into effect, where there is minimal gain in the potential assignment grades from any further research.

I don't think I struggle in finding the reading. What happens is I find too many readings, then because I want to include everything, I always end up writing a lot more than I should. I don't want to get rid of that idea.

(Angela, MSc HRM)

Whilst every assignment is different, the process to search and select texts follows a similar basic structure. You need a reliable process that you can apply again and again to effectively *deselect all but the most relevant texts*. This is summarised in the framework shown below in Box 4.2, which is designed to save you significant time and effort.

Box 4.2   Five-stage model of effective academic reading

1 **Establish an explicit purpose** for your reading. In the early stages, this will be to research ideas *to answer a specific question* that has been set for a tutorial/seminar or a written assignment.
2 **Identify several different texts** that may be relevant to your question. Select only the most important of these by *skimming* through the key sections, e.g. abstract, summary.
3 **Scan** these texts quickly to *highlight only* the sections that relate directly to your specific reading purpose.
4 **Read in detail** those highlighted sections of writing. You are seeking to understand in depth *only* these key points so that you can apply your interpretations into tutorial discussions or your assignment writing.
5 **Turn the reading into writing**, either directly into drafts for assignments or notes for tutorials.

The following sections explain the first two stages of this model, which are designed to enable you to find a shortlist of relevant texts as quickly as possible. The final three stages of the model are covered in the next chapter on reading texts efficiently.

Stage 1: establish your reading purpose

There are two main reasons for any academic reading related to your taught programme:

1 Preparing ideas for tutorial discussions.
2 Gathering information for coursework.

As so much assessment in business and management studies involves coursework, your reading purpose is most likely to be researching ideas for a particular essay question. Every assignment title in your assessments has been deliberately set by the tutor to *focus your research* on specific topics (the key concepts), probably within a certain business context. You must identify these key concepts and that research context *before* you can begin looking for relevant sources in the management literature. These enable you to establish a clear purpose targeted to the reading for each assignment. An example of this principle is shown below, followed by an activity on the next page for you to practise the process:

*Provide a **reflective account** based on comparing and contrasting*
***your own employability skills** with **those required by graduate employers**.*

The research context within which the essay must be written is that of a reflective account. The tutor explains that, in this case, it means comparing or contrasting your own skills set with that required by an employer. This means that *every paragraph* must somehow relate your capabilities to the ideal range of employability skills. You need to keep all your writing within this context – showing how you already meet employers' skills expectations and the gaps which you need to fill with further personal development.

The key concepts in this example are: (a) your employability skills; (b) employability skills sought by employers. For the former, you have the advantage of being the source of your data yourself. So your 'research' into this key concept is to reflect and capture your significant experiences that have developed relevant soft skills. For employers, though, you need to conduct external research into their recruitment needs, which is likely to come from sources such as HR reports and career development textbooks, among others.

ACTIVITY 4.1

Critically analysing an essay question

Identify the key concepts and research context in the following assignment question from an International Business Management programme:

> *'Countries may claim political justification for intervening in their foreign trade. Discuss the legitimacy of such arguments with reference to examples involving trade between the US and a developing country.'*

Answer the following questions to break this assignment title down into its significant components:

1 What are the key concepts in the essay title?

2 What is the specific context for your research into those concepts?

See the Activity Answers at the end of this chapter to check your ideas.

You can 'interrogate' most assignment titles using the above two questions. They remind you to identify the key concepts in any given title and ensure you limit your research to the specific context set by the tutor. As we have done here, it is critical that you first spend time pinpointing these parameters. In this case, we see that the question seems to be calling for research into the two variables of *political intervention* and *foreign trade*.

However, even more important than the key terms themselves is the *relationship* between those concepts. A great deal of academic research into business and management subjects explores the ways that one variable affects another. In other words, the process of *cause and effect*.

In this case, the implied relationship is that foreign trade can somehow be *dependent on* political intervention. The questions that critically analyse this relationship must be:

A. *How* do countries intervene politically in foreign trade?
B. *How* do these interventions affect that trade?
C. *Why* might these interventions be justifiable?

These questions direct your research to specific data and ideas on *how* governments intervene in foreign trade, and *why*.

Stage 1 summary: setting your research focus

- You must carefully analyse the assignment question to identify the key concepts.
- It is often the relationship between these variables that provides the main target of your research.
- You can critically analyse that relationship through a series of *how* and *why* questions that focus your research even more precisely.
- You must keep all of your assignment writing within the appropriate research context.

Stage 2: find the texts that *directly* address your reading purpose

Starting your research trail with the basic set of core texts

When you set out to research a new assignment topic, you must ensure that you are following the right direction. In Stage 1, you have established this specific purpose by identifying the key concepts in your essay or tutorial question. In Stage 2, you now need to develop a fundamental understanding of that topic from a set of core texts that cover the current debate around that.

Study the process illustrated in Box 4.3 for guidance on how to achieve that essential, solid foundation for your subsequent assignment writing:

Box 4.3   Establishing a basic understanding of your research topic

1 *Which lecture(s) referred directly to your research topic?*
  A. Look in the tutor's slides for any of the assignment keywords.
  B. Search especially for any mention the tutor made of the relationship between those variables.
  C. Read these selected class materials carefully until you understand the concepts presented by the tutor about this topic.
  D. If there are terms or concepts you are still uncertain about from the lecture materials, consult some general reference sources (these may be dictionaries/encyclopaedias/core textbooks) to clarify your understanding.
  E. Create a document on your computer as a template for your essay. Write about the variables' relationship from the understanding in your mind that you have gained by studying the tutor's lecture(s).
  F. Do not worry about editing these ideas at this stage; you are only aiming to get words onto the page as an initial draft.

2 *Which other materials has your tutor provided on this topic?*
  Review the resources that the tutor uploaded for this module on your university virtual learning environment. These could include videos, podcasts and additional readings. Whilst you may have already reviewed these as you went through the course, now you know your assignment title, you can read and review with a more focussed purpose.
  Repeat stages A to E above with these further sources of core ideas on that topic.

3 *How about the textbook?*

Consider your core textbook in a similar way to the above. Search in the Contents page, or if necessary in the Index, for the keywords from your topic. This will lead you to a certain chapter, perhaps even a specific section within that. Again, read that carefully to find the relevant ideas, following steps A to E as above.

You should attain a basic understanding of the required topic from this initial search of core materials. This stage should identify most, if not all, of the major issues that directly address the question focus, and these can then provide sub-headings for an essay template. These first few texts therefore provide early ideas for some draft writing within those identified essay sections. This means that your word count steadily accumulates in parallel to the early stages of your reading. This, in turn, spurs your interest into further reading and writing.

Developing your research beyond core texts

Each of the core academic sources identified above will, of course, include plenty of citations to their primary sources. *These represent the signposts to your further research.* Look for the authors they seem to notably cite as experts on the topic in question. Keep remembering to only focus on those citations relating to that reading purpose. These will lead you along the research trail *one step at a time*.

This *inductive* approach to research avoids you casting your net too widely and being overwhelmed by a multitude of choices at this early stage of research. You need to bear in mind that the sources cited in any text will have been written before that publication, of course. So it is helpful to conduct this type of research trail from texts that are as up to date as possible. At some point, you will still have to search databases for more recent sources. That *deductive* stage of research is covered later in this chapter.

The inductive stage of your research enables you to find a reasonable number of relevant texts that could contribute some useful information for your essay. This is about building your confidence in your knowledge of the topic as quickly and directly as possible.

The next step is to assess the value of these in terms of your reading purpose. You must have a way of doing this quickly, simply and *ruthlessly.* The following two activities show you some helpful techniques to select the best sources from the different possibilities that confront you at this stage:

ACTIVITY 4.2

Selective reading: choosing texts by their titles

Remember your reading purpose for the above assignment question, i.e. *Analyse political interventions in foreign trade between the US and a developing country.*

Consider the following list of four possible sources for that academic research. The type of publication is shown in brackets after the reference for each source. From the list of titles, tick those sources which you believe would be worth reading for this assignment:

☐ **1** Vorton, J. (2010) Government Intervention in International Trade Business: Political and Economic Motives. (Website – www.insidebusiness360.com)

☐ **2** Hill, C.W.L. (2014) *International Business: Competing in the global marketplace.* (Textbook)

☐ **3** Bis.gov.uk (2014) Notice to Exporters 2013/22: Changes to EU sanctions against Syria and Burma and related UK legislation. (British Government website)

☐ **4** Bulkeley, W. (2009) IBM to Cut U.S. Jobs, Expand in India. (Financial newspaper: *The Wall Street Journal*)

After you have made your choices, check the Activity Answers at the end of this chapter for further explanation on which texts appear to be most relevant, *and why*.

Checking titles is just the first step in your selection process, and mainly for the purpose of dismissing the least relevant sources. For texts with promising titles, you then need to look further into their suitability. This next stage is explained below, and illustrated in Activity 4.3.

For many of your management assignments, you are asked to discuss the theoretical views of researchers in a particular business field. Textbook chapters and journal articles are two main sources of your academic reading for this purpose. However, these academic texts are long and can easily consume too much of your time in trying to digest their complex ideas in full. Fortunately, chapters and articles have important, short sections at the beginning and end that summarise their key points. In books, these may be an 'Introduction' at the start or a 'Summary' at the end of each chapter. In journals, there is a separate section at the start of the article, before the Introduction, called the 'Abstract', and a 'Conclusion' at the end. Reading these summaries should usually enable you to decide whether *or not* to engage in the much more time-consuming task of reading the full text.

ACTIVITY 4.3

Selective reading: choosing texts by key extracts

As before, the reading purpose is to research texts that directly address the assignment question:

> *Countries may claim political justification for intervening in their foreign trade. Discuss the legitimacy of such arguments with reference to examples involving trade between the US and a developing country.*

Here are the abstracts from three articles on international trade. Skim read these quickly to decide which would be worth reading in detail to answer the essay question. Try limiting yourself to only one minute per abstract:

1 *USTR: United States Trade Representative (2015) United States Moves Forward to Assert US Trade Rights in Disputes with China and Indonesia. Washington D.C. USTR Press Office, Press Releases, April 2015.*

US Trade Representative, Michael Froman, announced today that the United States has moved forward in two offensive World Trade Organization (WTO) disputes with China and Indonesia. In both of these disputes, the Office of the US Trade Representative (USTR) is seeking to unlock economic opportunity for American workers, farmers, and businesses by challenging policies leading to unfair competition, and removing unwarranted barriers to US exports in key Asian markets. With regard to China, USTR has requested that the WTO establish a dispute settlement panel concerning China's export subsidy program. This program appears to grant unfair, prohibited export subsidies to a large range of Chinese manufacturers and producers.

2 **Teagarden, M. (2015)** *Globalization Challenges and Controversies.* **Thunderbird International Review. 13 February 2015.**

The term globalization is surrounded with definitional challenges and operational controversies. It is commonly conflated with internationalization, where internationalization is trade that crosses national boundaries for sale in a relatively small number of countries with similar consumer behaviours. An example is Mexican food products like Bimbo bread being sold in the US and Central America. Globalization, on the other hand, is trade of standardized products and services for consumption by any customer around the world. An example is Apple that sells iPhones and similar standardized products around the world. The difference between these terms is one of geographic scope and of consumer tastes and preferences.

3 **Baldwin, R.E. (1989)** *The Political Economy of Trade Policy* **Journal of Economic Perspectives 3(4) 35–43.**

International trade seems to be a subject where the advice of economists is routinely disregarded. Economists are nearly unanimous in their general opposition to protectionism, but the increase in US protection in recent years in such sectors as cars and textiles shows that economists lack political influence on trade policy. The type of protectionism chosen does not follow economists' advice, either. Generations of students have correctly pointed out that the equivalent of the domestic tax revenues raised by a tariff is transferred as a windfall gain to foreign countries when voluntary export-restraint agreements (VEAs) are introduced. However, these agreements are now the preferred means by which countries pursue protectionism.

As soon as you have read each abstract *once only*, write a brief reason below why you would or would not choose to read their full texts:

Article 1:

Article 2:

Article 3:

After making your choices, check the Activity Answers for further explanation of how to avoid wasting a great deal of time on a detailed reading of texts that are not directly relevant to your reading purpose.

Deselecting texts in this way before reading them fully may seem a risky research strategy. How can you be sure you will not be losing valuable sources of information?

The answer is simple; there are lots of other, more relevant academic sources waiting for you. The main challenge in academic research is never a lack of sources. On the contrary, your problem could rather be summed up as 'Too much information, too little time'. This is the main reason for suggesting the above *inductive* approach of following a single lead from one highly relevant text to another.

Matching different types of sources to business and management subjects

Business degrees cover a wide range of modules that draw on quite different types of research texts. As a starting point to consider the implications of this for your own research, here is an example of three references that were prominent in an MBA Managing People essay – a subject that requires students to draw mainly on theoretical concepts from management research:

Box 4.4   Typical sources for a theoretical management subject

Judge, T.A., LePine, J.A. and Rich, B.L. (2006) Loving yourself abundantly: Relationship of the narcissistic personality to self- and other perceptions of workplace deviance, leadership, and task and contextual performance. *Journal of Applied Psychology* 91 762–776.

Khoo, H.S. and Burch G.St.J. (2008) The dark side of leadership personality and transformational leadership. *Personality and Individual Differences* 44 86–97.

Robins, R.W. and Paulhus, D.L. (2001) The character of self-enhancers: Implications for organizations. In Roberts, B.W. and Hogan, R. (Editors). *Personality psychology in the workplace*. Washington, DC: American Psychological Association. 193–219.

These references for this theoretically derived module are for journal articles (the first two) and a chapter from an edited book (the last one). These are the types of academic sources that cover the theoretical debate on a particular topic, and so are commonly used for such subjects.

However, different types of sources are needed for the more factually based modules that you will also be studying each year on your management degree. A sample assignment extract from Business Economics is shown in Activity 4.4 below. Can you guess which types of sources the citations refer to?

ACTIVITY 4.4

Choosing relevant sources for different business subjects

Read the extract below, which is followed by a list of sources. Your task is to match the citations in the extract with the correct sources.

The issue here is of significant increase in cotton prices and its impact on clothing companies. Due to floods in Pakistan, an Indian export ban, cold weather in China and *storms in US, supply of cotton has decreased thereby creating a shortage in the market (Hall 2010). At the same time, demand for textile products has recovered faster than expected. Due to this lower supply and higher demand, cotton prices have increased to above $1 a pound for the first time since 1995 (Cancryn and Cui 2010).*

Low cotton prices in recent years had resulted in farmers reducing their cotton acreage leading to lower supply of cotton in 2010. Production for 2009/10 crop year has been 15.3 per cent lower than in 2004/05 (Cotton Incorporated 2010a). However, due to price increases, farmers tend to grow more which can be seen in USDA forecast of 10.6 per cent increase in world cotton harvest from 2009/10 to 2010/11 (Cotton Incorporated 2010b). Therefore, in the long-term, if supply increases as predicted, prices of cotton may move down to the average value.

Match each of the four citations with the most likely source from the following list by writing that source key letter against each citation. There may be more than one example of any of these sources:

Possible type of source:

A. Textbook
B. Market report
C. Financial newspaper
D. Company website
E. Journal article

CITATION	SOURCE LETTER (e.g. A for textbook)
Hall (2010)	
Cancryn and Cui (2010)	
Cotton Incorporated (2010a)	
Cotton Incorporated (2010b)	

Check your matches against the Activity Answers.

You will see from the answers to Activity 4.4 that quite different types of sources are used for an Economics assignment compared to those that were shown in Box 4.4 for a Managing People essay. A more factually based subject like Economics will rely mainly on up-to-date economic information in sources such as financial media and industry/market reports. In this example, the former are represented by financial reports from reputable daily newspapers in the US and the UK. The latter are represented by an online data provider, which describes its purpose as:

> *'The mission of Cotton Incorporated is to increase the demand for and profitability of cotton. The Cotton Incorporated Lifestyle Monitor™ helps fulfil this mission, by providing a range of marketing data and analyses to better inform decision makers on the global cotton supply chain.'*

(Cotton Incorporated 2017)

Additionally, you will be asked in Economics assignments to show your understanding of key principles, e.g. elasticity of demand; most of these can be learned and then cited from a single core textbook. This type of more factually based assignment is therefore likely to need fewer academic sources.

Overall, then, you need to consider each assignment title very carefully before you begin your research to ensure that you investigate only those sources that will yield relevant data for your reading purpose. Activity 4.5 helps you practise that. Try this exercise to compare typical sources used for different reading purposes across a range of business and management subjects:

ACTIVITY 4.5

Matching reading purpose to relevant sources

Which of these sources could be used for the reading purposes shown below?

A. Textbooks
B. Government reports
C. Journal articles
D. Lecture slides
E. Trade magazines
F. Newspaper
G. Companies' websites and annual reports
H. Electronic database
I. Official organisations' websites and reports (e.g. OECD, ACCA)

Write the letters (A, B, C, etc.) in the right column for the type of sources you consider worth consulting for each reading purpose. There could well be more than one source option for each type of reading purpose:

READING PURPOSE	POTENTIAL SOURCES
1. Explain or define a concept/model.	
2. Present similar (or different) views on theoretical ideas.	
3. Support an argument with primary research findings.	
4. Find real-life examples to support and/or critique theories.	
5. Examine a particular industry, sector or product.	
6. Show an understanding of geographical trading conditions.	

Check your matches against the Activity Answers.

Stage 2 summary: finding texts for your research purpose

- Establish a basic understanding of your topic from core module materials: Start with the relevant lecture slides, related VLE materials, core textbook chapter and/or perhaps a relevant journal article.
- Select only the sections from within these sources that specifically discuss the relationship(s) between the question keywords.
- Widen your search inductively to cited sources from the core research texts.
- Conduct a preliminary review of these potential texts' titles, summaries and abstracts. If you do not immediately see the main context or concepts of your reading purpose in these overviews of longer texts, then you can confidently discard the full text, without reading further.
- Focus only on those further texts that directly address your reading purpose.
- Many management subjects, e.g. Operations and HR, require multiple sources of theoretical research, notably textbooks and journal articles.
- More factually based modules, particularly Finance and Economics subjects, may draw mostly on a single, core textbook, plus relevant market or company reports.
- You should check which are the most appropriate types of sources with the subject tutor, librarian or from past, high-grade students' assignments.

Library resources

Having identified a specific text that you believe may be relevant, you can search for it within your university library. The library will have a finding tool like a **catalogue or search engine** which will help you discover the resources. You should check with your library which sources of information are available to you and how to search them. However, the following basic rules apply to all library search tools:

1 Enter some key information from the source you are trying to find – that may be the author's family name, the title of the book or article.
2 If the item is in your library, you should then get a link to the full text if it is an eBook or article. If it is a physical book, you will be given a call number which will help you find it on the shelf.

It is worth spending some time at the start of your course getting to know how the library works to search for resources. You should also physically check out the basic layout of the library and how those books are arranged on the shelves. **Ask a member of the library staff** for a quick demonstration of the catalogue or search tools as they will be pleased to help. They are there to guide you through the labyrinth of physical and electronic information.

Your initial, inductive search, described in Stage 2 above, will have generated references to some texts that you will be able to most easily access electronically. For example, the *Wall Street Journal* cited in Activity 4.2 is a major source of global, financial news. It is likely that your university will subscribe to this electronically. You will be able to **access the full text of the relevant article online**, and then email or download it to a folder that you create for potential assignment sources.

There may come a stage in your research when you perceive the need to consider **a wider choice of sources**. This could be where a *deductive* approach may be useful. Business and management tutors are looking for you to build essay arguments based on the theoretical views and other information from a wide range of academic sources. Books and journal articles are important sources of this type of management data, for example. University libraries subscribe to a range of **electronic databases** that allow students to access these academic research texts.

There are lots of different databases you may have access to, and Box 4.5 gives a list which might offer some starting points, depending on what you are looking to include.

Box 4.5   Types of information sources

Generalist search sources

a. University library search tool (e.g. Catalogue, Summon, Discover)
b. Google Scholar
c. Scopus/Web of Science

Business and management journal sources

a. ABI inform
b. EBSCO Business Source
c. Emerald
d. ECONLIT

The good news – and the bad news – is that these databases can lead to millions of journal articles and hundreds of thousands of E-books. You need a process of searching as efficiently as possible through these massive electronic databases, by quickly filtering these down to the most relevant texts. There are some ways you can improve your search by using specific characters or terms in the search box, as illustrated by the various choices shown in Box 4.6. However, do not try and use all of these in one search. Start by experimenting with one or two at a time.

Box 4.6   The language of searching

1 *Need to make your search more specific?*
   Add another term, connecting both terms with the word, AND, which will return only results containing both terms.

2 *Are your terms expressed as phrases?*
   By putting the phrase in 'quotation marks' you will search for all those words in exactly that order. For example: 'export license' will search for that specific phrase rather than returning results including the two words where they are not connected.

3 *Do you have you lots of variants of a term you want to include?*
   You can search for the root of a word and all terms which come after it by using an asterisk*. So Politic* will search for politics, political, politically, politicised and so on.

4 *Need to broaden your search, e.g. to include other similar terms?*
   Add these synonyms with OR (you may need to put the OR parts of your search in brackets).

Filters

Most search tools have filters which allow you to screen your results by criteria such as date, discipline area or type of material. These can be really useful to reduce your number of search results.

There is no such thing as the perfect search – try varying the terms you enter and the filters you apply. After each change, look at the results you return. Quickly evaluate the first few from the titles and abstracts as explored in Activities 4.2 and 4.3 above. What is missing from those results? Explore further possibilities with some of the other search tips above.

Your own library will have a somewhat different set of electronic resources and search functions. So you will benefit from some customised guidance by your university's library staff. In addition to attending any library workshops on electronic resources, make a point of arranging at least one individual consultation with a librarian. If the library does not have a management subject specialist, ask any member of library staff for some guidance, and they will point you to someone who can help. Take along a specific assignment title that you are currently researching, and ask them to show you how they would find relevant texts for this reading purpose. The librarian will discuss how you can refine your electronic searches within relevant databases to the potential sources aligned to that target. An example of a deductive research trail is given below, based on a search through one UK university library's electronic resources. This provides a useful model for you to get an idea of that deductive process.

The deductive search process is explored below in Box 4.7.

Box 4.7   Deductive electronic library searches

Research purpose: Find academic sources to analyse political interventions in foreign trade between the US and a developing country.

1   Open the Library home page on your university website. This will probably present you with a search engine prompt for all the library's academic resources (in effect, your university's version of Google).

2   Type in your key concepts, removing words like 'and' and 'in', i.e. *political intervention foreign trade*.

3   This yields over 200,000 possibilities. Clearly, you need to narrow that down to the most useful target selection. Depending on which functions are available on your university search engine, you could use the following criteria to significantly reduce the number of potential sources:

   A. Specify definite variable phrases, i.e. 'political intervention' AND 'foreign trade' = 1538 (the use of 'quotation marks' around each of the terms creates a searches for those words together as a phrase.)

   B. Full text available online = 1034

   C. Publication date in the last ten years = 607

   D. Disciplines: Economics; Business; International Relations = 334

   E. Journal articles = 65

This is now a much more manageable number, from which you can select a few articles using the filters practised in Activities 4.2 and 4.3 above. Keep the key variables' relationship – *political intervention in foreign trade* – at the forefront of your mind as you skim read quickly through the list of potential assignment sources.

In this particular search, for example, the first four titles can be quickly dismissed as irrelevant to that reading purpose for quite obvious reasons:

1 *'Ungleichgewichte im Außenhandel: Wie können Handelsbilanzsalden abgebaut werden?'*
2 *'The importance of talent management: A study of Chinese organisations.'*
3 *'Germany's solar cell promotion: Dark clouds on the horizon.'*
4 *'Demand-oriented innovation strategy in the European energy production sector.'*

This deselection of irrelevant sources by their titles alone need only take seconds. However, the fifth one, shown below, seems to match the required criteria well enough to suggest this article to be worth adding to a list to save or download for further study and reference:

Balbuena, S.S. (2016) *Concerns Related to the Internationalisation of State-Owned Enterprises: Perspectives from regulators, government owners and the broader business community.* OECD Corporate Governance Working Papers: 54.

Some students recommend initially considering up to ten texts at a time from this type of search. You can then reduce these down to the two or three most important by the skim reading process. A quick skim through the abstract and introduction from the above text soon yields the following paragraphs shown below in Box 4.8.

A further scan through this section to simply spot any mentions of the key variables only takes a few minutes at the very most. The points that seem to particularly relate to our reading purpose can then be underlined, as shown here:

Box 4.8   Identifying potential research ideas from scan reading: Balbuena's working paper extract

'Trade policy perspectives. From a trade perspective, it would appear that public ownership is a more defining factor with regard to distortions in the marketplace. Over 80 per cent of respondents consider that State Owned Enterprises (SOEs) are favoured by their governments (emanating more often than not from the local or sub-national governments), and more than 46 per cent report that SOEs are more prone to receiving advantages compared with privately owned enterprises (46 per cent). 73 per cent of respondents consider that such benefits can have an impact on international trade in goods and services. All forms of preferential treatment cited in the survey were selected to be of 'some' or 'strong' concern in both the goods and services markets. Finally, the advantages granted by SOEs were also considered to impact the playing field.

SOE (or government owner) policy perspectives. From an SOE (or government owner) perspective, most respondents do not consider that particular hurdles in their overseas operations are related to their public ownership status. At the same time, respondents report that their overseas operations can be met by recipient countries with political unease due to i) the presence of the government as a shareholder; and ii) perceived competitive advantages.'

It can be seen from this scan reading that several points relate to your reading purpose. Remember that this is for the following assignment question:

'Countries may claim political justification for intervening in their foreign trade. Discuss the legitimacy of such arguments with reference to examples involving trade between the US and a developing country.'

- **Paragraph 1**

The first three sentences provide empirical evidence that governments favour SOEs, which can be construed as political intervention in trade. The next three sentences emphasise that these interventions do impact on international trade. It could be argued from this study that these are politically justified as the government is a stakeholder in the SOE business, and their intervention will be mutually beneficial.

- **Paragraph 2**

This raises a potential concern from the overseas markets about the SOEs' government involvement in the trade deal. Whilst this offers competitive commercial advantages for the SOEs' foreign trade, it may conversely cause some political resistance in that market. That is a useful analysis showing two theoretical sides to the political argument. In your essay, you may then be able to illustrate this in real-life terms with examples from your other research into the two selected trading countries.

Sources of factual data

Not all the information that you include in your essays will necessarily be theoretical ideas, models and perspectives. In some subjects, such as Marketing, Accounting or Economics, the tutor will be expecting to see hard evidence of current facts and figures.

Fortunately, your university library will again have this well covered. Two major areas of business information, accessible by electronic databases, are especially important for you: market data and company financial data. Again, the specific sources to which your library has access will vary depending on your institution, but some common options are shown below:

Box 4.9   Business and management information sources

Market information:

  a) Mintel
  b) Marketline
  c) BusinessMonitor
  d) IBISWorld

Company information:

  a) Datastream/Eikon
  b) Bloomberg
  c) FAME/ORBIS/OSIRIS
  d) Mergent

Check out the most relevant, available databases for hard business information at your university by again consulting with a librarian in the first instance. Once you are familiar with the scope of these resources, you can then search independently with confidence.

Summary: developing a research trail from library resources

- **Make yourself familiar with the library's layout** – where your core subject's texts are based and their physical organisation.
- The library's electronic databases have a wealth of information for your assignment and tutorial questions. But these can be overwhelming, so:
  - ○ **Look out for library workshops** on research and other library skills.
  - ○ **Your management subject librarian or other library staff** will be able to help you select which of the available resources are most suitable for your needs, and they will also help you get the most useful data from those.
  - ○ Then try out those **electronic searching** options yourself for your next piece of research. Go back to check anything you are still not sure about with the librarian.
- Save an initial set of up to ten potential sources, and then filter those down by **skim reading** to the two or three most important at a time.
- Engage in a more **detailed reading** process of those selected texts. This is explained in the next chapter.

Activity Answers

Activity 4.1: Critically analysing an essay question

1 The two key concepts in the title are: *political intervention and foreign trade.* This question is asking you to explore *the relationship* between the two, i.e. *how justifiable* is the political influence on foreign trade.
2 The specific context is: trade between the US and a developing country.

Activity 4.2: Choosing texts by their titles

The texts worth further research for the given essay title would seem to be: **1; 2; 4.**

The clues are in the essay titles. The key terms identified in Activity 4.1 enable you to eliminate **Title 3** easily because you can see that this government source is concerned with UK legislation and European Union sanctions, whereas the question asks about US trade with one developing country.

Title 1 indicates the *political context to business* that the essay question specifies, so this sounds worth a closer look. **Titles 2 and 4** also sound promising for the required international trade issue, but you cannot be sure yet if these relate to *governmental intervention.*

So note that this does not mean you should immediately read the full text of any of those three possible sources. This first step has only taken you to the next step of (de)selection illustrated in **Activity 4.3.**

Activity 4.3: Choosing texts by key extracts

From the abstracts, the texts that would seem to be worth reading are: **1; 3**.

Abstract 2 may at first have seemed useful for this assignment because it refers to global trade and some specific examples of developing countries such as Mexico trading with the US. However, a careful reading shows that this online article seems to be concerned mainly with the nature of globalisation and international trade, but **not** with political intervention in these. This major omission is enough for you to eliminate this from further reading.

Abstract 1 clearly offers promise because of the US Government source and its references to political action concerning trade issues with two developing countries. The further detail on China specifically suggests this also has potential to be the developing country choice in your essay.

Abstract 3 sounds encouraging as this also refers to US political trade measures. Although this does not yet go into particular country examples, this still seems to offer useful points about the main issue of the essay title.

These latter two texts would therefore seem to be worth considering reading in full. That is when the serious, time-consuming reading really begins. This is covered fully in Chapter 5.

Activity 4.4: Choosing relevant sources for different business subjects

Here is the reference list for the citations in the Activity extract.

Cancryn, A. and Cui, C. (2010) Flashback to 1870 as cotton hits peak. *Wall Street Journal*, 16 October, B.1.

Cotton Incorporated (2010a) Framing the cotton pricing discussion. http://lifestylemonitor.cottoninc.com/Supply-Chain-Insights/Cotton-Pricing-Discussion/Cotton-Pricing-Discussion.pdf Accessed 22 November 2010.

Cotton Incorporated (2010b) Monthly Economic Letter. http://lifestylemonitor.cottoninc.com/MarketInformation/MonthlyEconomicLetter/1110mel.pdf Accessed 25 November 2010.

Hall, J. (2010) Clothing prices to jump 10pc as cotton soars, warns Next. *The Telegraph Online*, 4 November. http://www.telegraph.co.uk/finance/newsbysector/retailandconsumer/8108336/Clothing-prices-to-jump-10pc-as-cotton-soars-warns-Next.html Accessed 22 November 2010

So the correct answers were:

Citation	Source letter
Hall (2010)	C (Financial newspaper)
Cancryn and Cui (2010)	C
Cotton Incorporated (2010a)	B (Market report)
Cotton Incorporated (2010b)	B

N.B. Two different references are given for two different pages of the Cotton Incorporated website as these can be distinguished by the URL address. This helps a reader to access these directly if required. They are denoted in the Harvard format by a letter after the date in both the citation and the reference.

Activity 4.5: Matching reading purpose to relevant sources

The following list shows type of sources that are most likely to be useful for the range of reading purposes. The sources are also reproduced below to remind you.

Reading purpose	Potential sources
Explain or define a concept/model.	A C (D)
Present similar (or different) views on theoretical ideas.	A C (D)
Support an argument with primary research findings.	A C (D)
Find real-life examples to support and/or critique theories.	A C E F G I
Examine a particular industry, sector or product.	B F G H
Show an understanding of geographical trading conditions.	B E H I

Sources key:

A. Textbooks
B. Government reports
C. Journal articles
D. Lecture slides
E. Trade magazines
F. Newspaper
G. Companies' websites and annual reports
H. Electronic database
I. Official organisations' websites and reports (e.g. OECD, ACCA)

Notes:

- Reading purposes 1, 2 and 3 all need to explain academic ideas and discuss their merits/limitations. Theoretical sources, i.e. textbooks and journal articles, are the best sources for these.
- Relevant lecture materials (D) are also suggested in brackets as an important starting point for 1, 2 and 3, but use these to gain a basic understanding and then as signposts to a wider reading of other academic texts.
- The more factually based purposes in 4, 5 and 6 generally require more 'official' reports.
- Do be wary of relying too much on a company's own websites for product/company information. These are inevitably biased towards a positive, corporate view and must be balanced by more objective data from other, independent sources.

5

Efficient Reading Strategies

Chapter 4 introduced the first two stages of the five-stage model of effective academic reading, covering how to quickly find the right texts for your reading purpose. This emphasised that a major challenge of independent learning at university is that tutors expect students to *'read widely but also deeply'*, which implies that you should not only consult many different texts but that you must then study each of these thoroughly. Yet this is likely to become too time-consuming, even for students with English as a first language.

This chapter now explains the three subsequent stages of the five-stage model, which enable you to assimilate the important ideas from your chosen texts into analytical writing as efficiently as possible. The model is presented again below in Box 5.1 as a reminder of the full process:

Box 5.1   Five-stage model of effective academic reading

1 **Establish an explicit purpose** for your reading. In the early stages, this will be to research ideas *to answer a specific question* that has been set for a tutorial/seminar or a written assignment.
2 **Identify several different texts** that may be relevant to your question. Select only the most important of these by *skimming* through the key sections, e.g. abstract, summary.
3 **Scan** these texts quickly to *highlight only* the sections that relate directly to your specific reading purpose.
4 **Read in detail** those highlighted sections of writing. You are seeking to understand in depth *only* these key points so that you can apply your interpretations into tutorial discussions or your assignment writing.
5 **Synthesise the reading into writing**, *either* directly into drafts for assignments *or* notes for tutorials.

If you are not yet familiar with the first two stages of the model, it is recommended that you go back to Chapter 4, and study carefully how to pinpoint key texts for your assignment or tutorial reading. Otherwise, read on to discover in the next section how to undertake Stages 3–5 of the model to optimise your academic reading efficiency.

Stage 3: selective reading to find the relevant ideas within a text

Even when students have found potentially useful sources, they still report further significant barriers to reading those texts *efficiently*. The main reason for this is *slow reading speed due to the student's belief that s/he needs to understand every word of every recommended text.*

This (mistaken) belief may be based on previous experience of other types of reading. But for academic reading, this is a myth. You can study more effectively by adopting a highly selective approach to academic reading – dismissing large sections of any text that are not directly related to your purpose. This is the case for all but a small minority of assignments involving critical review of a single journal article and seminal texts for a dissertation.

Scanning

A first step in this selective reading process is to *scan read* your chosen text. This involves reading quickly and continuously, *only* looking for words or phrases that 'jump out at you' because they connect directly with the key concepts of your reading purpose. You simply highlight those relevant sentences and move on – always reading forwards and never looking back to try to understand these yet. Your only objective during scanning is to capture the important points that you can revisit later to study more carefully for full understanding.

The example below considers the reading purpose of preparing for a tutorial in the module 'Organisational Design'. The module leader has set the following question for students to research and then discuss at the tutorial:

'What are the advantages and disadvantages of the co-owned business model?'

Box 5.2 shows a text in which relevant points for the tutorial question have been highlighted from a scan reading and explained further in the notes that follow that. The chosen text is:

Cuthbertson, R. (2004) Quality Fresh Opinions, Honestly Given: Interview with Mark Price, Selling and Marketing Director, Waitrose. *European Retail Digest* 43 18–25.

Box 5.2   Journal article extract for potential tutorial reading

This year Waitrose will turn over about £300 million, we will have 168 shops and we employ about 33,000 partners. We are part of the John Lewis Partnership and so we work along the same constitutional lines, and we have the same values as John Lewis. Waitrose became the dominant player in the Partnership in 2000 when for the first time we made more sales than John Lewis, and last year for the first time made more profit than John Lewis. All the people who work in Waitrose are owners in the company and every year we share the profits of working in the company. More than that, the Partnership owns country houses and yachts for partners to use, and that helps provide us with a fantastic amount of loyalty and commitment.

We have the lowest staff turnover levels of any food retailer in this market and we have the highest level of longevity. It is not uncommon for people to stay with us for 20 to 30 years. All our heads of buying have worked in the business for more than 25 years, and you will find that most people at senior levels have spent a long time with the Partnership. Commercially, that gives us huge strengths because there is a consistency to our operation. People instinctively know our customers, and what is right and what is wrong.

In addition to getting a share of the profits, our partners have a say in the way the business works; we are a democratic business. Partners are elected to a council and so they get a vote on major trading issues. Day-to-day, managers run the business but they are held accountable by the democratic bodies.

As well as having a say in the way the business works, we also give the people who work in Waitrose unprecedented levels of information about how their business is operated because it is their business! So we are very open with information and our partners tend to be very knowledgeable. That unique combination of sharing profits, having a real say in the way the business is developed and having an intimate knowledge of how the business is doing gives us a huge commercial advantage because we tend to get happier, more loyal, committed partners.

In turn this tends to lead to higher levels of productivity and better levels of customer service. As a consequence, we have the best levels of customer service, and therefore the most loyal customers of any supermarket in the UK, and we tend to be the most profitable grocery retailer by square foot (our shops are not as big as some of the competitors, though they are becoming bigger). We think we have a virtuous circle between looking after our partners and looking after our customers.

Notes (numbers refer to paragraphs in the above extract):

1   This provides the company context. It does not yet offer any pros or cons for the co-ownership business model but does include a definition of that. That is important for your understanding of the core issue in the tutorial discussion.
2   This presents staff characteristics of the co-owned business in a positive light, i.e. starts to show some HR advantages of that model.
3   This provides more useful information about the way a co-owned business works to supplement those in paragraph 1. Again, this is important for you to show your knowledge of this organisational design (remember the module you are studying this for).
4   This focusses on the *internal advantages* for staff working in a co-owned business.
5   This complements paragraph 4 by identifying the *external advantages* to the organisation working within a co-owned business framework.

You can see that this text provides a useful *starting point* for your research. It gives you a simple description of that business model and a number of benefits relating to that. You only need to take those key points forward into your tutorial preparation. So this has already reduced the amount of text directly needed to less than half the original, even from this short journal article.

In fact, this extract is only the first, short section from a much longer article. This shows how you can often obtain all that you need from a text in its introduction and/or conclusion. That can optimise the use of your limited time for reading the many different texts required for successful higher education study.

Reading for note-making

The choice of whether to make notes or not depends entirely on your reading purpose. In this chapter, our main research purpose example is to prepare ideas for a tutorial discussion. Tutorial research may well be best summarised in note form for the following reasons:

Box 5.3   Note-making for tutorials or seminars

- It is valuable communication skills practice in tutorials to use (only) brief notes/ bullet points as prompts from which you explain your deeper understanding of an issue.
- Do not read verbatim from a prepared script of full sentences and paragraphs. Other students will pay much more attention when you speak directly from your understanding of the subject.
- Seminar tasks may also be the tutor's way of helping you to prepare for exam questions as they often base those on tutorial topics. Brief notes on these can provide memorable summaries of key issues for different exam topics.

Remember that our reading purpose for this chapter activity is to prepare for a tutorial discussion on the advantages and disadvantages of co-ownership. Box 5.4 shows some simple notes from the paragraphs highlighted earlier in Box 5.2. These notes have been produced in a visual form known as a 'cluster' (Rico 2000). Some people find this format easier for remembering and connecting ideas, so this could be one way that you try note-making at some point. The paragraph numbers have again been included for ease of reference to the sample text above:

Box 5.4   Visual note-making by clustering ideas

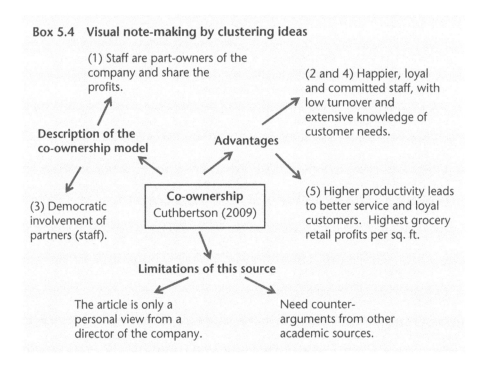

The two steps illustrated in this chapter so far – scan reading and simple note-making – have *quickly* distilled the key ideas needed from an original article of over 400 words to notes of less than 50 words. These are just the first steps of your research, though. As noted above, the article only reveals a partial view, i.e. the advantages of co-ownership. In order to engage in the critical reading expected by your business and management tutors, you need to show them that you have not simply accepted 'at face value' any single author's claims about a particular topic.

Most management research is concerned with debatable, evolving, theoretical ideas. You need to demonstrate an analytical approach to your academic reading by **comparing and contrasting different authors' views** on the same topic. In the above example from Cuthbertson, we now need to find some relevant academic articles that present counterpoints to his argument, i.e. that *critique* the co-ownership model.

To do that, we can follow the library database search process summarised below in Box 5.5. If you are not yet familiar with that, it will be helpful for you to first go back to the explanation of this process in Box 4.6.

Box 5.5   Library database search process

Stage 1: reading purpose

After reading Cuthbertson's article, we know that we are now searching for other academic views on the co-ownership business model, particularly relating to any perceived **disadvantages** of that organisational structure.

Stage 2: identify a relevant academic journal article

Library search: Here, we replicate the stages of narrowing down to a few sources as first shown in Chapter 4 by using various functions on the library search engine. This is an illustrative sample search from one UK university library. Your university's system would generate different results, but you can follow a similar process within your library's search engine or catalogue:

- Describing the topic of the search:

  Co-owned business = 5303

- Defining a key term. It can be worth trying to see if specifying an exact phrase with punctuation may yield helpful results: In this case, it proves to be a lucky guess:

  'Co-owned business' = 3

  And the second publication on that short list emerged as:

  Cathcart, A. (2013) Directing democracy: Competing interests and contested terrain in the John Lewis Partnership. *Journal of Industrial Relations*, 55(4) 601–620.

This clearly sounds well worth looking at and leads onto the next step shown below.

Our first step with a journal article is to consider the abstract. This provides a short summary of the research focus and some key findings, enabling you to decide if the article is worth reading more fully. Cathcart's abstract is shown below in Activity 5.1.

Scan reading to find key points within a journal article

You can practise scanning in this activity by *reading the text below quickly, moving continuously forwards*. Do not stop or check back to verify your understanding. Simply highlight any points that instinctively seem relevant to your reading purpose, and then move on. You should easily find three points indicating potential disadvantages of co-ownership. *Aim to reach the end of this extract within two minutes, highlighting key points as you do so.*

Journal article abstract

The John Lewis Partnership is one of Europe's largest models of employee ownership and has been operating a form of employee involvement and participation since its formation in 1929. It is frequently held up as a model of best practice (Cathcart, 2013) and has been described as a 'workers' paradise' (Stummer and Lacey, 2001). At the beginning of 2012, the Deputy Prime Minister of the UK unveiled plans to create a 'John Lewis Economy' (Wintour, 2012). As John Lewis is being positioned at the heart of political and media discussions in the UK about alternatives to the corporate capitalist model of enterprise, it is vital that more is known about the experience of employee involvement and participation within the organisation.

This article explores the ways in which the practice of employee involvement and participation has changed in John Lewis as a result of competing employee and managerial interests. Its contribution is a contemporary exploration of participation in the John Lewis Partnership and an examination of the ways in which management and employees contested the meaning and practice of employee involvement and participation as part of a 'democracy project', which culminated in significant changes and degeneration of the democratic structures.

Check the Activity Answers to see if you found the same points of relevance to the tutorial question. The points highlighted in the model answer provide enough indicators that the article is worth reading further for a counter-argument to the Waitrose article's affirmation of the co-ownership model.

However, we do not then just start reading the whole article. This is well over 7000 words of complex, academic research. *And remember that we are mainly now looking for the disadvantages of co-ownership in quite simple terms for tutorial discussion.*

So you can short-cut the process by going straight to the article's **conclusion**. This is where academic writers need to capture the key findings of their research, which, along with the abstract, will sometimes be all that you need for your reading purpose. An abridged version of this conclusion is shown below in Activity 5.2.

Detailed reading for deeper understanding of key points

See the text below for Cathcart's (2013) article conclusions. Some key points have already been highlighted for you. Your task is now to *read only those sections carefully* to make some appropriate notes for a tutorial discussion.

N.B. Paragraphs have been numbered for ease of reference in this exercise and the answers. This will not normally be the case in academic journal articles.

1   *A key lesson from the analysis of the JLP is that democratic functioning, even when protected by a Constitution and legal framework, remains vulnerable to challenges from people who seek to constrain and direct it in ways that meet instrumental ends. There are* **signs of degeneration** *in the JLP ranging from* **the increases in the maximum pay ratio** *from 25:1 to 75:1 and* **the growing reliance on non-Partners** *to deliver services such as cleaning (Pooler, 2012), through to the* **removal of voting rights** *in the majority of Branch Forums.*

2   **Donaghey et al. (2011: 167)** *note that* **much of the research** *on non-union forms of employee representation has been characterised by portrayals of* **'omnipotent management dominating an acquiescent workforce'**. *In short, management never intended to share power, but simply to inform and communicate. Here, it is argued that the unitarist perception of participation as a win–win scenario leading to happier, more engaged, productive employees (Cloke and Goldsmith, 2002; Mintzberg, 1983) dominated discussions in the JLP. Participation was supported by management as a mechanism for facilitating high employee involvement as a means of sustained competitiveness. Collective rights were always subordinate to those of the business and* **the language of industrial democracy was co-opted to create cultural control (Stewart et al., 2004).**

3   *There is certainly evidence here of a push by management to redefine democracy in ways that* **privilege business interests and managerial prerogative**. *However, the struggle to direct democracy in the JLP is not yet over.* **In April 2009, the John Lewis Council refused to approve a new proposal that would have cemented the practise of 'consulting with Partners in Branches' rather than allowing Partners to make decisions through democratic structures** *(John Lewis Focus, 3 April 2009). The Business Committee had put forward a proposal that decisions on trading hours should rest with the head of Branch, after input and influence from the Branch Forum. At the meeting, Councillors from the eight Branches that had chosen to retain their decision-making power during the trial objected to the proposal on the grounds that it meant that the Branch Forum would lose the vote. After a long discussion, Councillors voted against the proposal.* **A successful challenge was made to the 'seemingly incontrovertible truth' (Alvesson and Willmott, 1992: 435) that Partners did not want democracy.**

4   *Democracy continues to be a contested terrain, and the definition and purpose of democratic participation is the subject of ongoing debate and conflict. The process of 'democratic renewal' undertaken by the* **JLP has redefined participation in a way that undermines employee interests and closes down the possibilities for mutual gains**. *Although this definition is not irresistible or final, it does indicate the need for closer scrutiny of the claims made about the organisation.*

Make your notes on a separate piece of paper or device. You could produce these in the visual format illustrated in Box 5.4 above, or you could choose a linear format (bullet points) if you prefer.

Compare your notes against the example in the Activity Answers.

You can see that an article's abstract and conclusion yield a rich set of ideas for your reading purpose. These sections alone can enable you to begin Step 4 of the effective academic reading model: Developing in-depth understanding by reading in detail. The Activity 5.2 Answers show how a deep understanding of the topic concepts enables you to start paraphrasing those into your own words – even in note form. The answers also highlight how one source offers signposts to further relevant sources on your research trail.

Box 5.6   Top tip for reading concentration

Set a relatively short time for focussed, active reading, and then take a break (UNC 2019). Your concentration decreases beyond a certain time limit – estimates vary from 25 to 45 minutes – and you need to find what works best for you. Use your breaks for something quite different from mental study, e.g. physical exercise, refreshments, social media.

Researching an assignment question

The chapter has so far covered reading and note-making for tutorial questions, but a greater proportion of your academic reading will be for producing written assignments. **In the case of assignment preparation, it is recommended that you do not make notes,** but instead *summarise and paraphrase your understanding directly into an essay draft.* You do this by creating an 'essay template' with sub-headings that you guess will provide a relevant structure. You can always change these at a later stage, and in the meantime, you draft your interpretations of researched ideas straight into the most appropriate sections of this outline structure.

The **'direct drafting' approach of reading and writing in parallel has certain benefits:**

- You capture your understanding of a topic as soon as that is clear in your mind by immediately drafting full sentences and paragraphs into the relevant section of your essay template.
- This 'short-cuts' the process by omitting the time-consuming stage of making notes, which would not have a value beyond the assignment preparation. You continue making sense of the topic through the process of writing directly into the essay draft.
- You are unlikely to need revision notes for the assignment topics as they will not be repeated in exam questions.

The process of summarising and paraphrasing your business research into management degree-level academic writing is discussed fully in Chapters 6, 7 and 8, but an example of draft writing is given in Box 5.7 to show how you could have produced a section of a draft assignment from reading the two journal articles discussed earlier in this chapter.

Box 5.7   Interpreting academic reading directly into draft writing

Assignment title:

'What are the advantages and disadvantages of the co-owned business model?'

The following extract of text for the above assignment has been synthesised from points identified in the above Waitrose (Box 5.2) and JLP (Activity 5.1) articles, without the need for an intermediate note-making process:

Managers working within co-ownership organisations such as the John Lewis Partnership (JLP) acclaim multiple HR benefits of this alternative organisational structure, e.g. employment longevity, happy and loyal staff (Cuthbertson 2004). These, in turn, are asserted to lead to improved business performance, including better customer service and higher profitability. Other academic research has also commended the democratic principles of sharing profits and decision-making among the employee owners (partners) of the business, with some describing this a 'workers' paradise' (Stummer and Lacey 2001 in Cathcart 2013: 2).

However, Cathcart's review of other academic research into co-ownership (see Stewart et al. 2004; Donaghey et al. 2011) also points out that the rhetoric of employee involvement may actually disguise a culture of managerial control. Examples of the degeneration of a truly democratic process in the JLP co-ownership model include widening pay gaps between managers and workers, out-sourcing of services to non-partners and cases of voting rights being confiscated. This suggests that whilst the co-ownership organisational structure, in theory, offers significant opportunities for partners and customers, the reality of that may be less sustainable, at least in current practice.

Chapter summary

- When first considering an academic text as a potential source for detailed reading, start with the introduction to a textbook chapter or abstract to a journal article. These indicate the topics covered in the rest of the text.
- Quickly skim through these introductions for the key variables of your reading purpose.
- If you do not see explicit reference to these variables, then you can safely discard that possibility and move on to the next potential source.
- If you do identify a potential value to a text, then go straight to the summary or conclusion.
- Study these introductions and conclusions carefully to ensure you have a clear understanding of what they are proposing about the topic of your reading purpose.
- You can then write up these ideas, paraphrasing from your own understanding.
- This writing could be in note form, e.g. visual prompts for a tutorial preparation. Or you could produce full draft writing directly into an essay template for assignments.

Activity Answers

Activity 5.1: Scan reading to find key points in a journal article

There are some early points in Cathcart's article (*highlighted below in italics*) that provide further support for Cuthbertson's positive view of co-ownership. *However,* the **points in bold** highlight conflicts between management and employees that are undermining the democratic aims of co-ownership, i.e. **disadvantages of that model**.

So this suggests the article will provide helpful research in a continuing exploration of the two sides to this argument.

Journal article abstract

The John Lewis Partnership is one of Europe's largest models of employee ownership and has been operating a form of employee involvement and participation since its formation in 1929. *It is frequently held up as a model of best practice (Cathcart, 2013)* and has been described as a 'workers' paradise' (Stummer and Lacey, 2001). At the beginning of 2012, the *Deputy Prime Minister of the UK unveiled plans to create a 'John Lewis Economy' (Wintour, 2012)*. As John Lewis is being positioned at the heart of political and media discussions in the UK about *alternatives to the corporate capitalist model of enterprise*, it is vital that more is known about the experience of employee involvement and participation within the organisation. This article explores the ways in which the practice of **employee involvement and participation has changed in John Lewis as a result of competing employee and managerial interests**. Its contribution is a contemporary exploration of participation in the John Lewis Partnership and an examination of the ways in which **management and employees contested the meaning and practice of employee involvement and participation** as part of a 'democracy project', which culminated in significant changes and **degeneration of the democratic structures.**

Activity 5.2: Detailed reading of highlighted points for deeper understanding

Linear notes from Cathcart's conclusion could look like this:	His sources that you could research further:
Undermining of democratic principles at JLP evidenced by: a. growth in the difference between lowest and highest pay from a ratio of 25:1 to 75:1. b. Some jobs, e.g. cleaning, now being outsourced to non-partner workers. c. Loss of voting rights at JLP branches.	Pooler (2012)
Other research suggests non-union participation means management domination ... a managerial agenda of cultural control that is undemocratic.	Donaghey et al. (2011) Stewart et al. (2004)
However, JL Council rejected a plan to remove voting rights, so still recognising democracy at some levels.	
Overall view that JLP has 'redefined participation in a way that undermines employee interests and closes down the possibilities for mutual gains' (617).	

Cathcart (2013)

Academic Writing

Essentials of Academic Writing

This chapter presents the basics of writing: how to construct clear, fluent sentences; how to develop these into a coherent paragraph; how to link those together into a logical argument. It shows you how to:

- Recognise the **specific characteristics of written expression in business and management studies** so that you can tailor your assignments to the tutors' assessment expectations.
- Convey your subject understanding explicitly through **well-structured sentences and paragraphs**.
- Develop **logical arguments** that directly address the tutor's question.
- Create a distinctive impact in your **introduction** and a clear position in the **conclusion**.

Academic writing style

There are many different facets to writing style, but the principles shown in Box 6.1 are fundamental. Each of these is discussed with examples below.

Box 6.1   Linguistic style in academic writing – four key principles

1 Be objective
2 Be cautious
3 Use formal language
4 Most importantly, be concise, specific and clear.

Be objective

The majority of your writing in management essays and reports should be *based on others' ideas and information*. You need to show the tutor that you have assimilated a set of data from credible academic sources that are all relevant to your assignment question. This has important implications for your writing style:

- You must include a citation every time you bring in an externally sourced idea (see Chapter 7 for a detailed explanation of referencing).

- You generally need to use objective language, avoiding first person – 'I' or 'We' – unless the tutor has specifically requested you to reflect on your own experience (see Chapter 9 for examples of reflective writing).
- Your writing is not based on your original opinions, but rather on your *representations* and *interpretations* of others' published research findings. These are fundamental aspects of academic writing, and therefore considered in more detail below:

Representing authors' views and data

Firstly, you show the reader what you have learned about the topic by faithfully and accurately reporting relevant authors' views using the objective language referred to above. In its simplest form, this could just state the author's claim, followed by the citation, e.g.

> *Building an internationally inclusive campus nurtures cross-cultural learning and global citizenship (Guo and Chase 2011).*

For the purpose of developing a fluent writing style, though, it is helpful to vary the way that you present management researchers' views. Some further examples are shown below in Box 6.2.

Box 6.2   Sample phrases for representing academic ideas objectively

- *Some researchers such as Carroll (2005) and De Vita (2008) have observed that ...*
- *Fama (1988) proposed that ...*
- *However, it has since been suggested that ... (Pike et al. 2012).*

Interpreting authors' views and data

Once you have presented some key findings from your researched sources, *only then* can you bring in your interpretation of those. This must show your understanding of what those authors' findings mean for your assignment. An example of how you can signal your interpretation of others' ideas is shown below (underlined) in a sample paragraph from an essay addressing the question, '*How important will offshoring be to the future of emerging economies?*'

Box 6.3   Sample phrases for showing your interpretation of academic ideas

Offshoring is defined as the assignment of business activities to a foreign location (Levy 2005). Linares-Navarro et al. (2014) explain the value of this as a means of sub-dividing the firm's value chain activities for maximum efficiency, whilst Oshri and Van Uhm (2012) argue that this also harnesses the skills and expertise of the workforce from different countries. From the host developing country perspective, although the majority of activities performed tend to be low to medium value added and routine operations, this can often represent the largest source of private employment, and a major source of foreign exchange remittances, as in the case of the Philippines (Kleibert 2016). It is therefore clear that offshoring has major mutual benefit for both parties, and this seems likely to continue as a major provision of emerging economy development.

It can be seen that the academic writing style involves representing your research findings, *followed by* your interpretations of those for your essay title, *all expressed in objective language.* In management assignments, this is the way that you develop what is sometimes referred to as *the student voice.* This is *not* about expressing your preconceived opinions but instead emerges from your selection and presentation of other authors' views and your understanding of what those mean for your assignment topic. This process is captured in the series of steps below:

Box 6.4   Developing your voice in an assignment

1   Targeted selection of certain ideas or other data that *you* have deemed important for your reading purpose.
2   *Your* interpretation of the meaning of this information for that reading purpose.
3   Summarising those ideas *in your own words.*
4   *Your* skilful integration of these with other authors' ideas on the same topic.

Box 6.5 offers some more examples of objective language for you to start using in your business and management assignment writing. This is not a comprehensive list, so experiment yourself with other similar phrases too:

Box 6.5   Objective language for expressing your interpretation of the significance of authors' findings

INAPPROPRIATE, SUBJECTIVE EXPRESSION	APPROPRIATE, OBJECTIVE LANGUAGE
I will explain how ... **X**	✓ *The essay will show that ...*
I believe that ... **X**	✓ *This means that ...*
In my opinion ... **X**	✓ *It therefore seems that ...*
I think this shows that ... **X**	✓ *It can be argued that ...*

Reflecting your own experience

Note that an exception to the general principle of using objective language is for personal development modules, e.g. Employability and Enterprise, in which you are asked to write reflectively. In these cases, the use of first person is essential in order to relate your own experience, as shown in the example below:

When two team members did not turn up for an important meeting, I felt disheartened because I could not see how we were going to complete our assessment group-work project on time.

It is only for this kind of self-reflective writing that subjective, first person language should be used (see Chapter 9). For all other academic writing, follow the more objective style illustrated above.

Be cautious

Most business and management subjects you are studying will involve considerable debate among the researchers in that field. This is the nature of the social sciences, in which ideas continue to evolve through academic research. Each new development stimulates further counter-arguments or qualifying propositions.

As you will see from your own research in management journal articles, for example, the debatable nature of the subject material results in a cautious language style. Some examples are shown in Box 6.6 as guidelines for your own assignment writing.

Box 6.6   Cautious language in academic writing

Avoid superlatives, e.g.	**Possible alternatives:**
Brilliant … excellent … superb …	*Effective … productive … improved …*
(Such exaggerated vocabulary can be typical of corporate websites. Be especially careful not to 'regurgitate' these PR messages unquestioningly.)	(These are more precise, but you need to check carefully that their meanings accurately reflect the specific ideas you are describing.)
Avoid absolutes, such as:	**Use relative terms**, e.g.
Never … always … the most … the least … constant … best …	*More … less … fewer … often … a majority of …*

It is usually better in academic writing to use exact facts and figures, e.g. *productivity increased by 50 per cent in the six-month period between January and July 2019.* Aim for this level of precision wherever possible in your assignments to establish credibility to your research.

Use formal language

Academic writing is quite different from conversation, email or other informal dialogue such as social media. You need to use a more formal style in your coursework for submission to tutors, as shown in Box 6.7:

Box 6.7   Academic writing style

Avoid contractions, e.g.	**Use the full form instead**, e.g.
don't	*do not*
it's	*it is*
they're	*they are*

Avoid conversational, personal or emotive style, e.g.	**Use precise, neutral language instead**, e.g.
So, it's sort of like …	*This typically represents …*
The organisation doesn't really care about whether people want to work.	*The organisation does not seem to be concerned with employee motivation because …*
I deplore how MNCs exploit globalisation for their own use	*This essay argues that multinational corporations (MNCs) aim to increase profitability through globalisation, sometimes using ethically questionable methods.*

Be clear, specific and concise

It is a common misconception among business and management students that writing academically means using complex sentences with lots of interconnected ideas to sound 'intelligent', 'professional' or, indeed, 'academic'. However, this is certainly not the case, and can easily result in the opposite effect as exemplified in the short extract below from a student's essay:

> *Lloyd (2002) is critical of the established literature on how the training and development skills problem has not been actively dealt with in the UK, there have been several minor level schemes that were adapted but nothing chiefly effective has resulted, there has been a major emphasis on its failure due to the lack of knowledge companies possess, specifically senior managers who are unaware of the opportunities available for fellow employees.*

Clearly, the main problem here lies in the student writing 71 words in one, very long, complicated sentence. The next section of this chapter explores some simple principles to avoid this kind of confusion.

Sentence structure

Appropriate sentence length

a) How many different ideas can you count in the example sentence of student writing on training and development above?

b) What is the ideal length of a sentence? Tick your chosen option below:

    A. Less than 15 words

    B. 15–25 words

    C. 25–35 words

    D. More than 35 words

Check your answers against those at the end of this chapter.

Box 6.8 suggests a way of making this student's sentence more readable:

Box 6.8   Helping the reader by creating short, sharp sentences

Lloyd (2002) is critical of the established literature's reasons for why the UK training and development (T&D) skills problem has not been addressed. There have been several minor-level schemes that were adapted but nothing chiefly effective has resulted. The failure has been mainly attributed to the companies' lack of knowledge, specifically senior managers who are unaware of the T&D opportunities available for employees.

This has split the original, long sentence into three separate ones. The new paragraph is easier to follow, and word count has been reduced. The principle of constructing effective academic writing is to use short, clear sentences containing two, or at most three, connected ideas. Try that for yourself now in Activity 6.2.

Simplifying sentence structure

Simplify this extract from a Global Business Environment assignment (final year undergraduate). Create three shorter sentences from the long one so that there are just two, or at most three, connected ideas per sentence:

> It is undeniable that Vernon's Product Life Cycle theory was justifiable at that time when a large proportion of the world's new products came from the US (UKessays

Online 2013), as well as the forms of FDI was conventional that mainly refers to multinational corporations (MNCs) from developed countries to invest in developing ones in the forms of physical facilities and so on like factories, which was also in line with the contents of such theory.

Write your revised, simpler version comprising three sentences here:

You can find a suggested rephrasing of this extract, with detailed explanation, in the Activity Answers.

Accurate sentence structure

English sentences (and each clause within them) generally require a *Subject – Verb – Object (SVO)* structure. You need to use that quite consistently, otherwise your writing may confuse the reader. Actually, this last sentence was a good example of the active form in SVO structure:

You [S] need to use [V] that [O] consistently, otherwise [linking word] the writing [S] really confuses [V] the reader [O].

Here is another example, this time from a business studies context:

Box 6.9   Creating well-structured, active sentences

BMW [S] is [V] an example of an organisation [O] that [S, i.e. organisation] has responded [V] well to the negativity [O] which [S, i.e. negativity] surrounds [V] organisations and unsustainable operations [O].

Notice how the object of one clause (part of a sentence) becomes the subject of the next with the use of relative words such as, 'which' or 'that'. You can also create the same effect by using the connecting word 'to' in the same way, as in the following example:

Managers (S) will exercise (V) coercive power (O) to (S, i.e. the act of exercising coercive power) threaten (V) individuals with demotion and redundancy (O).

ACTIVITY 6.3

Identifying SVO structure in sentences

In this next activity, identify which words or phrases are subjects, verbs or objects in each clause of the sentences. Write S, V or O above the appropriate words:

a) *Firms do not pay taxes on income earned abroad, until it is brought back into the*

 United States (Altshuler 2010).

b) *Current business production is at 54.3 per cent of target, and attempts to*

 encourage sales have not resulted in increased business so far (Canada Life 2014).

c) *MNCs revise their strategic methods to stimulate competitive advantage in order to*

 maximise profits and productivity.

ACTIVITY 6.4

Reorganising sentences into SVO structure

Rewrite this confused sentence from a student's essay into an appropriate SVO structure:

 However, the most important aspect to build its competitive advantage and Lego had underestimated was the supply chain.

Write your suggested answer here:

A possible alternative is given in the answers at the end of this chapter.

Summary: writing style and sentence structure

- Use objective, cautious, formal language.
- Be clear and concise:
  - Keep most sentences within 15–25 words.
  - Generally, use SVO structure within each clause.
- Be specific and precise – ensure the tutor understands exactly what you mean.

Paragraph structure

If we think of writing an essay like building a house, each word can be thought of as a brick, and each well-constructed sentence as a row of bricks securely joined together. These rows of bricks are built up into a wall, of course, and these walls form the rooms of the house. Its strength is determined by how soundly each wall has been constructed, and how well these fit together.

And so it is with the paragraphs in an essay. Each paragraph should convey a single idea of its own (*Unity*), which also then connects clearly to the next (*Coherence*). For the reader, working through the essay should be like walking through a house where each room interests you in a memorable way and makes you want to see more.

Coherence is covered in the later section on essay structure. Unity is considered below:

Box 6.10   The TEEE framework for paragraph unity

- **Topic sentence:** This presents the key idea of the whole paragraph.
- **Explanation:** How that idea relates to your assignment question.
- **Evidence:** Citations to others' research that supports or challenges the idea.
- **Examples:** Real applications of the idea in the business world.

Box 6.11 gives an illustration of the TEEE framework from a Capital Markets module assignment entitled:

'I'd be a bum on the street with a tin cup if the markets were always efficient' (Buffett 1995). Discuss.

Here is a sample paragraph from a student's essay addressing that question:

Box 6.11   Sample TEEE framework paragraph

Information is not always accessible to all investors immediately. It takes time for them to attain and process newly received information regarding their investment (Van Bergen 2017). The variability of these interpretations results in different trading decisions of investors (Pike et al. 2012; Asness and Liew 2014). This could account for the fluctuations of stock prices in the short term.	**Clear *Topic sentence*. Further *Explanation* of the topic over two sentences with academic citations (*Evidence*). Writer's interpretation.**

This short paragraph shows you an example of the first three elements of the TEEE framework in a logical sequence. There is no real-life example given in this extract, so the final aspect of the model is missing. However, this does not necessarily detract from the value of this single paragraph. Perhaps the next one in that essay would give just such an illustration so that the essay writing development covers the four dimensions of the TEEE framework across more than one paragraph. In other words, the TEEE framework is a guideline, not a prescriptive formula.

The example of the framework in Box 6.11 is further complemented by a short interpretation from the student of the academic ideas they have collated around the topic. This relates to the point made earlier about developing your voice through an essay by making these kinds of interpretations after synthesising other sources' views in each paragraph. Another way of thinking about this is to consider these as extending paragraph structure with a single sentence *summary* – so you might find it helpful to think of the framework as TEEES.

ACTIVITY 6.5

Evaluating paragraph structure

Here are some examples of paragraphs from students' essays on the topic of Operations Management. Consider how well each paragraph covers the four criteria of the TEEE framework (Remember: Topic; Explanation; Evidence; Example – not necessarily in that order).

Assign a grade to each paragraph: A, B, C, D or E (where A is highest, and E is a poor fail):

Paragraph 1:

Successful innovation gives nations, industries and organizations an edge in the highly competitive world today. A racially diverse workforce guided by an innovation-focused business strategy provides firms with an competitive advantage. The key component for a country's economic growth is productivity. The same is true for any company.

Globalization and technological progress are the driving forces for the increase in productivity by the process of creating new demands by introducing new products or improving the efficiency of the existing production process.

Your grade: _____

Paragraph 2:

Business Process Re-engineering (BPR) has attracted a lot of attention in theory and practice, raising the question of how usefully this information management system may be applied across different business sectors (Vakola et al. 2000). The basic concept of BPR is to make changes to existing business processes with the aim to improve business performance dramatically in a short time (Bertolini et al. 2011). BPR introduces innovative ideas to model ideal work processes (Choi and Chan 1997), but multiple studies showed that, on average, only 30 per cent of BPR implementation turned out to be successful (Revenaugh 1994). For example, Infosys Technologies failed in its human resource process re-engineering efforts – "IRACE" and lost thousands of valuable employees (IRACE 2010). However, King's College Hospital's BPR efforts not only improved performance but also produced a profit of £1 million (Patwardhan and Patwardhan 2007). So, these case studies still pose the question of whether BPR is universally useful.

Your grade: _____

Paragraph 3:

It is evident that television drama production in the UK exclusively uses the project process (Blair et al. 2001) to produce one-off, complex, large scale and high work content products (Matthias 2010). Television drama production displays all of the attributes assigned to project processes described by the product-process matrix model. Each drama is specially made and customised using a variety of skilled labour which needs to be coordinated to produce the finished product. As the process used is project-based, there is always a defined start and finish within production (i.e. "green-light" or release of funds for the start of preproduction, to delivery of programme to broadcaster) (Slack et al. 2009).

Your grade: _____

Check your grades against the Activity Answers, which also explain the strengths and weaknesses of the above paragraphs.

Essay structure

Coherence

Coherence is about paragraphs clearly and logically following one another. Each paragraph should build on the preceding one so that your argument unfolds explicitly in the mind of the reader.

There are various ways you can create this coherent flow throughout your essay. These are summarised below in Box 6.12.

Box 6.12   Developing coherence between consecutive paragraphs

Each of these ways to connect two paragraphs coherently is indicated by a sample first sentence for a new paragraph with an explanation of how this connects with the topic of its preceding one.

- **To elaborate on the same topic**
  E.g. These opposing views of emotional labour require further analysis.
  (The previous paragraph introduced the debate around positive and negative perceptions of emotional labour.)

- **To provide a case study example to illustrate the previous idea**
  E.g. Various organisations have embraced systems thinking as a strategy for remaining competitive in the market, and a prime example is Toyota.
  (The previous paragraph explained systems thinking in general terms.)

- **To 'funnel down' from a general idea into specific forms of that**
  E.g. There are four possible forms of market structure: perfect competition; monopolistic competition; oligopoly; monopoly (Begg and Ward 2013).
  (The previous paragraph described what is meant by market structure.)

- **To present a counter-argument to the previous topic**
  E.g. However, NPV is not flawless. Magni (2009) stated that this requires some guesswork about the cost of the capital.
  (The previous paragraph discussed the usefulness of net present value (NPV) for investment analysis).

- **To clearly indicate a new direction**
  E.g. The analysis of Samsung's market can now be applied to the development of an appropriate branding strategy for the next five years.
  (The previous paragraph completed the audit of Samsung's marketplace, ready to lead into a strategy discussion.)

Here is an example of coherence (shown in bold) between two consecutive paragraphs, taken from the PWO essay introduced earlier in this chapter:

Box 6.13   Coherence between paragraphs

'Personality is a pattern of relatively permanent traits and unique characteristics that give both consistency and individuality to a person's behavior' (Feist and Feist 2009: 38). Personality type refers to the preference behaviour of an individual in the processes of thinking, feeling and behaving. For selection purposes, HR managers may benefit from determining the personality type of each candidate so that they can appoint those people whose characteristics potentially match the role's person specification. **In order to do this effectively, HR managers use various techniques inspired by established theories about personality.**

   Firstly, there are trait theories of personality. One example is Eysenck's three-factor model, *which states that personality consists of one from each pair of three bipolar factors: introversion–extroversion; stability–instability; and psychoticism (Eysenck and Eysenck 1975). Another trait theory, the 'Big Five' factor model, suggests* *the OCEAN acronym: openness to experience, conscientiousness, extraversion, agreeableness and neuroticism, each of which constitute a different personality (Digman 1990). Nowadays, HR managers assess candidates' traits by using personality tests such as factor analysis in the selection process. They believe these can determine an individual's interests, interpersonal skills, emotional adjustments and attitudes towards specific work situations.*

The first paragraph defines the concept of personality type and highlights its potential value for the employment selection process. This process is noted at the end to be dependent on personality theory *generally*. The object of that last sentence – personality theory – then becomes the subject of the first sentence of the next paragraph.

This immediately establishes a direct link between the two by focussing on a *specific type* of personality theory used by employers for finding the best candidates. The overall theme of employee selection is maintained coherently through both paragraphs.

You can test your understanding of coherence in Activity 6.6.

ACTIVITY 6.6

Coherence through paragraphs

This exercise shows one paragraph from a student's essay and then two possible paragraphs that could come next. Read these carefully and select which paragraph you think follows the first one more logically, i.e. shows the most *coherence*. Choose paragraph A or B as the more coherent, subsequent paragraph to follow the first one.

China & EU bilateral trade

China is a tremendous opportunity for the EU. It is a rising economic power and is a dominant player in global trade. It is predicted that it will soon become the world's biggest economy, and the EU is already China's biggest trading partner. Bilateral trade reached €428.1 billion in 2013 (Europa 2015) and is expected to grow by 1.5 times to €660 billion in a decade (Hansakul and Levinger 2014). This highlights the increasing significance of EU–China trade and shows how important this trade partner is to so many European member states.

A. *European businesses have been finding it difficult to increase revenue in their own mature European market, and China has become the engine for growth. France's textile fibre industry, Britain's skin fur industry and the EU paper waste industry all rely on China for 50 per cent of exports. European industries have benefitted from trade between the EU and China being dominated by manufacturing, which accounts for 84 per cent of total EU exports to China (Hansakul and Levinger 2014). Trade with China accounted for 27 per cent of exports for Czech Republic and 20 per cent for Denmark, Hungry and Estonia, for example (Maxwell 2015). Bilateral trade has positively impacted on many member states.*

B. *Bilateral trade has positively impacted on many member states. Trade with China accounted for 27 per cent of exports for Czech Republic and 20 per cent for Denmark, Hungry and Estonia, for example (Maxwell 2015). European businesses have been finding it difficult to increase revenue in their own mature European market, and China has become the engine for growth. European industries have benefitted from EU–China trade being dominated by manufacturing, which accounts for 84 per cent of total EU exports to China (Hansakul and Levinger 2014). France's textile fibre industry, Britain's skin fur industry and the EU paper waste industry all rely on China for 50 per cent of exports.*

Check your choice against the Activity Answers.

Writing conclusions and introductions

Most of this chapter has concentrated on the body of the essay. Your overall assignment structure also requires an introduction and a conclusion, of course.

This section has been deliberately left to the end to mirror good practice in your essay writing, i.e. your conclusion *and then* your introduction should be the last sections that you write when creating your assignment. You cannot really produce these until you have finalised the body paragraphs, as the direction and content of the argument only emerge through the actual process of writing.

Boxes 6.14 and 6.15 summarise the key requirements of introductions and conclusions, with a high-grade example for each. When drafting your essay, the introduction should be the last part you actually write. This depends on knowing what follows throughout the essay, including the conclusion. For that reason, the boxes below explain how to write a conclusion first, followed by how to write an introduction.

Here is an example of a well-constructed conclusion from a student's Economics essay on international trade:

Box 6.14   What should be included in a conclusion?

- Only summarise the key themes from the argument that has already been developed in detail through the main part of the essay.
- One paragraph is likely to be enough to capture the position you have reached on the proposition in the assignment question.
- You must not bring in any new points that have not been covered before.
- This also means no citations. You will have assembled all the academic support you needed to establish your argument in the main body. These sources do not need to be cited again.

Essay question

Outline the Heckscher–Ohlin model of international trade and its relevance for understanding inequality between developed and developing countries.

Conclusion

In conclusion, then, this essay has acknowledged the contributions made by the H–O model to the theoretical understanding of international trade. It explains this from the view of a country's basic source advantages, and thus establishes a foundation to modern trade theory. This has been particularly valuable in predicting reductions in wage inequality in newly industrialised economies in East Asia. However, there are some drawbacks with this static model because of its assumptions that do not adapt to the most recent international trade developments, for example in countries which have changed their comparative advantage.

Here is an example of a well-constructed introduction for the same Economics essay:

Box 6.15   What should be included in an introduction?

The purpose of your introduction is to hook the reader's interest with a simple, clear statement of the following:

- **Your interpretation of the question**. In your own words, you need to show the tutor that you understand the key implications of the specific assignment title that they have set.
- **Why this is an important, contemporary topic**. This is your first chance to refer to up-to-date research – do not hesitate to bring in relevant citations even at this early stage.
- **What the essay covers** – a brief overview of the structure.
- An indication perhaps of **the key findings** that emerge in your essay argument. Plenty of students can miss this last point, so this may be a distinctive factor in creating a good first impression in the tutor's mind.

Essay question

Outline the Heckscher–Ohlin model of international trade and its relevance for understanding inequality between developed and developing countries.

Introduction

The Heckscher–Ohlin (H–O) model is a symbol of a change of economic thinking from classicism to neoclassicism and is perhaps the most well-regarded theory of international trade. This essay will outline the H–O model, and then discuss its utility in developing an understanding of some trends in wage inequality, particularly in emerging economies. This discussion will, however, also highlight some limitations to the model in terms of more recent developments in modern international trade.

It is also possible that you may define some key terms from the assignment title (with citations). However, these are more likely to appear in the next one or two paragraphs after the introduction.

Summary: paragraph and essay structure

- Ideal paragraph length: Typically, between four and seven sentences.
- Each paragraph covers only ONE idea *(Unity)*.
- The paragraph analyses this one topic in depth.
- Each paragraph follows a clear structure, such as the TEEE framework.
- One paragraph then leads logically to the next *(Coherence)* to consistently build a clear argument through the essay.
- Show your position on the essay question in the conclusion, which (only) summarises the key themes of the assignment body.
- Return full circle from the conclusion to create the introduction, which indicates the overall finding(s) that emerge in the essay.

Evaluating and editing your draft writing

This chapter has been concerned with helping you to create, develop and refine your own written work. The advice and activities will all help you to reach the stage of a fully drafted essay argument. However, this first draft requires further reworking if it is to really justify the effort you have already expended.

The next stage – *editing* – requires you to carefully review your draft against the main criteria that have been covered earlier in this chapter. In summary, this extensive process should therefore include:

- Structure, e.g. a skeleton analysis of paragraph coherence (see below).
- Writing style, e.g. sentence clarity and conciseness – you can read any questionable sentences aloud either to yourself or a friend to hear if they make immediate sense.
- Accuracy, e.g. sentence grammatical structure, appropriate vocabulary, punctuation – this is the final proofreading stage.

You can do this yourself; by this point, however, you are likely to be so immersed in the content that it can be difficult to recognise any problematic patterns in your own writing. It is possible that your module tutor or academic skills unit may provide some formative feedback on sections of your writing. If this kind of external support is available, it is well worth taking that up in the mid to late stages of your writing. Alternatively, you could consider asking a friend or family member to read your draft. It can be surprising how a perspective from a non-expert will enable you to improve that piece of work in ways that you would not have recognised yourself.

This can be especially useful for your first assignment(s) at university as you can then apply those principles to future writing by yourself. Seeking help in this way is still all part of the process of becoming a truly independent learner. However, as your ultimate aim is to become self-sufficient in this respect, the following sections do offer further guidance on certain aspects of editing that you may find helpful to try yourself.

Improving your assignment's coherence

It is perhaps inevitable at some point in the writing process that you get caught up in the details and lose sight of the overall structure. Once you have a first rough draft, it can therefore be helpful to put that aside for a day or two and then reconsider how coherently (or not) your paragraphs flow into one another.

A good way of achieving that more detached view is to strip the essay down to its 'bare bones'. This involves summing up the key point of each paragraph in just a few words and isolating these topic phrases as the 'skeleton' of your essay. This is illustrated in Box 6.16 below in a sample essay from a first-year undergraduate module 'People, Work and Organisations'.

Note that for the purpose of this example, we are not concerned with the quality of the content, but rather with the *structure*.

Box 6.16   A skeleton analysis to check paragraph structure and coherence

Essay extract paragraphs	Skeleton topics
HR management is important in ensuring that employees are highly efficient and effective (Kehoe and Wright 2013). This can be achieved when workers are well aligned with their job roles, working environment and organisational policies. HR managers can use the theories of recruitment, selection and personality to employ workers with the desired attributes. Recruitment and selection is a process of employing new workers into an organization or promoting the existing ones. It is a crucial process for the HR managers, because this can result in immense long-term costs or benefits for the firms. HR managers need to determine the personality types of the candidates so that they can employ those people who are likely to sustainably fulfil the job requirements.	Crucial importance of three factors in HR management: Recruitment; Selection; Personality.
Recruitment can be defined as a process of attracting a pool of capable candidates with desired skills and knowledge for a specific job (AHRI 2015). Recruitment can either be external or internal. Internal recruitment is characterized by attracting the existing employees of the firm for upcoming posts, which has the added motivational benefits of promotion or new jobs for interns. Many devices, such as job notice boards, email flashes and intranet are used for internal recruitment. External recruitment is a strategy by which the managers attract people with fresh ideas and energy from outside the organization. This can be achieved through direct advertising or recruitment agencies, for example. However, internal recruitment is more beneficial for any organization as it reduces the cost of training and development (Applegate 2015).	Recruitment: The pros and cons of two main types.

Essay extract paragraphs	Skeleton topics
Following recruitment, suitable applicants will go through a selection process in which the best applicant with desired knowledge and skills is selected for a specific job (AHRI 2015). Potential candidates are first screened by examining their CVs for required skills and knowledge. Selected applicants are then invited to the organisation for further evaluation. This may take the form of an assessment centre for examining candidates' interactive skills such as group working and problem-solving, and/or candidates will be interviewed individually.	Selection: How the process works.
'Personality is a pattern of relatively permanent traits and unique characteristics that give both consistency and individuality to a person's behavior' (Feist and Feist 2009: 4). In order to determine personality types for selection purposes, HR managers use various techniques inspired by established theories about personality. These may also help employers to understand what motivates their employees to become effective in their work. In some cases, a psychometric test may be conducted. In this test, personality factors such as emotional stability, extroversion and agreeableness can be assessed. Nowadays, modern organizations are increasingly using online testing for this type of selection process, because it has a comparatively low cost and also saves time by conducting many tests simultaneously (Spicer and Lee 2014).	Personality types: How these are involved in the recruitment and selection process.
Businesses like McDonald's need effective and efficient staff to fulfil their established priority of customer satisfaction. For this purpose, they use a comprehensive recruitment and selection strategy. This specifies the duties, responsibilities, relevant experience, skills and knowledge required for every job, which is promoted through websites, recruitment agencies and job notice boards in restaurants. In the case of crew members and maintenance staff, selection interviews are conducted to predict the future behaviour of the candidate and rate each of them according to predefined personality criteria (Business case studies 2014). For managers, candidates are firstly assessed by a psychometric test and then an initial interview. Those with higher test ratings are then offered 'on job experience' for assessing their performance and then selection is finalised in a further interview. Even then, managers are further assessed for three weeks to make sure that they are displaying appropriate workplace behaviour before being assigned a permanent job (Business case studies 2014).	A business case study illustrating how the three factors identified in the first paragraph are operationalised in a workplace.

You can see that these five paragraphs show strong coherence. There is a logical development from identifying three factors in the introduction, each of which is then explained in its own subsequent paragraph, leading to an example of how these are all implemented in a real-life case study.

Next time you have produced a draft version of an essay, try this skeleton analysis exercise. As well as checking for *coherence* between paragraphs, it will enable you to check whether each paragraph shows *unity* by covering only one topic, which is consistently developed or illustrated through every sentence.

If you find it difficult to summarise the paragraph in one short phrase, then you may well need to split the paragraphs. Also, remember the principle noted above for paragraph length of between four and seven sentences as modelled in the Box 6.16 examples.

Further editing procedures

One common problem with early essay drafts can simply be too many words. University assignments stipulate maximum word counts, and you need to convey as much relevant information as possible while respecting the word count you have been given. To achieve this aim requires ruthless editing of every sentence.

This book cannot prescribe a generic method of editing for all your assignments, as every one of these is a unique production. However, to give you some idea of how you might go about that editing process, one example is shown below. This particular extract is an introduction to an essay for the module People, Work and Organisations. The student's original writing has been edited in the second version. Referencing issues requiring further attention are noted in bold.

Box 6.17   Editing your writing for clarity and conciseness

Original extract from the student's essay:

HR management is one of the few most important issues for any organization. Every organization wants its human resource factor to be highly efficient and effective, all the time, for its benefit. This is only possible if the workers in that organization are perfectly feasible with their work, working environment, organizational policies and are continuously being motivated to do their designated job. HR managers use the theories of recruitment, selection and personality to employ workers with desired skills, knowledge, thinking, feeling and behavior. They use famous motivation theories to motivate workers to continuously work efficiently and effectively. This essay discusses all those theories and look out for their application and implication to some specific organization's examples.

(116 words)

Edited version:

HR management ensures that employees are highly efficient and effective **(needs citation)**. This can be achieved when they are well aligned with their job roles, working environment and organisational policies. HR managers can use the theories of recruitment, selection and personality to employ workers with the desired skills, knowledge, thinking, feeling and behaviour. They also need to be continuously motivated to enjoy their designated job **(citation?)**. Motivation theories, for example, may be applied to increase workers' productivity **(needs citation)**. This essay discusses such theories' applications to specific organisational examples.

(83 words)

In addition to making the writing more concise, this has highlighted where the student is missing important academic support for debatable claims. Furthermore, reviewing the logical flow of ideas in the paragraph resulted in changing the sequence of two sentences so that the need for motivation and then theories of motivation directly follow one another.

Activity Answers

Activity 6.1: Appropriate sentence length

a This sentence contains up to eight separate ideas, as noted by the numbers below. This is clearly far too many to digest together without the punctuating signals of full stops to separate this into manageable chunks for the reader.

> Lloyd (2002) is critical of the established literature [1] on how the training and development skills problem [2] has not been actively dealt with in the UK [3], there have been several minor level schemes that were adapted [4] but nothing chiefly effective has resulted [5], there has been a major emphasis on its failure [6] due to the lack of knowledge companies possess [7], specifically senior managers who are unaware of the opportunities available for fellow employees [8].

b The single sentence above has 71 words. This is clearly far too long to follow. An ideal sentence length for academic assignments is around 15–25 words per sentence (Answer B), to help your tutor get your points quickly and easily.

Activity 6.2: Shortening sentences

Numbers have been inserted into this revised version to point out key improvements, which are then explained in the following notes.

> *(1)* Vernon's Product Life Cycle (PLC) theory was justifiable at that time when a large proportion of the world's new products came from the US (Wild and Wild 2008) *(2)*. Multinational corporations (MNCs) from developed countries typically invested *(3)* then in developing nations in the form of physical facilities such as *(4)* factories. *(5)* This was the context of place and time in which Vernon developed his PLC theory *(6)*.

Notes:

1 Remember that academic language in the social sciences is cautious. It is understood that most ideas are arguable, and need to be expressed tentatively. So avoid absolute terms, such as 'It is undeniable ...'
2 This is the first opportunity to split sentences for easier comprehension. Full stops signal a pause for the reader to digest each concept, before moving on. It is also important to note that UKessaysonline is a commercial source, and therefore unreliable. A credible, textbook citation has been used here instead.
3 Grammatical change to produce a more straightforward sentence structure.
4 Academic writing is formal. Avoid casual language such as, 'like ... and so on'.
5 By inserting a full stop here, you break up the ideas even more clearly.
6 Emphasises the main point of the paragraph as a final, single sentence. A citation to Vernon would be useful here to indicate key research has been conducted on the author of the theory.

Activity 6.3: Identifying Subject Verb Object (SVO) structure in sentences

a   *Firms (S) do not pay (V) taxes on income earned abroad (O), until it (S, i.e. foreign income) is brought back (V) into the United States (O) (Altshuler 2010).*

There are two clauses in this sentence, each following the SVO structure.

b   *Current business production (S) is (V) at 54.3 per cent of target (O), and <u>attempts to encourage sales</u> (S) have not resulted (V) in increased business (O) so far (Canada Life 2014).*

Subjects can sometimes include a combination of nouns and verbs to create a 'whole concept' such as that underlined here.

c   *MNCs (S) revise (V) their strategic methods (O) to (S, i.e. revising strategic methods) stimulate (V) competitive advantage (O) <u>in order to</u> (S, i.e. stimulating competitive advantage) maximise (V) profits and productivity (O).*

When used correctly, connecting words and phrases such as 'in order to' maintain a clear, logical flow to a sentence by indicating that the object of one clause has become the subject of the next.

Activity 6.4: Clear sentence structure with Subject Verb Object

You could have restructured the example into this sentence, by using SVO:

Lego [S] had underestimated [V] the supply chain [O], which [S] was [V] the most important aspect [O] with which [S] to build [V] its competitive advantage [O].

You can see that this has split the sentence into three clauses, each with its own SVO structure.

Activity 6.5: Evaluating paragraph structure

Paragraph 1

Original paragraph	Comments and grade
Successful innovation gives nations, industries and organizations an edge in the highly competitive world today. A <u>racially diverse workforce</u> guided by an innovation-focused business strategy provides firms with competitive advantage. The key component for a <u>country's economic growth</u> is <u>productivity</u>. The same is true for any company. <u>Globalization</u> and <u>technological progress</u> are the driving forces for the increase in <u>productivity</u> by the process of creating new demands by introducing new products or <u>improving the efficiency of the existing production process</u>.	It seems the paragraph *Topic* could be innovation linked to competitive advantage. However, several other, major business concepts then emerge (underlined), and each *without any further Explanation*. So, there is no development of a single theme, and the paragraph becomes a confusing mix of disparate ideas. There are no citations (*Evidence*) or *Examples*. **Grade: D/E (fail)**

Paragraph 2

Original paragraph	Comments and grade
Business Process Re-engineering (BPR) has attracted a lot of attention in theory and practice, raising the question of how usefully this information management system may be applied across different business sectors (Vakola et al. 2000). The basic concept of BPR is to change existing business processes to improve performance dramatically in a short time (Bertolini et al. 2011). BPR introduces innovative ideas to model ideal work processes (Choi and Chan 1997), but multiple studies showed that, on average, only 30% of BPR implementation turned out to be successful (Revenaugh 1994). For example, Infosys Technologies failed in its human resource process re-engineering efforts – "IRACE" and lost thousands of valuable employees (IRACE 2010). However, King's College Hospital's BPR efforts not only improved performance but also produced a profit of £1 million (Patwardhan and Patwardhan 2007). So, these case studies still pose the question of whether BPR is universally useful.	The *Topic* focusses on how universally useful BPR may be across different businesses. An *Explanation* over two sentences shows a further understanding of the aims and approach of BPR. A meta-analysis (summary of multiple studies) shows BPR potential for failure with a real-life *Example* from one sector. This is contrasted with another positive *Example* from a different sector, thus showing critical analysis by presenting two sides to the argument. Every point is supported by academic *Evidence* (citations). **Grade: A/B (high pass)**

In addition to closely following the TEEE framework, this shows strong theoretical knowledge as each sentence is derived from a different academic source. Many tutors will mark this highly for its demonstration of wide, relevant reading, well-integrated into a cohesive paragraph.

A possible qualification to that could be the perception that this continuous series of others' ideas lacks interpretation on the part of the student. A more interpretive approach is illustrated in Paragraph 3 below, albeit with fewer sources than the above example.

Paragraph 3

Original paragraph	Comments and grade
It is evident that television drama production in the UK exclusively uses the project process (Blair et al. 2001) to produce one-off, complex, large scale and high work content products (Matthias 2010). Television drama production displays all of the attributes assigned to project processes described by the product-process matrix model. Each drama is specially made and customised using a variety of skilled labour which needs to be coordinated to produce the finished product. As the process used is project-based, there is always a defined start and finish within production (i.e. "green-light" or release of funds for the start of preproduction, to delivery of programme to broadcaster) (Slack et al. 2009).	The *Topic* is TV drama production being a project process as defined by two different academic sources *(Evidence)*. This is related to a specific theoretical focus (model). A quite detailed *Explanation* then follows of how the TV production process illustrates the theoretical model in practice, further supported by a citation *(Evidence)*. TV drama production has become the real-life *Example* running through the paragraph. **Grade: A/B (high pass)**

The interweaving of theory and practice throughout this paragraph embodies a different approach to that shown in Paragraph 2 above. Instead of synthesising a series of theoretical research findings, Paragraph 3 repeatedly applies a single model to a single example – more like a case study approach.

This could possibly be criticised for the academic ideas being rather general, so each of these two approaches has its own merits, and their use will depend on the exact nature of your question. Both examples demonstrate a sound academic structure and logical development within the TEEE framework, hence the indicative high grades.

Activity 6.6: Coherence through paragraphs

Paragraph B provides the most coherent continuation from the first paragraph. This is because it begins by developing the general theme of how EU member states have benefited from bilateral trade – the finishing point of the previous paragraph. After these first two sentences, paragraph B then 'funnels down' to focus on specific industries' reliance on EU–China trade. This deductive approach to writing (moving from the general to the specific) within each paragraph tends to be typical of academic writing structure.

Understanding Referencing

Referencing is the process of signposting readers to the research sources that you have used in your assignments. It is your critical analysis of their data and ideas that accounts for a significant amount of marks in most module assignments. Essay arguments based on your pre-existing opinions will not be viewed as academically credible. Instead, these *must be derived from, and directly reference*, sources such as management journal articles and textbooks, as well as topical data from business databases and media.

Broadly speaking, there are two main types of referencing systems, each including several different styles:

1   **Name/date**, e.g. Harvard; APA; MLA.
2   **Numerical**, e.g. OSCOLA; MHRA; Chicago.

One version of the name/date style has been applied throughout this book, and that is Harvard. This is the one most commonly used in social sciences such as business and management. However, please note that even if your programme does use Harvard, there are many subtle variations of this style. *You must fully acquaint yourself with the guidance that your university provides on the exact formatting they require.*

This chapter explains the following:

- **Referencing appropriately and accurately**
  - How to use in-text citations as signposts to the sources of the ideas and data within your essays.
  - When to use citations to show the sources of your management ideas and business information.
  - How to present a full list of references at the end of your assignment.
- **Avoiding plagiarism**
  A major contention of this chapter is that you will avoid any risk of plagiarism if you follow the referencing guidelines rigorously. To be doubly sure, major forms of plagiarism are reiterated here so that you can recognise and pre-empt these accordingly.

How to produce citations (in the Harvard style)

Referencing systems have two elements:

- A citation (partial reference) within the text of your writing.
- A full reference list at the end of your assignment.

As an example of a name/date system, Harvard's format for citations simply requires the author's name followed by the year of publication. Let's look at two examples of Harvard citations from a financial management essay in Box 7.1.

Box 7.1   Citation format examples

Dichev et al. (2013) exposed the main motivations for companies to misrepresent their economic performance as the incentive to influence stock price followed by the pressure to hit earnings benchmarks. Although there are arguments advocating the use of stock options as a tool to lead to companies' success, 'the likelihood of managerial impropriety rises with the strength of the inducements' (Harris and Bromiley 2007: 352).

Do not worry if you cannot easily understand the subject content of this paragraph, which is from a final year undergraduate module. Our primary interest here is in the way that citations have been integrated into the sentence structure. This extract illustrates two ways of including citations in the text – at the beginning or the end of the sentence. Citations can actually appear at any point in the sentence, but while you are developing your academic writing skills, it is a good idea to practise integrating these either at the start or the finish of sentences, as these are where they are commonly found. These two citation placements are therefore discussed in more detail below:

Starting a sentence with a citation

The first citation, 'Dichev et al. (2013)', is used at the beginning of the sentence. In this way, it is integrated into the grammatical structure, i.e. the authors become the subject of the sentence, which must then be followed by a verb, in this case 'exposed'. When you start a sentence with the citation, as here, you *include only the date in brackets*.

Note: The Latin term 'et al.' is an abbreviation simply meaning 'and others'. This is *indicating there are more than two authors* of this publication. The Harvard convention is that this full list of authors does not appear in the citation, but is given in the referencing list (see Box 7.5, p. 107). *Double-check that your university follows this same 'et al.' convention.*

Ending a sentence with a citation

You can see from the second citation in Box 7.1 that you can alternatively insert these at the end of a sentence. This placement requires that *names and date are both set within the parentheses (brackets)*. As you are setting the citation at the end, there is no need to integrate this into the sentence with the use of a verb. *Note the importance of placing the citation before the full stop so that it is within the relevant sentence.* This makes it clear which idea is attributed to which source.

Showing page numbers in a citation

As an example of a name/date referencing system, most Harvard citations only require those two elements. However, there are two instances when you need to add page numbers into a Harvard citation:

1   **Direct quotes**
2   **Secondary referencing**

1   *Direct quotes*

Referring back to Box 7.1, you can see that the second citation gives a page number after the date (Harris and Bromiley 2007: 352). This is because the sentence includes a direct quotation, indicated by the 'speech marks' around the text. The Harvard style has a convention of showing the page number of verbatim quotes like this. It is possible that your university referencing system may have a slightly different way of depicting page numbers in citations, e.g. 'p. 352'. *Check this specific formatting detail with your departmental guidance.*

However, as explained in Box 7.2, tutors will view excessive use of direct quotes as poor academic practice, and these should therefore be kept to an absolute minimum in your assignment writing.

Box 7.2   Avoid using direct quotes wherever possible

- *Direct quotes should only be used sparingly* – perhaps just two or three in a typical assignment, for example, to define key terms which need to use the author's exact words.
- *The vast majority of your academic writing* should be formed by summarising and paraphrasing, i.e. making the writing your own. This is because the tutor needs to see your understanding of authors' meanings from the way that you interpret those to your assignment topic.
- As these crucial techniques of *summarising and paraphrasing* are such predominant elements of your assignment writing, they are covered in depth in the next chapter.

---

2   *Secondary referencing*

There is one other main reason for using page numbers in citations. This is for secondary referencing – when you are referring to an idea or information from a (secondary) source that has been cited by the author of the text you are actually reading (your primary source). This is illustrated in the following example:

Box 7.3   Secondary referencing example

Quality gurus like Feigenbaum extended principles developed in production settings to services operations and developed definitions of quality such as the following:

'The total composite product and service characteristics ... through which the product or service in use will meet the expectations of the customer.' (Feigenbaum 1983 in Brown et al. 2000: 194)

When presented clearly in this way, it is easy for the reader to understand that the student has found an original idea from Feigenbaum in the book that s/he was reading by Brown et al. In this case the idea has been reproduced directly as a quote.

The disadvantage to secondary referencing is that you are trusting your primary source's interpretation of another author's idea. If that idea seems relatively important to your assignment focus, consider consulting the original source. That, after all, is the basis of a sound research trail – following your key sources' own sources.

However, your tutor also understands that at some point you have to stop reading. Some secondary referencing will therefore be allowed. In the assignment overall, though, you must show plenty of primary sources as evidence of your wider reading.

Citing sources which do not have identified authors

In business and management assignments, you will often need to refer to information obtained from corporate, governmental or other organisational sources that do not show a personal author. This does not change the basic name/date principle of your Harvard citations. In these cases, you simply use the organisation's name for the author. An example is given below from a student's module report:

Box 7.4   Citations for organisational sources

Principle 4 from the Agenda 21 Principles states that 'In order to achieve sustainable development, environmental protection shall constitute an integral part of the development process and cannot be considered in isolation from it' (UN 2011: 16). It could be argued that this approach to sustainable supply chain management has been successful at BMW, which insists that its suppliers throughout the supply chain implement social, environmental and governance standards (BMW 2015).

References:
BMW (2015) Emission-free into the future: Sustainability and BMW i. http://www.bmw.com/com/en/insights/corporation/bmwi/sustainability.html Accessed 14 February 2017.
UN: United Nations (2011) *Review of implementation of Agenda 21 and the Rio Principles.* Department of Economic and Social Affairs Division for Sustainable Development.

In both cases in Box 7.4, the organisation's name has been used for the citations. The first example is taken from an intergovernmental organisation, and the second is from a corporate website. The reader can determine the exact nature of the source from the corresponding references. These can then be followed up by your tutor if s/he would like to check out your information sources further.

Box 7.4 also shows the first two examples of a full reference in this chapter. You can see immediately that far more information is required than for citations. The next section tells you more about this second part of the referencing process.

How to produce references (in the Harvard style)

Full references appear in *one alphabetical list* at the end of your assignment. These show the types of sources you have consulted and therefore the academic credibility of that research – an important criterion for the tutor's grading. For example, in Box 7.4 above, they are likely to be somewhat sceptical about the use of a corporate website to affirm that company's sustainability credentials. This may well be accepted as a starting point, but some more independent sources will be required in other paragraphs to substantiate the BMW claims. In contrast, the UN will naturally be regarded as a far more reliable source of objective information or a policy statement such as that provided in the citation.

Learning how to format your full references

References include far more information than citations. As a case in point, take a look at the references for the citations that were shown earlier in Boxes 7.1 and 7.3.

Box 7.5   Examples of full references for different types of sources

Brown, S., Lamming, R., Bessant, J. and Jones, P. (2000) *Strategic Operations Management.* Oxford: Butterworth-Heinemann.
Dichev, I.D., Graham, J.R., Harvey, C.R. and Rajgopal, S. (2013) Earnings quality: Evidence from the field. *Journal of Accounting and Economics* 56 1–33.
Harris, J.D. and Bromiley, P. (2007) Incentives to cheat: The influence of executive compensation and firm performance on financial misrepresentation. *Organization Science* 18(3) 350–367.

The first example is a textbook source for the citation in Box 7.3. The second and third are journal article sources for the citations in Box 7.1. Note that these have been compiled into a **single alphabetical list**, regardless of the type of source – as you must do for the all the references in your final list.

If you also compare these with the different sources from Box 7.4 – a company website and an official report – you can see that every type of source requires somewhat different information. These illustrate the variations in detail for referencing different types of sources, and it is unlikely that you will be able to remember all of these.

You therefore need to **check your university's detailed guide** for all these sources. Each time, check the relevant example in the guide and copy across the specific details of your source into that format in your reference list. Do this each time you bring in a citation so that you do not lose track of any sources.

References or bibliography?

All *references* must be cited at least once in your assignment. If you include sources at the end that you do not use directly with a citation, these constitute a *bibliography*. This shows a list of texts that you have read, that have provided ideas to inform your understanding of the topic, and yet you have not included those ideas in your essay.

But why spend time studying ideas that you will not actually use? You have limited time for your reading and limited word count for your writing. For these pragmatic reasons, the reading that you do for that assignment needs to contribute directly to your essay argument. These sources then need citations and a corresponding reference in your list at the end of the assignment.

It is therefore strongly recommended that you only show a list of references for your assignment, and not a bibliography. However, it is possible that your tutor may still like to see a bibliography, and this is a simple question to ask them to ensure that you are meeting their expectations.

Summary: how to format citations and references

- **A citation is a pointer in the text of your work,** saying that you are using someone else's ideas or data. The formatting for these is quite simple. After reading this chapter, you should know how to cite your sources and be able to create these easily in your text.
- **The reference gives the full details of where the information came from.** This sits in the reference list at the end of your work. As the formatting of these is more complicated, this chapter does not show you how to do that comprehensively. Instead, you need to methodically follow your own university referencing guidance for the correct formatting in your assignments.

When to provide citations

The previous section has explained in detail *how* to cite and reference your research sources. The issue that needs more thinking about is *when* to reference. Take a look at an extract of student writing below, which is from an Operations Management assignment:

Box 7.6   Multiple citations in management essay paragraphs

Business Process Re-engineering (BPR) has become a popular concept among business management and information systems (Vakola et al. 2000). The basic concept of BPR is to make changes to the existing business with the intent to improve business performance dramatically in a short time (Bertolini et al. 2011). BPR focusses on introducing creative and innovative ideas to model the work (Choi and Chan 1997), but multiple studies showed that on average only 30 per cent of BPR implementation turned out to be successful (Revenaugh 1994). For example, Infosys Technologies failed in its human resource process re-engineering efforts – 'IRACE' – and lost thousands of its valuable employees (IRACE 2010). However, King's College Hospital's BPR efforts not only improved the hospital's performance but also generated a profit of £1 million (Patwardhan and Patwardhan 2007). These case studies pose the question as to whether BPR is applicable in all organisations. Is it a universally helpful theory in every situation?

The business tutor marking this essay regarded this paragraph as an example of good academic writing, *especially commending the amount of research evidenced by the number of relevant citations shown.* Students can sometimes be surprised to see so many citations within model paragraphs like this. They may think this breaks up the fluency of the writing and resorts to an over-reliance on others' ideas rather than their own.

Yet the tutor graded the full essay at over 70 per cent. **Feedback commended the use of multiple sources** to present the purpose and value of BPR and especially affirmed the integration of two empirical research studies to show the opposing experiences of BPR implementation. This is just one example of the generally applicable principle that tutors are looking for *the majority of your academic writing to be based on other authors' research.* This means that most paragraphs in many of your management assignments should contain multiple citations to those external sources.

Test your understanding of this principle in the following exercise, which shows an extract from a case study assignment in the module 'Managing People'. A case study presents a business situation and requires you to analyse that with reference to theoretical ideas from other authors. You are likely to come across this type of assignment in various subjects during your management degree.

ACTIVITY 7.1

Citing ideas from other authors

The student's assignment extract below should include a number of citations to external sources of theoretical ideas used to analyse the case. These have been removed, and **your task is to tick all the sentences that you believe require a citation** where the student would have brought in those other sources, i.e. NOT from the case study:

   Initially, Manager A displayed several positive personality traits. However, it became apparent that this style of leadership was not effective across the business. During highly stressful situations, the charismatic style slipped and a more narcissistic personality appeared. It is suggested that this personality 'is typically described in relation to charismatic leadership'.
   Narcissistic individuals have overrated views of themselves, and this includes their self-evaluation of their work capabilities. This became clear as the business performance dropped, evidenced by one of the worst internal financial audits in the company's history. Throughout this period, Manager A continued to rate himself highly on the criterion of personal task performance. As a result of such behaviour, the followers of Manager A questioned his capability. That response seems to be supported by the notion that narcissism is positively related to managers' self-evaluations, yet is negatively related to their subordinates' feedback on the managers' leadership capabilities. During many discussions at the time, there was an air of denial from Manager A of the issues that the company faced. Such a refusal to acknowledge personal shortcomings is characteristic of a narcissistic personality.

Check the Activity Answers to see where the student actually used citations.

Summary: when to provide citations

1 To inform the reader of sources of tables, photos, statistics or diagrams presented in your assignment.
2 When describing a theory, model or practice associated with a particular writer.
3 When giving emphasis to a particular idea that has found a measure of agreement and support among commentators.
4 To inform the reader of sources of direct quotations or definitions in your essay.
5 When paraphrasing another person's idea or definition that you feel is particularly significant or likely to be a subject of debate.

Avoiding plagiarism

If you follow all the referencing guidelines above, you will not fall into the plagiarism trap. As well as satisfying the university's regulations, accurate referencing also meets your tutor's academic expectations, and therefore achieves higher grades for your assignments. That is why this chapter has concentrated so far on the positive value of referencing, rather than the 'dark side' of plagiarism. However, for the sake of absolute clarity, Box 7.7 lists the ways that you could fall into the plagiarism trap, perhaps even inadvertently.

Box 7.7   The main causes of plagiarism and poor academic practice that you must avoid

You have committed plagiarism if you:

- Pay another person to produce your assignment, whether that is a friend or an online 'essay mill'. This is the most serious offence, and you would be punished severely by the university.
- Copy another student's work and submit that as your own. Again, the intent here is to deceive, which would result in major penalties, potentially even expulsion from the university.
- Allow another student access to your work, which they copy and submit. You may well be deemed by the university to be as guilty as the offender, unless you can prove that they submitted that copy without your knowledge.
- Copy statements exactly from a source without showing those are direct quotes, i.e. without 'speech marks', and do not give a citation.
- Summarise or paraphrase ideas from a source into your essay without citing the author.

Poor academic practice (a lesser, but still significant offence) occurs if you:

- Copy statements exactly from a source without showing these are direct quotes – even if you give a citation.
- Import ideas from a source, only paraphrasing these slightly – even if you give a citation. See Chapter 8 for guidance on paraphrasing.

Some further, cautionary points are included in Activity 7.2 to check your understanding of the potential risks of plagiarism or poor academic practice, and how to avoid those.

ACTIVITY 7.2

Avoiding plagiarism

Tick the appropriate column, indicating whether a reference is needed or not:

SITUATION	REFERENCE?	
	YES	NO
1. When quoting someone directly from a website.		
2. When using statistics or other data that are freely available from an encyclopedia or reference book.		
3. When summarising the cause of past events, where there is agreement by most commentators on cause and effect.		
4. When paraphrasing a definition found on a website and when no writer, editor or author's name is shown.		
5. When summarising the ideas of a particular author, but which have been paraphrased by another person; for example, when author A paraphrases what author B has said.		
6. When summarising, in the conclusion, the themes that you discussed and referenced earlier in your assignment text.		
7. When including in your assignment photographs or graphics that are freely available on the Internet and where no named photographer or originator is shown.		
8. When paraphrasing an idea you have read that you feel makes an important contribution to the points made in your assignment.		
9. When summarising undisputed and commonplace facts about the world, past or present.		

Check your decisions in the Activity Answers.

These quiz answers show that every time you bring an idea, fact or figure from an external source, *you must cite it.* The only exceptions occur when ideas are established, common knowledge, although as that can be difficult to judge at times, the golden rule is: *If in doubt, cite it.*

Plagiarism is a serious breach of university regulations, and this will lead to major penalties in your programme assessments. Formal disciplinary committees examine significant cases of plagiarism, which can bring about loss of degree qualification or expulsion for those cases involving a deliberate intent to deceive. Even minor cases of poor academic practice will result in deducted or zero marks from module tutors. This latter problem commonly and inadvertently occurs for students who have not yet mastered the referencing principles explained in this chapter. *You must study these carefully in conjunction with your own faculty's localised guidance for good academic practice.*

Checking for plagiarism

Your university will use some form of plagiarism detection software to check the originality of your written coursework. The most common version is Turnitin, and you may well be required to submit your assignments via this system electronically. Turnitin automatically checks your writing against its database and other websites to generate a report outlining how much of your work matches with all such Internet sources. This is represented as a percentage in the similarity index of the report.

Your faculty may allow or even require you to submit a draft of your assignment *before* your formal deadline for the express purpose of obtaining a Turnitin report, which provides helpful academic quality assurance, and is therefore to your advantage. This procedure is set up to enable students to check for instances of plagiarism or poor academic practice so that you can summarise, paraphrase and reference your research accordingly. A lower similarity index will also then be produced in your final submission report.

To help you start learning how to interpret Turnitin reports accurately, two extracts are shown below from business students' reports.

Turnitin originality reports

What does a Turnitin report show?

The top section of the report shows the total *similarity index, i.e. the percentage of the essay that matches texts found by Turnitin on the Internet*. However, in itself, this is not the decisive factor for a tutor identifying a definite problem of plagiarism or poor academic practice. This overall figure will include some **legitimately matched texts** such as your list of references, figures, models and other data that may need to be shown as they are in the original source. That is why the report requires more detailed evaluation.

The next section of a report provides a **full list of sources** from which Turnitin has matched sections of your text. Each of these is normally shown in a different colour, but these are depicted in bold in the examples below.

The most important section of a Turnitin report, though, is the **copy of the full essay, with all the matched sections indicated in boxes** separated out from the student's own words. Each box is 'coded' by its colour and relevant number in the list of sources. Again, the book example here shows all of these in bold. The student's own words, i.e. those that have not been detected by Turnitin anywhere on the Internet, are shown as continuous text outside the boxes and in normal type.

This all means that you (and the tutor) can immediately see at a glance how much of the essay you have copied directly from other sources and how much you have summarised and paraphrased into your own words.

Sample Report 1

Similarity Index

50%

Sources

For the purpose of this book example, only those sources relating to the sample paragraph of students' writing shown below are included here:

31.	< 1% match (student papers from 06 May 2014)
	Submitted to Manchester Metropolitan University
84.	< 1% match (student papers from 17 Apr 2012)
	Submitted to University of Bristol
103.	< 1% match (Internet from 15 Feb 2014)
	http://wat2146.ucr.edu/papers/02a.pdf
121.	< 1% match (Internet from 26 Sep 2014)
	http://www.nssa.us/journals/pdf/NSS_Journal_41_1.pdf
125.	< 1% match (student papers from 16 Feb 2013)
	Submitted to Sim University

Extract from full essay reproduced in the Turnitin report

(Matched text shown in bold)

The more the extrinsic and intrinsic rewards associated with a particular

> 121 **identity, the higher** *that* **identity in the** *prominence* **hierarchy; the**

> 103 **more prominent a role identity, the more likely it will be** *invoked* **in a situation**

(Burke and Stets, 2009). Social self-categorization theory (SCT) (Turner, 1987) also makes a great contribution to identity research. Turner and his colleagues regard self-categorization and depersonalization as cognitive processes and ensure

> 84 **that cognition is always shaped by the social context in which it takes place (Turner et al., 1994).**

SCT proposes that different levels

> 125 **of self-categorization** *distinguish* **personal and social identity and**

gives a clear conception to

> **31 *personal identity*,** *which* **refers to self-categories that define the individual as a unique person in terms of his or her individual differences from other (in-group) persons.**

How would a tutor interpret Report 1?

The tutor will be alarmed by this report. The pattern of 'copying and pasting' complete phrases and sentences illustrated in this one paragraph is actually repeated throughout the essay. So most paragraphs contained boxes of matched text like those shown above. This is what mostly accounts for the 50 per cent similarity percentage to original source texts that Turnitin has found on the Internet.

Referring back to the list shown in Box 7.7, there are actually examples of both types of academic regulations breach in the above extract:

- *Poor academic practice*

The first three sentences will be categorised as *poor academic practice* because they have a continuous series of words quoted directly from the original sources, *even though the authors are cited*.

In the first two boxes, only one or two words have been changed, and the third box is entirely verbatim. Although these are interspersed with a couple of short sections of the student's own writing, the amounts of frequently copied text show that the student has been copying too much from the original source, rather than paraphrasing and summarising (see Chapter 8).

These repeated examples of using direct quotes, rather than the student's own interpretation of their meaning, will result in the tutor deducting significant amounts of marks for poor academic practice.

- *Plagiarism*

Even worse though, the next sentence is copied almost entirely from other sources *and without any citations*. The latter point means that this section of the essay text will constitute plagiarism. Without citations, the student is in effect passing this off as their own work.

When this problem of direct, unattributed quotes is repeated a number of times throughout an essay, the tutor will have no choice but to report the student to the university for plagiarism, which is likely to result in severe penalties as noted above.

Overall, the frequent recurrence of long chunks of matched text, including several without citations, resulted in the tutor referring this assignment to the university academic affairs committee for investigation. This led to a zero mark and formal warning for the student, who had to then undertake a plagiarism awareness course with the library before being able to submit any further assignments.

Sample Report 2

Similarity Index
15%

Sources
For the purpose of this book example, only those sources relating to the sample paragraph of students' writing shown below are included here:

1. Submitted to University of Bradford Student paper	2%
18. ar.scribd.com	1%
20. Submitted to London School of Economics and Political Science Student paper	1%
22. fr.scribd.com	1%
23. en.wikipedia.org Internet source	1%

Extract from full essay reproduced in the Turnitin report

*Huawei, established in 1987, is the biggest Chinese private enterprise in 2016. This company focused on manufacturing telecommunication equipment and has become the biggest global company since 2012 (Economist, 2012). They have also expanded by providing smart phones and just [20] **beat Apple to become the second largest smartphone** manufacturer in the world (Guardian, 2018). They also provide [23] **operational and consulting services and equipment to enterprises** globally. Huawei has over 170, 000. They have expanded their service to over 170 countries and covers one third of the global population. The net profit for Huawei was US$7.3 billion in 2017 (Huawei, 2017).*

Competitive positioning

*If an organization finds a strategy which they can create value from, and they do apply it, strategic competitiveness is obtained (Hitt et al., 2016). Porter (1980) pointed out that there are [1] **three generic strategies of successful companies** which **are focus, differentiation and cost leadership. This model can be used to** analyse Huawei. Huawei is a typical example that combines different strategies together in a harmonious way.*

[22]	PRESENT PRODUCT	NEW PRODUCT
PRESENT MARKET	*Market penetration* *1. Continue to increase the market share in the global view.* *2. Acquire more customers.*	*Product development* *1. Use business reputation for the product advertisement.* *2. Use its competitive advantage for high-tech product.*
NEW MARKET	*Market development* *1. Continue to expand in other countries by setting up more centres.* *2. Increase its brand loyalty in China.*	*Diversification* *1. Other fields in electronic devices.* *2. Vertical integration.*

Corporate level

[18] Corporate level strategy is an action taken to gain a competitive advantage through choosing the market and industries. The Boston Matrix is used in this part to analyse Huawei. In the whole industry for Huawei, the smart phone market is seen as a question mark. The market share, as shown, is not very high compared to other mature companies like Samsung, but the trend is growing and Huawei is developing a higher market share. Star product can be seen as the operator network. Huawei has its own technique and is a world leadership firm in this field. It has generated three times as much revenue as Ericsson did in 2016.

How would a tutor interpret Report 2?

The tutor was not concerned by this report. The paragraphs reproduced above were virtually the only ones in the full essay in which matched text appeared. So most paragraphs contained only the student's own wording.

You can also see that even the matched text above constituted only a minority of the full paragraph in each case. The tutor will immediately recognise that the student has worked hard at summarising and paraphrasing his research, rather than reproducing large chunks of sourced material. This Strategic Management assignment was awarded a mark of 67 per cent.

In more detail, the tutor is likely to make the following observations:

Paragraph

1 This provides **descriptive facts** about the company. It is inevitable that some of this will have appeared in that form somewhere on the Internet. Providing this has not been reproduced in full, the tutor will allow these kinds of brief, matched statements for the sake of accurate reporting.
2 The section of matched text refers to an **established theory** from Porter, so again some direct reproduction of the 'technical' terminology from that theory will be expected by the tutor. It could be argued that the names of the three strategies should be in 'speech marks', but as these are clearly the main dimensions of a cited theory, the tutor is unlikely to be concerned.

    The table is a good example of where category titles in most kinds of **figures** may well be picked up by Turnitin. The important issue for the tutor is that the student has applied the theoretical framework to the specific company. To be strictly correct, the student should indicate this with a citation beneath the table as 'Adapted from …' followed by the source name and date.
3 Again, this shows only a small proportion of matched text within the paragraph. This first sentence is a **definition** – one of the few instances in which a direct quote would be appropriate. However, that would then need to be shown in speech marks and given a citation. If this report had been generated by Turnitin from the student submitting an advance draft, they could then correct that direct quote error and citation omission before final submission.

Overall, this report shows that a similarity index rating of 15 per cent *or even higher* is not necessarily cause for alarm. There can be legitimate reasons for matched text in Turnitin reports, which require further interpretation as discussed in the FAQs below.

Box 7.8   Turnitin FAQs

Is there a definite threshold percentage for the similarity index that I must not exceed, e.g. 20 per cent?

No, it is not as simple as that. The similarity index is only a starting point for further evaluation of the report. Turnitin will include some legitimate sources as direct matches, e.g. your reference list, which could account for around 10 per cent similarity. Your assignment may include several figures, charts or graphs, which needed to be reproduced directly.

Isn't it a good thing to include plenty of quotes cited directly from my research sources so that I can show I'm reproducing other authors' work accurately?

No, this will result in the tutors marking you down for poor academic practice. Any student can copy and paste direct quotes without necessarily understanding what they mean for their assignment question. Tutors are looking for your interpretation of the subject material, through summarising and paraphrasing others' ideas (see Chapter 8).

The list of sources in the Turnitin report doesn't show the same ones I used for my research. Surely, it's made a mistake?

No, the information from the sources you used may appear in a number of different places on the Internet, e.g. other students' essays based on those same sources. Turnitin lists the sources where it first detects matches.

The important point here is that most of your essay needs to be in your own words. These must be derived from you thinking carefully about how other authors' data and ideas relate to your essay topic, and not by simply importing chunks of text from those sources.

Chapter summary

- **Referencing is integral to academic writing** and essential for passing any module assignment.
- **You must obtain your university's guide** to the appropriate referencing system for your subject(s), and follow this meticulously.
- Each system has two parts – citations within your text, and a reference list at the end.
- *Every time* you bring in any data, information or ideas from an external source of your research, *cite it.* This is a win/win scenario – **you will gain marks** for each relevant source that you cite as evidence of your wider reading, *and* you avoid marks being deducted for plagiarism. *If in doubt, cite it.*
- **Avoid using direct quotes,** even when these are cited and shown correctly in 'speech marks'. More than occasional use of these will still result in marks being deducted for poor academic practice. **The tutors want to see your interpretation of the research.**

- Many management subjects require extensive referencing to academic texts such as journal articles. Tutors expect **multiple source citations within most paragraphs**.
- Certain subjects such as Accounting may require fewer references. These are likely to be **factually based sources** such as financial reports.
- It is therefore important to gain as much guidance as possible from each subject tutor as to their recommended sources for your research.
- All students will encounter some instances where they are unsure about referencing. This could be simply how to cite an unusual source right through to interpreting a full Turnitin report with a worryingly high similarity index. If in doubt, always **seek help from appropriate university or faculty services, notably librarians or academic skills advisors.**

Activity Answers

Activity 7.1: Citing ideas from other authors

The student's actual assignment extract included citations at the points below. These show where the student has brought in others' theoretical ideas to justify their analysis of the case study. The citations clearly differentiate these externally sourced ideas from the issues the student has drawn directly from the case study itself:

*Initially, Manager A displayed several positive personality traits. However, it became apparent that this style of leadership was not effective across the business. During highly stressful situations, the charismatic style slipped and a more narcissistic personality appeared. **Khoo and Birch (2008: 35)** suggest that this personality 'is typically described in relation to charismatic leadership'.*

* **Robins and Paulhaus (2001)** suggest that narcissistic individuals have overrated views of themselves, and that this includes their self-evaluation of their work capabilities. This became clear, as the business performance dropped, evidenced by one of the worst internal financial audits in the company's history. Throughout this period, Manager A continued to rate himself highly on the criterion of personal task performance. As a result of such behaviour, the followers of Manager A questioned his capability. That response seems to be supported by **Judge et al. (2006)**, who point out that narcissism is positively related to managers' self-evaluations, yet is negatively related to their subordinates' feedback on the managers' leadership capabilities. During many discussions at the time, there was an air of denial from Manager A of the issues that the company faced. **Watson and Clark (1984)** confirm that such refusal to acknowledge personal shortcomings is characteristic of a narcissistic personality.*

Activity 7.2: Avoiding plagiarism

SITUATION	REFERENCE?	
	YES	NO
1. When quoting someone directly from a website. *Comment: The sources of all quotations should be referenced.*	✓	
2. When using statistics or other data that is freely available from an encyclopedia or reference book. *Comment: The sources of statistics or other data that you use in assignments should always be referenced.*	✓	
3. When summarising the cause of past events, where there is agreement by most commentators on cause and effect. *Comment: This can be regarded as common knowledge, which does not need to be referenced. However, the sources for any contested or contentious discussion of the same events would need to be referenced.*		✓
4. When paraphrasing a definition found on a website and when no writer, editor or author's name is shown. *Comment: If no named writer, author or editor is shown, you should cite and reference the name of the website, e.g. BMW (2015).*	✓	
5. When summarising the ideas of a particular author, but which have been paraphrased by another person; for example, when author A paraphrases what author B has said. *Comment: You always need to acknowledge your sources, even if they are secondary ones. However, it is advisable, whenever possible, to consult the main (primary) sources for yourself and to reference these.*	✓	
6. When summarising, in your conclusion, the themes that you discussed and referenced earlier in your assignment text. *Comment: New ideas should not appear in a conclusion. All sources should therefore have already been cited in the body of the essay.*		✓
7. When including in your assignment photographs or graphics that are freely available on the Internet and where no named photographer or originator is shown. *Comment: The photographs or graphics are the result of work by another person. In this situation, you should cite and reference the name of the website that contains the illustrations.*	✓	
8. When paraphrasing an idea you have read that you feel makes an important contribution to the points made in your assignment *Comment: This is an important reason for referencing, as it acknowledges the relevance of the source to the development of your argument.*	✓	
9. When summarising undisputed and commonplace facts about the world, past or present. *Comment: General public awareness of undisputed facts can also be treated as common knowledge (see also 3, above).*		✓

Critically Analytical Writing

What is critical analysis anyway?

Tutors' feedback on low-grade assignments usually includes comments such as: *'Not enough analysis'; 'Too descriptive'; 'Needs more depth'*. One way or another, such comments refer to a *lack of critical reading and writing*. Both of these interdependent processes of assignment production require an analytical approach, and this often represents the greatest and most challenging 'step up' in learning for many students making the transition to higher education.

So what do management tutors actually mean by critical analysis?

Pause for Thought

Which of the following do you think might best describe 'critical analysis' as required in business and management assignments?

(You can tick more than one box):

- ☐ A. Questioning what you read and hear.
- ☐ B. Summarising others' ideas.
- ☐ C. Paraphrasing others' ideas (in your own words).
- ☐ D. Comparing and contrasting others' ideas.
- ☐ E. Challenging others' views on a topic.
- ☐ F. Expressing your own opinion.
- ☐ G. Stating what a theory proposes.
- ☐ H. Exploring the debate around a topic.
- ☐ I. Developing strategic recommendations.
- ☐ J. Offering solutions for business problems.
- ☐ K. Applying theoretical ideas to business situations.
- ☐ L. Showing what happened in a business situation.

Check your thoughts against the suggestions in the Activity Answers.

The following forms of critical analysis are vital for high-grade academic writing:

✓ Questioning what you read and hear

A questioning attitude is fundamental to how you approach all of your academic reading and writing. In other words, you should not accept 'at face value' anything that you read and hear in your academic studies. When you are reading textbooks, and even listening to lectures, your tutors will expect you to continuously **evaluate** the arguments that are being presented.

'Critical thinking is a habit of mind characterized by the comprehensive exploration of issues, ideas, artifacts, and events before accepting or formulating an opinion or conclusion.' (Association of American Colleges and Universities 2016)

However, this 'explorer mindset' may be quite unfamiliar to you. Perhaps the teachers in your previous educational culture emphasised unquestioning belief in a single textbook or series of classes on a subject. So how can you begin to evaluate others' ideas more open-mindedly?

✓ **Summarising and paraphrasing others' ideas**

Module tutors introduce you to academic concepts, otherwise known as theories, principles, models or frameworks. You discover these ideas initially through their lectures, but tutors expect you to then conduct further, independent research, especially in textbooks and academic journals (see Chapters 4 and 5) to explore different authors' perspectives on the same topic.

The first steps of critically analysing these theoretical views involve you in *active reading.* You need to carefully study each relevant idea in the source text. Keep re-reading this until you really understand its meaning and relation to your assignment topic. Only then can you write this into your essay *from your own understanding,* i.e. without taking the language directly from the original. You can always then go back to the original source to double-check that you have faithfully captured the main idea(s).

This means you will be able to simplify the author's concepts and re-express these in ways that make sense for you (*summarising and paraphrasing*). The tutor who marks your final assignment will be able to immediately recognise that you have understood the theoretical ideas well enough to represent these authentically in your own words.

✓ **Exploring the debate around a topic by comparing and contrasting different ideas**

Once you have summarised and paraphrased one author's views on a topic, you need to then relate those to ideas on the same topic from other texts. You simply adopt the same process as described in the previous section for each author in turn.

You will soon begin to recognise how their ideas are **supporting or countering** each other (*comparing and contrasting*). You are exploring how different authors are agreeing or disagreeing with one another in any subject area. This means that you can then build each paragraph of your writing by **integrating several views** around the same topic (*debating*).

Academic tutors look for your understanding of the complex debates that characterise the social sciences such as business and management. You do not have to reach definitive conclusions on one side of an argument or the other. You may do so, but that should only emerge out of considered discussion of the different views around a topic. It is your intelligent appreciation of the debate that will gain you a considerable proportion of your assignment marks.

Tutors want you to develop critical thinking skills that are based on a relatively **open-minded and curious attitude** towards a range of differing ideas around each of the topics you study. They hope that you come to value the exploration of different possibilities more than necessarily reaching the destination of a 'right' answer.

These analytical functions are required in *some* assignments:

✓   Challenging others' views

Students can easily assume that critical analysis requires them to *criticise* others' ideas. This often means that they try to argue against an academic theory through their own existing opinions, or what they might think of as 'common sense'. Some textbooks, and even tutors, may seem to reinforce this by advocating a need for students to seek out flaws or fallacies in others' academic research. However, if this has been published in a textbook or journal article, then you know it has involved careful research, which will then have been reviewed by other academic peers before publication.

You should not feel pressured into immediately challenging the arguments you find in relevant academic texts. The starting position in your own research should rather be one of respect as you **first seek to understand** one valuable idea that is relevant to your reading purpose ... and then another idea ... and then another ...

You can think of each of these ideas as one piece of a jigsaw puzzle, and no one piece can provide the whole picture, of course. As a relative novice in this subject area, you are gradually creating the picture by finding how the ideas from different texts do and do not fit together. You are not trying to find fault with any one section of the picture while you are assembling it; you are just finding out 'what goes where'. So it is with academic research – you do not need to instinctively criticise any particular author's view.

Instead, you can challenge any theoretical perspective you are reading by **referring to other researchers' related work to show contrasting ideas.** It is these other perspectives from academic sources such as textbooks and journal articles that provide all you need to develop the different sides of an argument. You relate all of these to your question focus, evaluating how they either support or counter each other's claims concerning that topic.

✓   Applying theoretical ideas to business situations

Your tutorial and assignment questions are likely to demand all the above stages of critical analysis. In addition, *some* of these will require you to further demonstrate your understanding of academic theory by relating this to a single case study or perhaps a series of real-life examples from the business world. In this respect, critical analysis is about the **relationship between theory and practice**, not just describing either of these alone.

As with all other elements of critical analysis, a *questioning approach* is required to apply theory to practice. Once you have identified the particular theory and business situation that you want to analyse, then you can ask yourself questions about how they relate to one another. These could include:

- Why is this theory important for this type of business case?
- How does it apply to the specific situation you are analysing?
- How does it offer reasons for what is happening there?
- Has this theory been developed out of research into similar business cases?
- In which other business situations has this theory been applied?
- How are those situations similar to your scenario?
- How could those other research findings help you better understand what is happening here?

But remember, **any theory is just one part of a bigger picture**. It may not entirely fit your case study, as it will address certain issues but perhaps not others. So, you can sometimes *use business practice to critically analyse the theory* by asking the following questions:

- What might be the limitations of the theory for this specific situation?
- How is this case different from others that this theory has been related to before:
  - ○ A different industry/business sector?
  - ○ Another cultural context (geographical, organisational)?
  - ○ A distinctive, or more complex, situation?

Some tutors *may* require these analytical aspects in their assignments:

? Recommending strategies or finding solutions

It is advisable to check with your tutor whether they would like you to reach some recommendations for an effective way forward in the business situation you are exploring in your essay. It may not be necessary to even arrive at such a definite position. Instead, in some theoretical discussion subjects, such as Human Resources Management (HRM), Business Ethics or even Operations Management, it can be sufficient for you to show your understanding of the debate around a topic. In other, more applied modules, such as Marketing Strategy or Management Accounting, the tutor may well be looking for specific recommendations based on your assignment analysis. In these two module examples, such recommendations could respectively take the form of a corporate marketing plan or a decision on whether to invest in a company.

Overall, then, this is a possible requirement, but highly dependent on the nature of the specific assignment. This is an easy question to ask the module leader to ensure you are taking the right approach.

The following elements do *not* constitute critical analysis in business and management assignments:

✗ Stating *what* is proposed by a theory or *what* has happened in a business situation

When you simply state *what* has happened, you only *describe* the theory or situation. This may be a necessary, early element of your essay, but as soon as possible, you need to move on to *analysis*. This means addressing *how and why* questions, i.e. *how* does a theoretical idea that you have been studying explain *why* that situation occurred and *how* might that be tackled differently according to that theoretical view.

✗ Expressing your own opinion

It can be frustrating for students that tutors direct them to read so many other authors' ideas, rather than encouraging the expression of their own, existing views. The question can easily arise – where is the student's voice in the essay?

> *It is only by reading, thinking about what you have read and then connecting this reading to your own experiences, that you will begin to find your own voice* (Neville 2007: 2).

You will find opportunities in your writing to bring in *your interpretations* of the debate that you have already presented. But, please note, tutors will expect to see these more personalised views emerging only as **explanations of what you have come to understand through reading a wide range of other authors' ideas.** In other words, they are looking for substantial academic evidence in support of any opinions that you express in your essays.

This point covers the majority of your modules on a business and management degree. The exception to this principle is for reflective writing in certain assignments, particularly personal development or employability modules. This alternative, subjective style of writing is explained in depth in Chapter 9.

We can translate the above principles of effective critical analysis into a practical model of academic writing, shown in Box 8.1.

Box 8.1   A four-step model of effective academic writing

1 **Summarising and paraphrasing**
   Concisely expressing your understanding of an author's research in your own words.

2 **Synthesis**
   a) Building support by integrating complementary ideas or factual data from other authors.
   b) Developing debate around that topic with contrasting ideas and information from different sources.

3 **Interpretation**
   Explaining your view of that debate in terms of your assignment question.

4 **Application**
   Relating the debated, theoretical ideas to actual business practice.

Step 1: summarising an author's idea, and paraphrasing that to show your understanding

This is a tricky skill that takes some practice to develop, yet it is fundamental to effective writing in the discursive style of most business and management assignments. Inadequate paraphrasing can sometimes be the cause of students' poor academic practice at university, perhaps incurring penalties in their assessments. It can be tempting to copy across many of the words and phrases directly from the source – or simply change a few words here and there – because you believe it is not possible to express these ideas 'any better' than the original, expert author. That section of text is likely to still then show up in the report from the university plagiarism software with a high level of similarity to the original.

As it is imperative for you to become adept at summarising and paraphrasing, these skills are explored here in detail.

In the example below, the first text is taken from page 95 of the book: Thomas, A.B. (2003) *Controversies in Management* (2nd edition). London: Routledge. The second text has summarised and paraphrased the main points of the original one.

While many social scientists will continue to generate generalizations about behaviour and organizations, these will seldom if ever be so specific to the particular contexts of practice that they can be applied as if they are scientific laws.

Management today ... will always be based on improvisation. By that I do not mean simply making it up as we go along, but, rather, the activity of fitting together all the various sources of knowledge that can inform practice in fruitful and productive ways.

What distinguishes the thinking manager from the 'practical man' is not that the former applies the fruits of social science while the latter relies on more or less intelligent forms of guesswork. Both are engaged in improvisation. But the thinking manager incorporates the concepts, findings methods and attitudes of the social sciences into the process of improvisation giving them their rightful place among other sources of insight and knowledge.

(152 words)

Here is one way that this could be summarised into a more concise version that still retains the key points. You can see from the underlined vocabulary how few keywords needed to be reproduced exactly, with the rest having been paraphrased:

It seems there are no universal <u>laws</u> or rules which guide <u>organisational behaviour</u>. However, Thomas (2003: 95) suggests that '<u>practical' managers</u> can still become more '<u>thinking</u>' in their approach by integrating the learning gained from <u>the social sciences</u> into improving their practice.

(46 words)

Summary: principles of summarising and paraphrasing

- You produce a more concise version of the original text *without* losing the main points of that. In this example, the *summarising* process has reduced the word count to less than one-third of the original.
- You must fully grasp the main points so that you can explain these in your own words. *You can then express that understanding from your mind*, not directly from the original text.
- Skim read the original text *after* you have summarised and paraphrased the main idea(s) from your own understanding. You can check that your new version does faithfully represent the ideas of the original text.
- This intelligent *paraphrasing* only needs to retain absolutely necessary vocabulary from the original. You connect these using new phraseology that emerges from your own understanding of that.
- These four steps ensure the tutor immediately recognises that you do understand the concepts you are representing.

You can now practise summarising and paraphrasing in Activity 8.1 below. This is the first of a set of activities in this chapter that uses an example of the following coursework assignment title from a module, 'Cross-Cultural Management':

Analyse the cross-cultural factors affecting the negotiations for a new international joint venture with a domestic partner which is culturally distant from the home base of the multinational company (MNC).

ACTIVITY 8.1

Summarising and paraphrasing practice

Take your time to carefully read the selected extract below from a journal article by Tihanyi et al. (2005). Ensure that you really understand how this relates to the above assignment question. Note, for example, that this title includes the concept of 'cultural distance' – so the extract is a useful source for you to *show the tutor your understanding* of one of the key terms in the assignment question.

> *Cross-border business transactions involve interaction with different societal value systems. Adapting to local cultural values that are transmitted through nations' political economy, education, religion, and language may create an additional burden for multinational enterprises (MNEs) operating in different countries (Schwartz 1999). The study of principal differences in national cultures between the home country of MNEs and their countries of operation, that is, cultural distance, has gained a broad interest in international business research.*

(110 words)

Citation: (Tihanyi et al. 2005: 270)

Once you have a clear sense of what this text has to say about the idea of cultural distance, summarise that into your own words below. Aim for a word count of no more than half the original.

Check your summary against the suggested example in the Activity Answers at the end of this chapter.

Step 2a: synthesising different authors' ideas to present an argument and build support for that

> *'Synthesis: The process of combining ... ideas into a complex whole.'*
>
> (Collins English Dictionary 2018)

Tutors expect to find multiple citations within most paragraphs of your assignments. In other words, they want to see evidence of wide reading throughout your coursework. This requires you to bring together a number of different authors' views around the single topic of each paragraph. But this should not just be some kind of 'long-hand list' of their ideas. Actually, tutors expect you to skilfully synthesise these views in a meaningful way.

Pause for Thought

Why do you think tutors are so insistent on this *synthesis of different views* in students' academic writing? Write your thoughts in the space below:

Here are a few reasons why tutors place such importance on the integration of different authors' views on each topic:

A. To identify the extent of the research you have undertaken, i.e. the *quantity* of texts that you have read.
B. To establish the academic credibility of sources that you have researched, i.e. the *quality* of the texts that you have read.
C. To assess your capability to represent a variety of ideas that relate directly to the question.
D. To see your understanding of how different authors' views agree or disagree with one another.

Any of the above factors may be taken into account when tutors assign marks. However, they are especially interested in how well you can represent different views on the question topic (C). This helps them to see your understanding of the debate around this topic, i.e. *how and why* different authors agree or disagree (D). As the dictionary definition suggests, this *synthesis* has the potential to create a picture that reflects the complexity of debate around any contemporary management idea.

The first side of this story is to show the various sources of *support* for any particular idea. Box 8.2 shows an example of this in an early paragraph from an essay written by Sebastian on the above question on cross-cultural negotiation:

Box 8.2 Building academic support for an idea

Negotiation was often referred to as a three-step process in academic literature. It was clustered into pre-negotiation, face-to-face negotiation and post-negotiation (Graham, 1987; Brouthers and Bamossy 1997; Peterson and Lucas 2001). Cavusgil et al. (2013) revised the process in five more detailed steps: Offer, informal meetings, strategy formulation, face-to-face negotiation and implementation. All these stages require planning and preparation to succeed, and the academic literature in this field provides useful assistance in this respect (Kim et al. 2009; Cavusgil et al. 2013).

This extract is an example of good practice in academic writing because it achieves the following:

- Briefly describes a prevailing view in the literature on this topic over a significant period of time.
- Quickly moves on to qualify that view with more up-to-date research over the past decade or so.
- In one quite short paragraph, Sebastian has therefore *summarised* a breadth of research covering 25 years that captures the suggested theoretical stages of cross-cultural negotiation.
- Shows *some variation in those ideas* concerning the actual number of stages, *but builds a general case* for a sequential model of cross-cultural negotiation:

Sebastian seems to have established quite a consistent support across several different academic texts for a model of successful negotiation based on a number of successive stages. This illustrates the process of *synthesising* complementary ideas from several different authors.

However, he wanted to develop further critical analysis by continuing through the Four-Step Model to *debate,* which is illustrated in the next section.

Step 2b: developing debate to present different sides of the argument

Sebastian knew that he still needed the 'other half of the story'. He had to explore the relevant literature to find any perspectives that may *argue against* the above idea of a *universal theory* for cross-cultural negotiation. He wanted to find other views that challenged the above proposition of a standardised framework of sequential stages for negotiating business deals anywhere in the world.

He found several texts that presented such counter-arguments, and short extracts from three of these are shown in Activity 8.2. This provides an opportunity for you to practice the same process as Sebastian to summarise and synthesise these counter-arguments into a single paragraph:

ACTIVITY 8.2

Synthesising practice

Consider the following texts that Sebastian found as potential sources for his counter-argument. He realised that, in different ways, they are all making the same point. So read through the texts now, looking for **a single theme** that connects these three extracts.

Extract 1:

The cultural context of both sides of the negotiations also impacted on the exchanges. The Western European partners' negotiators wanted to work in small groups with different problems, while the Soviets worked in a more hierarchical way, which meant that all problems had to be approved by officials in the Kremlin.

Citation: Munns et al. (2000)

Extract 2:

A growing body of research has emerged over the past decade looking at cross-cultural differences in negotiation style (Fisher 1980; Tung 1984). These studies conclude that people of different cultures use significantly different negotiation approaches. These different approaches include communication styles used, persuasion strategies employed, and protocols followed.

Citation: Tse et al. (1994)

Extract 3:

In international business, we step into cultural environments characterized by unfamiliar languages and unique value systems, beliefs, behaviours, and norms. These differences influence all dimensions of international business. Often, they get in the way of straightforward communication …

Citation: Cavusgil et al. (2012)

1 What do you think is the common, single theme running through these three extracts?

2 Paraphrase and integrate the key, *connected* ideas from these extracts into a few sentences of your own writing. Remember that you are summarising a counter-argument to the claim that a generic framework can be applied in all cross-cultural negotiations.

Compare your paragraph with the example shown in the Activity Answers.

This activity demonstrates an important element of critical academic writing by highlighting potential exceptions to a generalised theory. The student gathered other authors' ideas to explain that there are likely to be cultural variations to universal claims in any management research. As noted in the example answer, this might be due to national, organisational or personal cultural influences. In your own essays, whilst you should show your understanding of a selected theory and its potential relevance, you should also consider its potential limitations.

Step 3: interpretation – explaining your own view of the debate that you have already presented (student voice)

As soon as you begin reading others' views, you inevitably start forming your own interpretations of their meaning. It is from this personal assimilation of others' ideas that *your own voice* emerges in your essay writing. This is not simply based on your previously held opinions but actually from a formalised, yet independent learning process. As an objective approach to interpretation is fundamental to business and management assignment writing, this process of developing the student voice is reiterated here in Box 8.3. You may remember this was first shown in Chapter 6 as an essential element of academic writing development.

Box 8.3   Developing your voice in an assignment

1 Targeted selection of certain ideas or other data that *you* have deemed important for your reading purpose.
2 *Your* interpretation of the meaning of this information for that reading purpose.
3 Summarising those ideas *in your own words*.
4 *Your* skilful integration of these with other authors' ideas on the same topic.

Written assignments require the extensive application of all the above stages. Your final essay directly reflects your personal journey through an academic landscape determined by your individual perception of that subject. And the more ideas you take from a growing number of texts, the more individualised your assignment will become. **Your own voice emerges distinctively from the unique way that you assimilate your research findings.** By the time you reach the end of that process, you will be submitting an essay that is absolutely distinct from that of any other student.

Your university tutors' assessments are based on how clearly you have shown your understanding of theories, models, concepts and other data from a variety of sources. Whilst the tutors are expecting most of those assignments to be based on extensive academic research, the *way that you have assimilated those views* is uniquely your own.

Box 8.4 shows an example of how Sebastian presented his informed position on the contrasting arguments in his essay. This indicates his critical assessment of the usefulness of academic theory in guiding cross-cultural negotiations.

Read this carefully, considering which side of the debate he seems to choose: Is he more convinced about the value of academic literature or practical experience for effective cross-cultural business negotiations?

Box 8.4   Summarising your argument and position on the question

In conclusion, academic theory that suggests a five-stage framework is found to be useful to prepare IJV negotiations with a culturally distant partner. This can provide a helpful overview of how the negotiation process might take place and gives insights into the necessary preparation.

However, caution is required because academic literature could be outdated and in some cases hardly realisable. Nowadays, in a global world, a clear distinction between cultures is becoming less likely. Business executives are more socially mobile, being educated or working abroad, thereby adopting some foreign cultural characteristics. A negotiation partner may well behave differently from academic prescriptions in cultural literature. Overall, it can be inferred that this cannot replace experience. Negotiators need personal expertise and/or local guidance to deal effectively with culturally distant partners.

Notes:

- Sebastian has only reached this stage of *interpretation* by the end of his essay. The majority of his writing has been based on analysing the findings of research from other authors. Academic tutors expect you to show this evidence of wide, relevant reading, rather than your opinions.
- His conclusion has captured the main themes of his preceding argument, i.e. a balance between both sides of the argument – theory and practice.
- However, Sebastian does indicate by the end of this final paragraph that he is more convinced by the arguments in favour of practical experience rather than academic research.
- He supports this position by reminding the reader of a key idea in his essay: Theoretical cultural differences are becoming less significant in an increasingly globalised business world.

Step 4: applying theory to business practice – illustrating your understanding with real-life examples

One way that you can interpret authors' theoretical ideas is by relating them to the business world. This section explores various ways that you can do that.

Pause for Thought

How do you think tutors expect you to apply theoretical ideas from your research to real business situations? Write your ideas in the space below:

Tutors will ask you to **apply your academic research to real-world examples** in plenty of your assignments. They expect you to do this in any or all of the following ways:

- **To explain why business situations occur in the way that they do.**
- **To compare the 'utility' (usefulness) of different theories for understanding a business case study.**
- **To recommend effective strategies for future business development.**

In any business and management assignment, the tutor is scrutinising how well you understand the implications of academic research for the corporate world. This highlights another major difference between low- and high-grade academic assessments:

- Lower-grade assignments will concentrate mainly on *describing what* a theory says and *what* is happening in a business situation.
- Higher-performing students use their essays to present *analysis* by *comparing and contrasting* different theoretical ideas and showing *how and why* they are relevant to real life or not.

These are all important aims of *applying management theory to practice*. Conversely, critical analysis can also involve looking at this process the other way around: Business practice may be used to *critique theoretical ideas* because, as shown throughout this chapter, no single theory can explain or predict every given situation in the real world. So a further purpose of critical analysis can be:

- **To use the specific, organisational situation to highlight the limitations of a generic theory.**

Summary: key principles of critical analysis in assignments

1   Establish **a clear purpose** to each reading and writing project, e.g. researching and discussing the relationship between two specified variables in an assignment question.
2   Develop **a basic understanding** of that topic by first reading materials from the relevant module lecture(s) and core textbook chapter.
3   Use that understanding to create an essay **'template' structure** with topic sub-headings.
4   As you go into further research, select only the most **relevant ideas and data** from these other sources (See Chapters 4 and 5).
5   Read those selected points carefully so that you gain a deep enough understanding to **summarise** them concisely but faithfully.
6   Once you fully understand an author's point, you can then **paraphrase** that straight into the relevant section of your essay template, i.e. without needing to make notes.
7   Search for other authors' ideas on the same topic. **Synthesise** in one or more paragraphs those that broadly agree with, or further develop, the first idea.
8   Gather **counter-arguments** or alternative views on the same topic from other authors. Synthesise these initially in a separate paragraph(s) to explore the current *debate*.
9   Find **real-life examples, facts and figures** that illustrate the theoretical ideas in practice. Use these to analyse why the theories may be important and how they explain what is happening in the business world.

10   You can edit the sequencing and combination of these paragraphs as much as you
     need to at a later stage.

This chapter now provides a high-grade exemplar of a student's essay that
objectively explores the different sides to a particular topic. This has been shortened
for easier reading and includes tutor annotations to illustrate each of the above stages
in critically analytical writing.

Sample essay

Why is successful repatriation problematical, and how can it best be achieved?

This essay addresses the issue of repatriation – how to make it successful. Generally,
most studies have focussed on how to train for successful expatriation; however, there
are only a few studies that have focussed on successful repatriation. The further
discussions will explain the need to address the issue of repatriation. A case study
analysis in the later part of the discussion will underline this need. A theoretical
framework is also presented to support the theme of this essay.

> Tutor Comment [TC1]: The essay is a critical piece of work from the beginning.
> The chosen topic questions the mainstream research and seeks to explore the
> gaps in our knowledge.

Need for the study of repatriation

Napier and Peterson (1991: 173) quote Dowling and Schuler (1990), defining
repatriation as, 'the process of return to the home country at completion of (an
international) assignment'. Lazarova and Cerdin (2007) explain that while globalization has increased the attention paid to an effective management of expatriate
employees, only recently has there been a focus on the global expertise that could be
accumulated by studies of successful repatriation. Hyder and Lovblad (2007) state
that it could be more difficult to readjust to the home country after the assignment
compared to original relocation in the host country. While the expatriation literature
discusses cultural shock, in the case of repatriation, there is a corresponding phenom-
enon called "reverse cultural shock" (Rodrigues 1996; Baruch and Altman 2002).

> TC2: The author of this essay did not identify the 'critical' topic by herself, but drew it
> from the reading of academic literature. This wider reading, going beyond basic
> textbooks and mainstream articles, is needed. Importantly, this integration of different
> ideas [Synthesis] makes a strong case for the study of repatriation.

Hyder and Lovblad (2007) present data from The Global Relocation Trends
2003/2004 Survey Report (GMAC 2004) depicting 13% of repatriates resigning
within a year after returning home and another 10% leaving in the subsequent year.
They also present the data of Baruch et al. (2002), whose analysis shows 50%

resignations within a few years of returning and data from Vermond (2001) who reports that 49% of repatriates leave companies within two years of repatriation. Solomon (2001) also emphasises one of the most important aspects of returning home as being the career management process. Hence there seems to be a growing need to examine this issue of repatriation.

> TC3: The author draws on the literature to provide practical evidence of why repatriation is an important issue. These examples support the arguments in the articles reviewed previously [Synthesis].

Repatriation: An organisational effort

Napier and Peterson (1991) propose that repatriation in an organisation is a three-stage process: the initial stage of expatriate selection and training for the assignment, the overseas assignment, and the expatriate re-entry into the home country [TC4]. Martin and Anthony (2006) find that the selection process is a major factor contributing to successful repatriation and retention. They give an example of Sun Microsystems, which reduced its 62% repatriate turnover to 13% through careful screening of expatriate candidates. Klaff (2002) supports this by mentioning that the repatriation process begins before the employees move to a foreign post. Organisations should be focussed on setting career expectations by defining assignment goals and clear specifications on how these goals would embed into the employee's long-term career plans [TC5]. This discussion shows that organisational efforts play an important role in successful repatriation and that it is crucial to begin the repatriation process at the very beginning of the expatriation [TC6].

> TC4: Here the author starts defining the concept of repatriation in more detail by referring to academic theory. Such detailed definitions are crucial for a critical understanding of any topic.
>
> TC5: In this section, the author identifies the most crucial component of the repatriation process ... A critical review of the literature is in part about identifying what is most important for your topic.
>
> TC6: Here the author draws a conclusion out of the above discussion, showing a particular understanding of the literature [Interpretation].

Repatriation: An individualistic effort

Another perspective on repatriation is the Protean Approach (O'Sullivan 2002) that focuses on the individual level of analysis. As mentioned above, organisations provide repatriates with more suitable post-return jobs (recognizing and rewarding their internationally developed competencies) and improved, formal post-return training (minimizing the reverse cultural shock for expatriates).

However, these approaches are basically top-down interventions consisting of a mix of information provision, financial perks and career planning, and the organisations, even after implementing these strategies, have high repatriate turnover rates. So O'Sullivan (2002: 602) points out a need to improve the transitions of repatriation by focussing on individual-level analysis:

'The protean approach reflects the presumption that career trajectories can, and often must, be actively influenced by an individual if the career is to advance to both the individuals and the organisation's satisfaction.'

TC7: Here the author cites a paper that provides a critique of the previously discussed theory. This shows that you do not have to rely on your own judgement to criticise academic theory – draw on other theories to do so.

Note that in this section and the previous one, the author identifies two directions in the theory – one pertaining to organisations and one pertaining to individuals. This shows a critical and analytical approach to theory, as opposed to a simple description of who wrote what.

Overall, both organisational and individual efforts are required to reduce the repatriation turnover. Future literature may develop new frameworks that include the nuances of both – reducing repatriation turnover and enabling repatriates to successfully further their careers.

TC8: A summary statement to indicate the most important conclusions from the above discussion [Interpretation].

Case study example: Process of repatriation during expatriation

Klaff (2002) gives an example of the repatriation process in AT&T – an American telecommunication giant. The first stage, called a 'safety net', is conducted before the overseas assignment. The employees and their families are counselled by a psychologist specially trained in repatriation issues. This professional guides the expatriate family on a spectrum of issues that might arise – for example, the problems with expatriate spouses finding jobs and children adapting to the new environment. Moreover, the expatriate and family are entitled to call up this professional at any time during the overseas assignment.

Throughout the assignment, AT&T offers a mentor programme which helps the expatriates to stay connected with their colleagues and home organisation developments. This includes home office visits periodically for meetings. About six months before the end of the overseas assignment, they go through the 'journeying home' programme where the psychologist and an HR representative visit the family and prepare them for the return. They help to update the expatriate's CV, plan further career development and arrange the logistics for relocation, schools and housing. One month after the expatriate's return, a 'welcome home' seminar is held. In addition to this, AT&T provides bonuses for repatriates who stay for six months with the company after returning home.

Klaff (2002) reported that companies with such repatriation programmes have only 5% of repatriates resign within a year compared to 22% in other companies. This case shows the importance of concurrence in the repatriation and expatriation process.

TC9: Here the author provides a case study of a successful repatriation process. Practical evidence is crucial for both deeply understanding and critically supporting the theory [Application].

The above discussions summarised the need for addressing various aspects of repatriation. Organisational efforts play a vital role in the repatriation process, which needs to be addressed in concurrence with the expatriation process. Individual efforts also play a big role in successful repatriation, hence there must be an appropriate mix of both. This benefits both parties – the organization by reducing its losses (both financial and knowledge) due to turnover and individuals by enabling them to have a lucid and comprehensible career path ahead. It could be concluded that repatriation turnover rates can be reduced by treating repatriation as a process from the beginning of expatriation and with proactive organizational and individualistic efforts.

TC10: A conclusion is made summarising only the key points of the preceding argument.

How is critical thinking useful for your future career?

Students can discover over time that they have developed the skill to critically evaluate competing sources of information on the same topic. This capability to discriminate between more or less useful viewpoints is fundamental in a modern business world increasingly characterised by increasingly complex information, fake news, constant change and too little time.

Employers need graduates who can **isolate and verify the important issues in complex situations**. Broadly speaking, these situations fall into two categories: problems and opportunities. The former require optimal solutions, and the latter demand innovative strategies. Whilst these potentially involve a variety of management subjects that you study on your degree, critical thinking is involved in the generation of *all* these solutions and strategies.

The development of this skill during your studies will have encouraged open-mindedness on your part – the willingness and capacity to **evaluate a variety of different business perspectives**. In each of these cases, you will have learned to consider the views of different individuals and organisations in relation to one another, and come to informed, rational decisions about the best course of action.

> *The U.S. Department of Labor has identified critical thinking as the raw material of a number of key workplace skills, such as problem solving, decision making, organizational planning and risk management. Good decisions require focusing on the most relevant information, asking the right questions, and separating reliable facts from false assumptions – all elements of critical thinking. And yet too few employees possess these essential skills.*

> (Pearson 2015)

To come back to your studies then, the principles of critical analysis challenge you to firstly question all viewpoints rather than accepting any one source of data or ideas, whether this be a website, a textbook or even your teacher. Essentially, this means that you do not simply accept others' views at face value – there is more than one useful side to any business and management issue.

Chapter summary

This chapter has outlined four main steps in developing critical analysis for your assignment writing:

1 **Summarising and paraphrasing**
2 **Synthesis**
3 **Interpretation**
4 **Application**

Key principles:

- The critical quality of your academic writing depends on adopting **a questioning approach** throughout your academic reading. This enables you to faithfully represent and fairly critique the key concepts directly related to your assignment.
- This **research needs to be extensive, but also highly selective**, so that you develop a clear enough understanding to apply the steps of critically analytical writing successfully.
- You need to **focus continuously on the essay question** to ensure every paragraph addresses that directly.

Activity Answers

What do management tutors mean by critical analysis?

The original list has been separated below into sections that show which factors constitute critical analysis in business and management assignments, and which do not. These are all discussed in detail at the beginning of the chapter.

Necessary, analytical elements in all your assignments:

- ✓ A. Questioning what you read and hear.
- ✓ B. Summarising others' ideas.
- ✓ C. Paraphrasing others' ideas (in your own words).
- ✓ D. Comparing and contrasting others' ideas.
- ✓ H. Exploring the debate around a topic.

Analytical functions required in some assignments:

- ✓ K. Applying theoretical ideas to business situations.
- ✓ E. Challenging others' views on a topic.

Some tutors may require these aspects in their assignments:

- ? I. Developing strategic recommendations.
- ? J. Offering solutions for business problems.

Descriptive writing, i.e. not critical analysis. This should only be briefly summarised early in the essay:

- ✗ G. Stating what a theory proposes.
- ✗ L. Showing what happened in a business situation.

Not critical analysis:

- ✗ F. Expressing your own opinion.

Activity 8.1: Paraphrasing and summarising

A suggested summary of the extract text has been paraphrased below:

Example answer:
(Vocabulary from the original has been underlined to emphasise how only a few key words need to be directly reproduced in this way.)

> _Cultural distance_ can create challenges for _multinational enterprises_ (MNEs). This involves _adapting_ their business operations to major differences in the _'political economy, education, religion, and language'_ of their home base and other countries _(Schwartz 1999 in Tihanyi et al. 2005: 270)._

Some important points to note from this activity are:

- The original text paragraph of 110 words has been reduced to 40 words. This _summarising process_ is crucial to take ideas from several, long texts, and condense these into your essay which has a much shorter word count than any of the original source texts.
- The new version has been paraphrased into simpler language that clearly shows the tutor that the student has written this _from his own understanding_, not directly from the source text.
- This example illustrates the principle of _secondary referencing_ (see Chapter 8): The student has cited Schwartz but clearly indicated that he has read this in the Tihanyi et al. article, not from the primary source.
- The summary also includes a short, direct quote. This has been kept in its original form because it lists specific terms that contribute to a definition of a key term. The vast majority of your writing should otherwise be in your own words, as shown in the rest of this paragraph.

Activity 8.2: Developing debate

To present a counter-argument, Sebastian could have written something along the following lines:

> _However, negotiation processes vary between cultures, e.g. Eastern and Western European countries (Munns et al. 2000). Different communication strategies and behaviours arise as a result of cultural beliefs and values (Cavusgil et al. 2013; Tse et al. 1994). This makes every negotiation preparation unique and only partially repeatable._

Some important points to note from this activity are:

- The writer has used different sources to establish the single theme – that negotiation processes may well differ across cultures.
- This demonstrates his understanding of the wider debate by clearly countering the argument made earlier in the essay for a universal theory of negotiation.

Reflective Writing

Reflective writing can potentially be specified as a requirement in any business assignment. For example, there is an increasing trend for management tutors to request a final section to some essays in which you report on the difficulties and breakthroughs you experienced through your assignment research and production. This encourages you to recognise your learning development throughout the business and management programme.

Mostly though, reflective writing is the domain of skills development modules, such as Employability and Enterprise, Personal Development Planning, and Work-Based Learning. At the core of these modules, there is a growing recognition that employers expect their graduates to embrace the concept of **continuous professional development**:

> CPD is the holistic commitment of professionals towards the enhancement of personal skills and proficiency throughout their careers. It enables learning to become conscious and proactive, rather than passive and reactive.

> (CPD Certification Service 2019)

You need a 'growth mindset' of openness to this continuous, **experiential learning** during your university journey (Dweck 2006) so that you are already equipped to meet the CPD expectations of your future employer. However, *thinking* about an experience is not enough in itself to consolidate your learning. You achieve that much more actively by *writing reflectively* about that experience. The process of writing becomes the active element of the learning. This chapter therefore covers:

- **What does reflective writing look like?** Recognise the key characteristics of the reflective writing style.
- **How do you do it?** Two popular models of reflection are explained in detail and illustrated by examples of students' coursework.
- **How does this relate to theoretical writing in academic assignments?** Deepen your analysis by combining the two main approaches of degree-level writing – academic and reflective.

Employers differentiate between graduate applicants on the basis of their employability skills, such as problem-solving, teamworking and leadership. Their recruitment processes challenge students to distinguish themselves from others by showing how they have grown through stretching experiences and can now demonstrate the relevant skills they have harnessed by reflecting on those experiences. The potential value of this process is well captured by Reid (2009):

Using self-awareness to move beyond limited knowledge acquisition enables a more profound form of learning to take place. The participant uses both acquired knowledge and reflection on experience to question their own taken-for-granted beliefs and behaviours. As their assumptions are challenged, they are able to become more ... effective by refining their understanding and ability to respond to the behaviour of others.

To demonstrate this process of conscious, proactive learning to tutors, you have to write reflectively about your university and workplace experiences. Many students' early attempts at this quite different style of writing turn out to be quite superficial – *what I did, what happened, who said what.* This chapter takes you beyond that descriptive writing into reflective analysis – *why this was important for me, how I have changed, how I am going to act differently in future.*

What is meant by reflective writing?

A simple framework to introduce you to the process of reflective writing is shown in the three-step approach suggested below:

Box 9.1   An overview of reflective writing

1   First of all, you do need to *briefly describe* the situation, i.e. *what* happened, and *what* your reactions were.

2   However, the main purpose of reflective writing is to explore *your* experience of that situation, i.e. *how* it affected you. From there, you can start to analyse *why* you reacted in the ways that you did, and *how* they were helpful or unhelpful for you.

These **how and why questions** take you beneath the surface level of description into the depths of *analysis*.

3   The third stage is to then project yourself into a similar situation in the future. You plan *how* you would like to respond differently next time, and *why* that will be more purposeful and constructive for you.

Reflective writing embraces both success and 'failure'

Although the aim is to show the reader how you are learning from your experience, this *does not* mean you always have to prove how successful you have been. Whilst you will perform well in some learning situations by drawing on existing strengths and qualities, other circumstances will challenge you emotionally and psychologically in ways that seem to block any apparent, immediate achievements. The objective in the reflective writing process is to show how you can grow through any situation, even one in which you might feel disappointed at the time.

The overall structure of any such assignment should therefore present a balanced view that recognises that any student's university journey is bound to provoke a mixture of positive and negative reactions. Here are some questions to consider when developing that general structure (Box 9.2):

Box 9.2   Creating a balanced view of your strengths and vulnerabilities

The challenges

- What personal and academic difficulties have you faced?
- How did these affect you …
   ○ How did you feel at the time?
   ○ What did you think/believe about yourself?
- How did you react …
   ○ What did you do?
   ○ How personally effective (or not) was that?
- How would you like to respond differently in future?

The positives

- What are the more enjoyable experiences of your learning journey so far?
- What qualities and capabilities have you discovered in yourself?
- How can you build on these existing strengths?
- What strategies have you developed to overcome future challenges?

The reflective writing style is quite different from traditional academic writing

As you have learned in earlier chapters, most of your business and management assignments require you to write in an objective, neutral way. This mainly involves paraphrasing the ideas and findings of other authors' research. In contrast, reflective writing adopts a subjective style (Box 9.3):

Box 9.3   Distinctive aspects of the reflective writing style

- You write mainly in the first person, e.g. *'This made me realise …'*, *'When that happened, I felt …'*.
- You reflect predominantly on *your* experience, not others' ideas.
- You use examples directly from *your own* experience.
- You explain how and why *you* felt, thought and acted in the ways that *you* did.
- You imagine a future scenario and suggest constructive strategies for how *you* will manage that.

Some aspects of reflective writing are still similar to your other academic writing. As part of your degree-level assessment, this still requires a rigorously academic approach. This means that you must continue to delve beneath *description* (what happened?) by moving into *analysis* (how did you respond, and, more importantly, why?). Furthermore, you may well need to relate the insights from your own experience to general, theoretical ideas that support these.

How to write reflectively

There is no exact formula for reflective writing. The following two models – linear and cyclical – each provide a set of stages that will help you to structure your reflective assignment. These share some similarities in aims and approach, so you can choose from either option or a combination of the two.

The linear approach to reflective writing

Box 9.4 suggests a simple structure for creating depth to your reflective writing by working through three levels. Each of these is then explained in more detail in the following sections.

Box 9.4   A three-step linear model

Level	Purpose	Questions to address	% of content
1	Description	What happened?	15
2	Analysis	How did I react and why?	70
3	Future planning	How would I like to respond in similar situations?	15

---

1. Descriptive writing

In traditional academic assignments, some descriptive writing is needed to relate *what* a theory claims or *what* is happening in a business situation. Similarly, reflective essays require some description, usually to introduce your experience in terms of *what* happened and *what* you and others did. As with academic writing, reflective description should be quite brief, but still explanatory:

✘   *We held a meeting to discuss the project. I made a presentation on the staffing structure.*

This is too brief – the reader is left with too many unanswered questions about exactly what you did, and what happened as a result. Instead, *some* more description is needed about what happened, as shown in the better example of descriptive writing below:

✔   *I made a presentation on the marketing plan. When I asked for feedback, there were some great comments, but this also suggested that the people at the back of the room couldn't hear me, and that I went through my PowerPoint so fast they struggled to keep up. I then watched the recording, and have to agree with what they say.*

Level 1 is just the introduction to your reflective writing. The problem in low-grade student essays generally is that they stay at this descriptive level. The reader is left without much idea of what was going on 'beneath the surface'. To move beyond simplistic description into *reflective analysis*, you need to explore three major aspects of your experience more deeply: *How did you feel, think and act?*

2. Analytical reflection

Reflective analysis requires you to address these questions:

a) How were you affected by what happened? (Feeling)
b) How did you make sense of that? (Thinking)
c) How did you then respond? (Acting)

Even more importantly, though, these *'How?'* questions lead into the deepest question of all in reflective writing – *'Why?'*

- *Why* did this situation affect you in that way?
- *Why* do you believe this means what you think it does?
- *Why* have you responded in the way that you did?

These are difficult questions because they challenge any of us to explore the unconscious drivers of our reactions to external circumstances. But this also means they can lead you on **the most rewarding learning journey of all** – your inner self. They will enable you to value and assert your positive qualities for sustainable self-confidence. Perhaps even more importantly, they present the opportunity to recognise the limiting self-beliefs that you want to change so that you can respond more purposefully to future challenges.

The extract below shows how one student explored an analytical approach to reflective learning development by addressing **how and why questions**. Read this carefully to then complete the question/answer matching exercise that follows (paragraphs have been numbered for the purpose of this exercise):

1 *Starting university again from undergraduate studies after a year's break has naturally been a high-pressure experience. Usually, with careful planning in past years of academia, I could reduce the pressure I was under, although this time I found I was struggling due to the magnitude of additional learning. It was difficult to ascertain what was causing my anxiety, hence I created a journal for a week to classify what situations within my environment created the greatest stress and how I responded (see Appendix 1). This really helped to clarify my thinking and unscramble my thoughts. It also helped me as I then started to take a note of my feelings, and if I had not written down these foundations of my predicament, I wouldn't have known what I was trying to deal with.*

2 *In accordance with Cartwright and Cooper (1997), I found that stress can be caused by lack of control, high workload, and change. Coming from a different professional background, HRM postgraduate study seemed alien to me in many ways as workloads were unquestionably different, and there was no familiarity, e.g. new teaching mechanisms. Having to meet many more deadlines put me under intense pressure and in turn caused me to feel increasingly anxious.*

3 *In summary, what I learnt was that the stress caused was not my fault or my personal failings, as I perceived it to be in the beginning. These failings were due to not having the correct knowledge on ways to overcome the new challenges, and I realised that I can learn how to do that.*

Appendix 1: Weekly stress journal

> *Day 3 ... The start of the lecture went well, and I could write down notes needed for the group work next week. The final hour of the lecture consisted of a seminar session answering questions and working with my friend besides me, I felt this went well. Towards the end the module leader started to speak about deadlines and assignment questions. Straightaway, I began to feel uneasy as I felt I may not be able to get the group study done around my job working hours. However, I convinced myself everyone else would probably be in the same boat as me, so I didn't think about this too much. I attended my last two lectures and prepared myself for the next day. When I got home though, I felt stressed looking at all my university books next to my work duty rota.*

ACTIVITY 9.1

Matching reflective prompts and answers

Remember the earlier prompt questions for good reflective writing. Some of these are listed again in the left-hand column below. The right-hand column shows answers to these questions from paragraph 1 in the above extract. Your task is to match each example against the relevant question. The first one has been completed for you:

Reflective question	Evident in paragraph 1
A. *How* did you react to this situation (what did you first think about that)?	*... I found I was struggling ...*
B. *Why* did this affect you in that way?	*... it was difficult to ascertain what was causing my anxiety.*
C. *How* did you then respond?	*This really helped to clarify my thinking and unscramble my thoughts.*
D. *Why* did you respond in that way?	*... the magnitude of additional learning.*
E. *How* helpful do you believe this kind of response is?	*... I created a journal ...*

Check your matches against the Activity Answers at the end of the chapter.

Identifying answers to reflective questions

Where in paragraphs 2 and 3 above can you see examples that further address each of these reflective questions? Write one answer in the right hand column against each question. Again, one example has been done for you:

Reflective question	Evident in paragraph number ...
A. How were you affected by what happened?	2: ... intense pressure ... caused me to feel increasingly anxious.
B. Why were you affected in that way?	
C. How did you perceive this situation (what did you first think about that)?	
D. Why do you tend to react in that way to that kind of experience?	
E. Why has this situation been useful for your personal development?	

Check your selection of examples against those in the Activity Answers.

3. Future generalisation

So far, we have considered reflective writing as a retrospective activity, i.e. reviewing past experiences. Whilst reflection is naturally about looking back over past challenges and successes, an important purpose is also to show how you are learning from those experiences to direct your future thinking and behaviour in more constructive ways.

Here is how one student extrapolated a strategy for her future participation in team meetings based on a recent group work challenge:

After realising more about my learning style (Honey and Mumford 1986), I reflected on our meetings, and could see how my strengths definitely lay in the practicality of application. I am very technically process-minded so could quickly point out problems with certain processes that others could not, especially when looking at implementation. This can be a strength as it results in me questioning processes, and therefore sometimes being seen as a natural project leader. However, I need to work on knowing when this is not possible, and not becoming stressed about the situation. If I were to attend the meetings again, I would try to be more open-minded to different solutions, and be more patient with others who might not necessarily understand the technical side of the project. They may have more holistic solutions and will bring different ideas to the table.

In this example from a first-year self-development module, the student shows the reader how she has identified relevant personal strengths through a theoretical model. She affirms those attributes in detail, but not in a way that arrogantly assumes they fully equip her for future group work. She is willing to take a proactive approach to overcome other limitations in her existing ways of thinking and acting.

An alternative, or perhaps complementary, approach to the linear reflective process can be to consider this in a more circular way.

A cyclical approach to reflective writing

It can be helpful to think of any writing task as a cyclical process – one that brings you back round to your starting point, but with informed insights that address the questions you began with. This is particularly applicable to reflective writing, which many consider to be a continuous learning process, as can be illustrated through Gibbs' (1988) model, shown below:

Box 9.5   Gibbs' Reflective Cycle

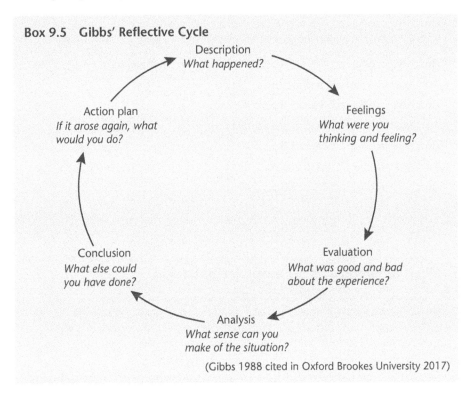

(Gibbs 1988 cited in Oxford Brookes University 2017)

The following prompts may help you to write reflectively by using this type of cyclic, developmental model:

1 One experience that changed the way I think was when … e.g. *I was rejected for a job.*
2 At the time, I felt … e.g. *disheartened.*
3 The problem was … e.g. *the way I was answering the interview questions too tentatively.*
4 I learned that … e.g. *I needed to 'think on my feet' more quickly.*

5 But the good thing was ... e.g. *this pushed me to seek advice from the interview experts in our university careers advice service.*

6 And I can handle this differently now by ... e.g. *being more confident as I know how to prepare myself for interviews.*

This process is actually just another way of conceptualising the three-stage sequence of reflective writing described in the first, linear model. The cyclical model simply provides you with another set of questions to focus your thinking into productive reflection. The sequential correspondence between the two reflective frameworks is indicated below:

Box 9.6   Cyclical and linear reflective thinking – two different ways to the same objective

Gibbs' cyclical question stages	Linear process levels
What happened?	1. Descriptive writing
What were you thinking and feeling?	2. Analytical reflection
What was good and bad about the experience?	
What sense could you make of the situation?	
What else could you have done?	
If it arose again, what would you do?	3. Future generalisation

---

Reflective writing as an employability skill

The modules involving reflective assessment help you explore and represent your experiences in the ways that you will later need for application forms, assessment centres and interviews. Throughout any employer's recruitment process, their assessors will expect you to *evidence* how you have developed your graduate attributes from experiences gained while studying at university.

One of the most useful ways that you can help yourself prepare for this is through the well-known STAR technique:

1 **Situation**
2 **Task**
3 **Action**
4 **Result**

As a general guide to the STAR approach for positive reflective writing, you can use the suggested structure in Box 9.7:

Box 9.7   The STAR technique for evidencing your experiential learning

SITUATION AND TASK (15%).
Introduce the challenge you faced:

- What was happening?
- What was the problem or opportunity?

ACTION (70%):
Explain *how* you responded to the challenge, and *why* you did so in that way:

- Demonstrate effective behaviour.
- Be specific – enable the reader to easily envision what happened, e.g. *I carefully studied the market analysis from the other team members to develop an initial list of strategic recommendations for further discussion.*
- Use first person singular, e.g. *I presented the strategic element of the report.*
- Write in full sentences and use action verbs, e.g. *I led the team meeting and invited each person in turn to give their view of the company problem.*
- Quantify/qualify your statements/answers, e.g. *I organised four group meetings over a three-week period culminating in the completion of a draft report within one month, and a week prior to the deadline.*

RESULT (15%)
Clearly explain the specific outcomes from your actions:

- How effectively did you resolve the problem or capitalise on the opportunity?
- What skills did you develop?

Note: The STAR process is designed to focus on positive outcomes. However, if you did not meet all your targets, you can still demonstrate your positive learning development, e.g. *The project was not entirely successful because ... However, I have learned the value of clear communication processes such as ... and I have become more confident in my capability to recover from setbacks.*
        (Adapted from: University of Bradford Career and Employability Services 2018)

You may also be able to show employers relevant, reflective learning from outside university. This will be especially helpful if it relates to some kind of work experience. Here is a brief example of how one student framed that through the STAR model to clearly demonstrate her learning development:

One area of the language school teaching programme experienced low sales figures (SITUATION). My goal was to improve these sales by raising student satisfaction (TASK). I improved operations by developing the focus of the programme and training teachers to be both more confident and competent in this area. I achieved this by increasing the communications between the management, Japanese sales staff, teachers and students and by forming stronger links with other schools. I worked with all these groups to design a 6-week action plan (ACTION). Under my management, sales increased from 50 to over 100 in only 2 months. I received positive feedback from my manager and the sales staff, whilst the engagement of students and teachers improved significantly too (RESULT).

The above example is based on a mature student's full-time work experience. However, your reflective STAR examples could be taken from all sorts of contexts – part-time work, volunteering or student societies. If you work at a supermarket, for example, they will have formalised systems of performance appraisal. These provide feedback that you can show to potential employers on the transferable skills you have been developing in the workplace, e.g. teamworking, time management, customer service. Here is another example for you to explore your understanding:

ACTIVITY 9.3

Using the STAR technique to show positive reflection

Read this student's attempt at writing reflectively about her part-time work experience. In this case, the STAR technique has not been so well applied, and your task is to suggest improvements to that.

> Although working at Debenhams throughout university has been a financial necessity and not due to any career aspirations, the job has provided a consistently challenging environment. The team is tight-knit and with constant challenges to achieve strict targets, efficient, friendly teamwork is always necessary. The biggest challenge is always the Christmas period which is exceedingly busy. I cannot claim that I have been key in the success of this year's Christmas effort (the busiest and highest selling yet) but all our hard work as a team achieved great results.

1. Where can you see *any* elements of the STAR model in this extract?

2. How could this piece of reflective writing be improved through the STAR technique?

Check the Activity Answers for some suggested answers to improving this student's reflective writing.

Reflecting on personal experiences from a theoretical perspective

So far, we have mainly considered reflective thinking expressed in the first person, e.g. *'I felt ...'*, *'This was important to me because ...'*, *'I realised that ...'* Tutors will certainly expect to see plenty of this personalised language in reflective essays, which require you to express *your* feelings, thoughts and actions.

However, they may also expect you to show some relevant research that theorises about this kind of personal experience. Such theories may identify strategies for developing the attributes that you have identified for improvement in your employability skills set. This is where reflective essays and the more traditional academic assignments converge – in the need to cite sources that present supporting evidence for the personal development points that you have been making.

The two extracts below, from the module 'Employability and Enterprise', show how students have managed to integrate theoretical ideas into their reflective writing:

> *It was important to establish a common understanding of the group tasks and how each student could contribute to those most efficiently (Scudamore 2013). One of the other members took this a step further by getting us to agree on a set of ground rules, e.g. respecting each other's ideas, and committing to meeting times as suggested by Carroll (2005). I felt relieved that the others seemed to be taking this team-working seriously, and it encouraged me to play my part to the full.*

> (Hassan)

> *Through this module I understood the importance of a team and the benefits of being part of a team. In order for a team to be effective it must be small, the members need to have common purpose, approach and specific goals and also they need to have complementary skills (De Vita 2001). According to Belbin's team roles (2007), in task-related or social-related situations, I found that I am the 'shaper' type as I am goal-oriented and dynamic, but also I have the disadvantage of offending people's feelings.*

> (Alexandra)

You can see that these students have considered a theoretical concept of personal development and applied that to themselves. It is worth checking directly with your tutor whether they prefer this approach of supporting your reflective writing with academic ideas. If in doubt, it is more than likely this will enhance the credibility of your assignment, and thereby, your grade.

Applying all the principles of reflective writing in a management assignment

Activity 9.4 below provides an opportunity to imagine you are the tutor, marking students' work against all the principles considered in the chapter so far. Read each extract carefully to look for examples of where the student may have applied each stage of the reflective writing process. If you are unsure about those criteria, refer back to the reflective questions in the Linear and Cyclical models above.

ACTIVITY 9.4

Putting yourself in the tutor's shoes: What's the grade?

Using the simplified marking system below, assign an alphabetical grade to each of the two assignment extracts, giving your reasons for that assessment:

Grade		%
A	=	70 +
B	=	60–69
C	=	50–59
D	=	40–49
E	=	30–39

Example 1

I was interested to learn more about motivational theories, as I have already completed the module Leading, Managing and Developing People, and wanted to learn more about the academic explanations of motivation. Overall, I found myself disappointed in the studies conducted, and feel that even Herzberg (1959) and Maslow (1954), who are more focussed on the humanistic side, often make the assumption that people are motivated by the same things. From my experience in various group work projects, I have seen that different people are motivated fundamentally by very different things. Some university peers, for example, seem quite prepared to 'ride on the back' of more conscientious students, and I have found this particularly frustrating as I strongly believe in the value of earning rewards through my own hard work.

However, I could generally relate to Maslow's hierarchy of needs, in particular the idea that the experience of self-actualisation can never be satiated. However, he uses this as an argument for long-lasting and effective motivation of people at work. This does not seem to fit with my experience, as I believe this 'never satisfied need' can become a source of stress in itself. I recognise this has resulted in me pushing myself further and further, sometimes with little gratification. I have come to understand that I may be continually trying to achieve something unattainable as the bar is always moving.

Your grade:

Reasons for that grade:

Example 2

In the Hexagon activity, I developed the skill of creative discussion as me and my team needed to plan an approach in 6 minutes on how to make six hexagons in up to 10 minutes without talking and we managed to complete the exercise first.

Furthermore, during this module I had many opportunities to develop skills like team-working, team-building, problem-solving, reducing conflict, etc. From the first day, we asked to form groups and my group was actually the most enthusiastic about getting to know each other so we formed a WhatsApp group. The group was made for this module specifically but we began to be closer and started to talk about other modules as well so it was more like a study group.

We arranged two hour meetings in order to help each other with the homework we had each week and it was really productive. We were discussing everything, and although we had many different opinions, we were reaching a conclusion through discussion.

Your grade:

Reasons for that grade:

Check the Activity Answers for suggested grades and explanations of those.

Sample reflective essay

This chapter finishes with a longer example of a student's reflective writing extracted from a full essay. Again, this is written in a theoretically informed way, but its high grade is especially due to the in-depth, personalised approach that really explores *how* the student has developed self-awareness through the module, and *why* this has been especially useful. Tutor commentary (TC) is given after each paragraph.

I have always been keen on self-development so I was very interested in this subject. At the start of the module, I recognised a need not only to learn more about personal development from my own perspective, but also, I saw that the more we understand about our own needs, personality types and learning styles, the easier it is to understand the needs of others.

TC: A helpful indication that the student recognises *why* a reflective approach to learning is important.

I found it interesting looking at the Honey and Mumford learning styles (1986). I had always thought of myself as an Activist as I prefer to try things out myself, and get frustrated when being told how to do something. I often struggle to remember instructions given verbally, but only need to try something once for the process or method to become completely absorbed. However, I did not relate at all to the general characteristics of these learners, and after completing the learning styles questionnaire, I found I am a Pragmatist learner. This suggests that although I am keen to test things out in practice, I do prefer to be shown the process by an expert first, and then have that expert check as I try out the process.

TC: Showing *how* a relevant theory illuminates her approach to learning *and* challenges her assumptions in the process.

My MBTI personality type is INTJ (The Myers and Briggs Foundation 2017). I was already aware of my general introversion, but reading further into the other aspects has helped me understand my personality more. This has enabled me to adjust some of these aspects so I play to my strengths and keep in mind areas that I may need to work on in the future. I have recently learned that I need to be more open-minded to other people's suggestions, and this is also reiterated with an INTJ personality type. As someone who prefers logic and rationality, I often forget to take into account emotional considerations. I need to ensure that in group discussions, everyone gets heard and their ideas considered.

TC: Again, this explains *how* another theory has helped the student to understand her typical responses and *how* this also established areas for improvement.

MBTI also highlighted my aversion to working in groups and my apparent lack of social skills. I have always been aware of this; however, understanding my personality type better has helped me appreciate why this aversion exists, and how I can adapt my practices when group work is necessary. It has also allowed me to understand my strengths as an individual worker – I am very independent and prefer using my own initiative. This results in a limited social life and when I was growing up, I often found this frustrating as I struggled to relate to others or quickly became bored with small talk or gossip. In more recent times, and as I have learnt more about my own personality, I have come to accept my preference for my own company, and rely less heavily on the social expectation of a large friendship circle.

TC: In-depth exploration of personal tendencies, perceptions and growth.

However, I have also learnt that this preference to working or being alone can sometimes stem from a fear of a new situation. As someone who prides myself on composure and capacity for decisive self-direction, being in a situation where I may not know what to say or how to act results in a high amount of stress. In such a position, I will often try to shape the situation so I can work independently. However, this potential problem is not so easily avoided in an academic environment or workplace, where group work is often encouraged. Starting university as a mature student, I found this hard to adapt to, and this quickly became an even higher source of stress than the workload itself. I found that I would prefer to do the work of four students rather than work in such a group.

TC: Opening up a current challenge that has arisen within university study ...

Surprisingly though, being pushed into these situations during this semester has allowed me to see the benefit of working with others, and how teamwork is not necessarily about just dividing the workload, but also about diversity of ideas and using people's strengths as a group. For example, last semester, we needed to conduct a group presentation, and we divided it according to our strengths. As someone who thrives in research and critique, I took this part of the project. This sharing of workload and specialisms helped me to see the advantages to working in a team and is something I have tried to replicate in the work environment.

TC: ... and explaining *how* she has learned to think and act differently.

Overall, I found this module, in particular the personality type questionnaire, to be quite helpful, specifically, learning how I can focus on my strengths rather than just overcoming my weaknesses. I have often tried to overcome my personality traits, for example, I will try to force myself to be more Extrovert as I am naturally more Introverted. However, we discussed in one lecture how, if I simply focus on overcoming my personality type, I reduce the impact of my inherent qualities. It is best to focus on building my current capabilities and finding situations where they can be utilised successfully, rather than solely forcing myself to try to be other personality types.

TC: Taking an overview of the learning development to pinpoint key learning outcomes of the reflective process.

This discussion has stuck with me throughout the semester and has been something I have applied to my personal, academic and work life with much success. I believe it has helped me stand out as I now focus more on playing to my strengths, rather than being average at both sides of the personality type. It has even helped reduce my stress levels by understanding and therefore accepting certain characteristics which I can use as qualities rather than viewing them as weaknesses and trying to push myself in the opposite direction.

TC: Returning full circle to the introduction, re-emphasising the value of reflecting honestly and optimistically on interpersonal experiences.

Activity Answers

Activity 9.1: Matching reflective prompts and answers

Reflective question	Evident in paragraph 1
A. How did you perceive this situation (what did you first think about that)?	*... I found I was struggling ...*
	... it was difficult to ascertain what was causing my anxiety.
B. On reflection, why have you tended to think that way about that experience?	*This really helped to clarify my thinking and unscramble my thoughts.*
C. How did you then respond?	
D. On reflection, why have you responded in that way?	*... the magnitude of additional learning.*
E. How helpful do you believe this kind of response is?	*... I created a journal ...*

Activity 9.2: Identifying answers to reflective questions

Reflective question	Evident in paragraph number ...
A. How were you affected by what happened?	2: *... intense pressure ... caused me to feel increasingly anxious.*
B. Why were you affected in that way?	2: *Having to meet many more deadlines ...*
C. How did you perceive this situation (what did you first think about that)?	2: *HRM postgraduate study seemed alien to me ...*
D. Why did you react in that way?	2: *... workloads were ... different, and there was no familiarity ...*
E. Why has this situation been useful for your personal development?	3: *These failings were due to not having the correct knowledge ... to overcome the new challenges, and I can learn how to do that.*

Activity 9.3: Using the STAR technique to show positive reflection

Your answer could have suggested that the Situation and Task are briefly alluded to in the *'challenges to achieve strict targets'*, especially at Christmas. However, the crucial Action and Result elements of the model are not really covered at all, to the point that the student even deflects this by writing, *'I cannot claim that I have been key in the success ...'*

This example could be significantly improved by much more detail about what the student actually did *herself* and specific data about the outcomes, perhaps including:

- Personal sales performance figures during that Christmas period.
- Increases in sales figures by the team against previous sales periods.
- Qualitative examples of team camaraderie and support.
- Personal reflections on how this experience developed employability skills.

Activity 9.4: In the tutor's shoes – what's the grade?

Extract 1
Grade: A

The first paragraph recognises the relevance of motivational theories across different subjects, emphasising holistic learning on a degree programme. The student then shows a keenly analytical mind by *critiquing some of those theories through her own experience*. She does so by explaining *how* others' actions have affected her and *why* this has been so.

In the second paragraph, the student really personalises a theoretical concept. She shows a profoundly honest self-appraisal in recognising *how* a tendency that many might regard as positive (persistence) actually affects her negatively. She also shows how that reflection has enabled her to delve deeper into understanding *why* she has repeatedly been acting in a way that she now sees as unhelpful rather than productive.

Extract 2
Grade: D

This is, at best, a low pass because the writing stays primarily at the descriptive level. In other words, this is mainly stating *what* happened in the team task. Although this is quite detailed, it becomes apparent that there is no explanation of *how* the experience impacted on the student, *how* the team achieved the developments suggested or *why* this particular way of team-working was developmental for the student.

Communication

Getting Started with Group Work

Business and management degrees involve numerous group work assessments designed to develop essential employability skills for working effectively with others. Graduate employers will expect you to demonstrate these skills at assessment centres – through role-plays, for example. At your interviews, they will often ask you to reflect on group work situations at university and how you have grown through those experiences (Targetjobs 2018). This chapter helps you understand how to:

- Identify what you personally want to achieve from the group work, and how you can most positively contribute to that.
- Establish group objectives and practical arrangements.
- Explore the need for a leader, and identify their responsibilities if appropriate.
- Practise discussion techniques that engage all members equally, especially in those groups with a typical mixture of dominant and quieter personalities.
- Use personality type assessments as a potential way of assigning group roles that best suit individual members' strengths.
- Organise the group project into relevant tasks. Delegate these realistically in ways that engage each member's commitment.

Employers in the increasingly competitive graduate marketplace value students' soft skills as much as their business knowledge. Even in the more 'technical' business fields such as accounting, for example, numeric ability and financial analysis skills are not enough in themselves to become a successful manager. **The capability to work effectively with others** is what will distinguish you during the recruitment process and later in the workplace itself.

Like many other soft skills, effective teamworking requires sustained practice and reflection to acquire the levels of proficiency demanded by graduate employers. This is a major reason for business schools using group work assessments across a range of management subjects. These typically take the form of a written report and/or class presentation, perhaps accounting for up to 50 per cent of the assessment in the module. They provide opportunities for students to develop collaborative skills in a relatively risk-free environment at university as a practical preparation for the less forgiving future workplaces.

Personal responsibility: group work starts with you

Whilst group working can be a challenging process for many students, that in itself offers great potential for personal growth. This requires a genuine intention and willingness to be a constructive member of the group – regardless of what happens. The extent to which you have *a positive experience* of group work depends primarily on how constructively you approach that situation. Activity 10.1 offers a helpful technique for guiding yourself into a positive mindset. You can use this anchoring process in various circumstances where you might find yourself out of your comfort zone. This can be especially helpful before you go into a new or challenging group situation.

ACTIVITY 10.1

Anchoring your positive self

Give yourself a few minutes to sit quietly without any distractions – switch off all devices. Re-read this script until you understand the process well enough to guide yourself through it with your eyes closed. Alternatively, you can listen to the recording on the companion website so that you relax fully into the guided experience.

1   Take a few, deep breaths, slowly and easily. As you do so, bring your attention into yourself ... notice what you feel physically – the floor beneath your feet ... the chair beneath you ... your hands in your lap ... the rise and fall of your breath ...

2   As your body softens into this self-awareness, allow your mind to drift back to an earlier, enjoyable experience with other people. Take your time – reflect on several experiences if necessary until you settle on one that feels very positive ... where you conducted yourself in ways that really showed others your personal qualities.

3   Spend some time reviewing what was happening at that time. What can you see ... look through your own eyes at that time and notice colours, surroundings ... really focus in on that. And what can you hear? ... the sounds of others enjoying themselves ... the pleasant tone of your own voice ... clear ... confident. How does that feel? ... settle into your body at that time ... re-experience the positive sensations of being there ...

4   What is the one word that captures the special capability that you were showing at that time? This really could be anything – *calm ... easy ... listening ... smiling ...* Keep repeating that word in your mind so that it becomes a 'verbal anchor' or reminder of the personal strength that you know you could easily bring into any future situation.

5   You can anchor that even more strongly by creating a physical reminder to help you reproduce the feeling easily whenever you need. Lightly clasp your hands together, for example, to imagine capturing that positive feeling in the future.

6   Once you know that you can apply those anchors to recreate the positive feeling in new situations, allow your mind to gently return to your present time and place. Open your eyes when ready to do so, remembering the unique capabilities that you bring with you.

(Inspired by Grinder and Bandler 1981)

When you do then go to your next group situation, know that all you really need to do is concentrate on being yourself. You will naturally and unconsciously find opportunities to contribute your positive qualities easily and confidently, especially when you use your verbal or physical anchor to remind you of those.

The following sections in this chapter introduce some vital ingredients for effective teamwork that have been reported by students from high-achieving groups. These will help you and your group members to organise yourselves effectively, produce quality outputs and hopefully also enjoy working together.

Gathering commitment to a shared goal

At the first meeting, you need to engage in an open discussion in which everyone is encouraged to express their views and reach an explicit agreement on the group work objectives.

ACTIVITY 10.2

Objectives for your first group meeting

What would be your top three priorities for the first meeting of any student project group?

List your ideas below:

1

2

3

See the Activity Answers for a helpful list of objectives for that first group meeting.

Everyone has a voice

An important purpose of academic group work is to provide an opportunity for each person to contribute their knowledge and skills to a genuinely collective effort. Every member of your group will have something valuable to offer if you can find the way to harness that. This includes you too ... whatever position you find yourself occupying in a group, you can contribute constructive ideas for how to get the most out of working together.

A potential problem at this early stage of working together is that one or two people can quickly dominate the discussion. We have all probably experienced this situation in groups before when someone, perhaps with the best of intentions, takes charge by expressing strong views as to what should be done. Other members may allow themselves to be directed by this apparently confident 'leader'. Such dominant personalities may assume that quieter colleagues have nothing useful (different) to say. This will usually be a most misleading impression, as these less vocal members often have a great deal of value to add to the project. They may simply be more internally reflective than others who 'think by speaking'. Each group member is a potential source of great ideas and other important, practical contributions.

How could everyone be enabled to actively participate in the first meeting?

Pause for Thought

Jot down your thoughts about how your first group discussion could be run to find out as much as possible about everyone's ideas:

A simple way to hear from everyone in the group is to allow each person to introduce themselves and say a little about their personal background. As in any other life situation involving teamworking with a group of relative strangers, the first steps are about **relationship-building**. It is helpful to know something of who your new colleagues are, where they come from and what experience they have to offer.

The first thing you can do is to **take turns to speak** until each member has had the opportunity to share something. If you like, you can make this into more of an **icebreaker** through one of the following quick activities:

- Pair off first of all to tell your partner about yourself. You then have to introduce each other to the group, rather than speak for yourself.
- Individually, think of something unusual from your earlier life that might surprise your colleagues. Once everyone has had a minute or two to prepare, then you each share that personal event or experience.
- Alternatively, ask everyone to share something positive about themselves – a passionate interest, a personal quality, an important belief, a significant achievement.
- Get each person in turn to recite the names of the members who have already introduced themselves, so that the last person has the whole group to identify.

Once everyone feels a little more engaged in the group, you can elicit the views of each member about your collective purpose. For example, this could be to produce a report that addresses a tutor's project brief such as the one shown below from a first-year undergraduate module 'People, Work and Organisations':

> *Use one example each of a successful and an unsuccessful organisation to demonstrate how the ideas/theories/concepts you have studied so far may explain why some organisations succeed whilst others fail.*

Considering this purpose carefully together is an important, creative stage of the group process. This is about **gathering ideas from everyone without censoring them** so that you can explore the project from all possible angles. You can then break this down into distinct parts. In the case of the above example, these could be:

- *What examples of successful organisations can we think of?*
- *What examples of unsuccessful organisations can we think of?*
- *Which theories have we learned about on the course so far that explain organisational success or failure?*
- *So, what do we believe constitutes success or failure in organisations?*

You could cluster (brainstorm) ideas for each of these in a 'free-for-all' discussion. This is a creative approach commonly adopted by groups. However, remember that people are still at an early stage of finding their comfort levels in the group situation. You could otherwise consider giving each person a few minutes to cluster their own ideas on paper. Then everyone can **share their thoughts in a turn-taking format**, with one person recording these on a flipchart.

How to enable everyone to 'stake their claim' in the group

Once you have created a set of potential issues for further research, members need to express their views about which are most important and how they could best be divided up in the group. You could try the following process to encourage constructive discussion. This is based on using a 'talking stick' to give everyone a voice in public gatherings, so someone needs to bring an item that will serve this purpose to the group meeting. This could be a natural object, such as a crystal, or something else that is easy to pass around.

One person takes the role of **group facilitator or chairperson** to govern the use of the talking object. They ensure that each person is allowed their say, and that their ideas are really 'heard' by everyone else. The facilitator establishes the focus of the discussion by specifying the required outcomes of the meeting. So, in the above scenario, this could be to choose the top four issues for research and allocate one of these to each member.

The chairperson then explains the 'rules' for the first phase of the meeting, as shown below:

Phase 1: Involve everyone by gathering first thoughts

- One person volunteers to start and is given the talking object. Let's assume this is a soft ball. They offer a view on the optimum research focus. The facilitator must ensure that *no-one else is allowed to interrupt* the person who has the ball.
- Once the first speaker has said all that they wish, then the ball is passed to the person to their left. A variation to this can be that the speaker chooses someone else and throws the ball to that person to speak next.

- This process continues until everyone has voiced their ideas. The facilitator then moves the discussion onto the next phase:

Phase 2: Affirm ideas from Phase 1

- The participants are given the opportunity to *show their support* for another's expressed idea from the first phase.
- One person signals their wish to speak by asking for the ball. This speaker *must first reflect* what they believe that other person had been expressing earlier. Then they explain why they agree with this view, and how it could be effective.
- Others then indicate their wish to speak in a similar way to show their agreement with any views from the first phase. They can do so, once they have been given the ball.
- It is important to focus on these *supportive views* first so that an atmosphere of *positive acknowledgement* is established first of all.

Phase 3: Consider alternative views and counter-arguments

- Someone may soon wish to challenge others' views that have been supported so far. This is when the facilitator's role becomes especially important. They must ensure that *every speaker first reflects their understanding* of another's statement that they are challenging.
- Needless to say, the facilitator must also keep order by immediately stopping anyone from interrupting whoever has the ball at that time.
- Once there seems to be some form of consensus emerging (general, but not necessarily unanimous agreement), the facilitator moves the discussion onto the next phase.

Phase 4: Establish a general course of action for the group and specific tasks for each member

- Hopefully, by this stage, a clear majority view has emerged of the main directions for the group research. The facilitator can summarise that, to confirm everyone's **understanding of the consensus** that seems to be emerging, and check that a majority of members are in agreement.
- The chairperson can then **summarise the key tasks** identified during the discussion. They could formalise this process of establishing group roles by writing up the tasks on a flipchart/whiteboard. This helps everyone to clearly visualise everything that needs to be done and to remember more easily what each other's roles are.
- It is typical at this stage to ask for **volunteers to undertake each of the tasks**. If everyone has been participating quite comfortably in the group discussion, they can simply explain why they think a particular task suits their strengths. If the facilitator feels that some students are still reticent in the group, they could then anonymously 'bid' for tasks by writing their name on a Post-it Note against the task number of their choice.
- An alternative, systematic approach to **assigning roles** is presented in the next section. This may better harness everyone's skills and commitment by connecting tasks to members' personality types from a self-assessment exercise such as the Myers–Briggs example shown below.
- The final stage of this first group meeting is to **agree on deadlines** for the assigned tasks, leading into a date for the next progress meeting:

Phase 5: Commit everyone to specific outcomes and future participation

- The facilitator role is crucial at the final stage too, when there is a risk that members may relax and leave without clear objectives or personal commitments.
- A final run-through is important to remind everyone of their agreed responsibilities. This means specifying required actions and precise objectives to be achieved by the next meeting.
- Finally, everyone must agree when they are free to attend the next meeting and commit this to their calendars.

Assigning team roles by personality type

An interesting exercise to undertake at the beginning of your group project is to consider which type of role each member can best play in your team. This may help you harness each person's strengths so that everyone has the satisfaction of being actively included and contributing effectively to a successful group outcome.

Try the Myers–Briggs self-assessment exercise in Activity 10.3 to find out your own personality type. This exercise is based on a theory developed in the 1940s by American psychologists, mother and daughter, Katherine Briggs and Isabel Briggs Myers, who had in turn based their work on the concept of psychological types proposed by the famous Swiss psychiatrist, Carl Jung (1875–1961). The Myers–Briggs system suggests there are sixteen different personality types, and that each person identifies significantly with one of these.

Box 10.1 and Activity 10.3 give you clear guidance on completing the Myers–Briggs self-assessment and relating your results to the likely role that you naturally find yourself enacting in teamwork.

Box 10.1   The Myers–Briggs Type Inventory (MBTI) exercise

This is based on the premise that everyone will incline to one end of a spectrum of response to each of these four basic aspects of personality:

How we interact with the world and where we direct our energy:
(E) Extraversion------------------------x--------------------------Introversion (I)

The kind of information we naturally notice:
(S) Sensing----------------------------x------------------------------ Intuition (N)

How we analyse and make decisions:
(T) Thinking----------------------------x---------------------------------Feeling (F)

Whether we prefer to live in a more structured way (making decisions)
or in a more spontaneous way (taking in information):
(J) Judging----------------------------------x------------------------------Perceiving (P)

Each of these terms is explained in more detail in Activity 10.3 below.

Everyone's personality will reflect all of these aspects to some extent. You use Extroversion and Introversion at different times, for example. However, you are likely to have **preferences** of response to situations generally. That instinctive preference will help you arrive at your MBTI profile. This personal profile falls into one of sixteen possible combinations:

ISTJ	ISFJ	INFJ	INTJ
ISTP	ISFP	INFP	INTP
ESTP	ESFP	ENFP	ENTP
ESTJ	ESFJ	ENFJ	ENTJ

Each of these sixteen types can result in a predisposition to respond in a particular way to situations such as group work. It must be stressed that these are not fixed – people can and do behave in unexpected ways.

Try the self-assessment now in Activity 10.3 to identify which one of these sixteen types best describes your interpersonal tendencies.

ACTIVITY 10.3   THE MYERS–BRIGGS PERSONALITY TYPES

Extroversion and Introversion

If you tend to seek out the company of others, and enjoy spending time interacting with them, you are more likely to be an *Extrovert,* denoted by the letter E. If, on the other hand, you are generally happy in the company of your own thoughts and ideas, then you are more of an *Introvert*, denoted by the letter I.

For example …

Extroverts:	Introverts:
Energised by being with others	Energised by spending time alone
Often think out loud	Think things through without speech
Share personal feelings easily	More private with their feelings
Talk easily and with enthusiasm	Listen more than talk

On balance, do you incline more to E or I? Write that letter here: ☐

The kind of information we naturally notice

Do you focus on 'what is' or 'what could be'?
If you process information in terms of facts and familiar terms, it is called *Sensing* (S). If you think in terms of possibilities, it is called *iNtuition* (the letter N is used to avoid confusion with I for Introversion).

Take a look at these examples:

Sensing:	iNtuition:
Trust what is certain and 'concrete'	Trust instinct and inspiration
Like new ideas only if 'practical'	Like new ideas for their own sake
Value realism and common sense	Value imagination and innovation
Like to use established skills	Like always to learn new skills
Oriented to the present	Greater emphasis on the unknown

On balance, do you think you incline more to S or N? ☐

How we make decisions

If you make decisions based on logical and objective considerations, this is called *Thinking* (T). If personal feelings are at the heart of your decisions, this is *Feeling* (F).

For example …

Thinking:	Feeling:
Step back from problems	Care how decisions affect others
Can analyse problems objectively	Value empathy and harmony
Truth more important than tact	Like to please others
Motivated by desire to achieve	Motivated by desire to be valued
Trust feelings only if they are logical	Involve emotions in decision-making

On balance, do you think you incline more to T or F? ☐

The way we organise our lives

How do you prefer to organise your life?
Judgement (J) type personalities like to take control over their lives by being decisive, and they experience tension until a final decision on an issue is made. *Perception* (P) types prefer to be flexible while they consider various opportunities and find it stressful to decide on action which eliminates other options.

Here are some examples …

Judgement:	Perception:
Happiest after decisions are made	Prefer to leave options open
Strong work ethic	Strong play ethic

Set goals to work towards	Enjoy adapting to new situations
Want to know exact implications	Cope well with ambiguity
Gain satisfaction from finishing tasks	Enjoy starting new projects

On balance, do you think you incline more to J or P? ☐

Working out your own personality type

List the letters you have chosen for each of the four dimensions

Your choice of letters: ☐ ☐ ☐ ☐

What does your Myers–Briggs type suggest about your ideal team role?

The main purpose of trying the MBTI questionnaire here is to see how your personality type connects with the role you might best play in a group. Box 10.2 shows the team role that is most likely to equate to your personality type:

Box 10.2   Myers–Briggs group working roles

COACH	ESFJ/ENFJ
Build team spirit and harmony. Harness everyone's contributions and facilitate positive relationships. Foster agreement by overcoming conflict.	
CRUSADER	ISFP/INFP
Passionate about personal values and certain ideas. Prioritise these emphatically in team discussions.	
EXPLORER	ENTP/ENFP
Think outside the box to discover other possibilities. Challenge existing ways of doing things to develop new potential.	
INNOVATOR	INTJ/INFJ
Carefully examine the situation to develop new insights from their observations to seek radical solutions to the current problems.	
SCULPTOR	ESFP/ESTP
Focussed on achieving immediate results. Confront the current challenges by harnessing their existing resources and spurring others into action.	

CURATOR	ISFJ/ISTJ
Examine all relevant information to establish clarity. Observe carefully. Focussed on detailed plans needed to achieve well-defined goals.	
CONDUCTOR	ESTJ/ENTJ
Well-organised, bringing a systematic structure and plan to implement necessary actions. Define responsibilities and apply resources.	
SCIENTIST	ISTP/INTP
Gather evidence to explain all aspects of the situation. Develop useful theoretical ideas and ways of making these work in practice.	

The above exercises on Myers–Briggs personality types have been adapted from the Bradford University Effective Learning Service booklet, 'Group Work' (Neville 2006).

You can read explanations of the personality types associated with your choice of letters at: www.personalitypathways.com/type_inventory.html or https://www.16personalities.com/. If you are interested in exploring the personality types concept further, you can also read the following sources on which the above exercise is based:

- Briggs-Myers, I. (2000) *Introduction to Type.* 6th edition. Oxford: Oxford Psychologists Press.
- Myers, K.D and Kirby, L.K. (2000) *Introduction to Type Dynamics & Development: Exploring the Next Level of Type.* Oxford: Oxford Psychologists Press.

Pause for Thought

How accurate do you feel this exercise has been in pinpointing your likely team role?

Very accurate -- *Very inaccurate*

Which aspects of your personality type would you most like to express in your next group project?

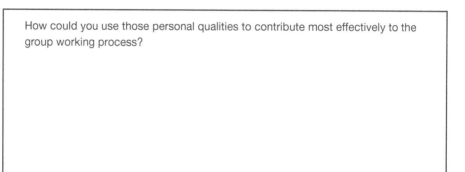

How could you use those personal qualities to contribute most effectively to the group working process?

How can personality types help your group work?

In group work, we may act unconsciously in ways that are influenced by the innate tendencies suggested by self-assessment exercises such as MBTI personality types. If you do think the results describe your character quite accurately, then you might like to suggest that other members of your group try the same exercise.

Students usually find a personality questionnaire quite entertaining, so if nothing else, it can be a light-hearted icebreaker to help build some group rapport. You can try suggesting this for group members to do after the first meeting, and bring their results to the following one, but without any serious pressure. You can compare notes at the next meeting, and discuss how this might help you work together by each member explaining what they understand about their natural tendencies in group work.

However, some see the concept of personality types as limiting because this can seem to categorise an individual into a definite identity. Most of us have the capacity to think flexibly and the potential to act unpredictably in different situations. Paradoxically perhaps, an important principle to therefore keep in mind during these self-assessment exercises is that we are all different. Each of us is literally a unique individual. No two people have an identical set of innate traits, background and experiences. First and foremost then, value yourself and the distinctive qualities that you bring to any group situation.

Are you the group leader?

You will doubtless study theories of leadership as an academic subject during your business and management degree programme. Group work provides an opportunity for you to observe those principles in practice. This is assuming, of course, that the group accepts the need for a leader at all. So that is the first question for you to consider:

Do we need a leader to co-ordinate our individual inputs to the group project?

If the answer to that is yes, your next question may well be:

'Do I want to be that leader?'

That is a question that only you can answer, of course. It may help to reflect on the pros and cons of this decision from the perspective of past students who found themselves in that position ...

I have done three group-works, and in all I consciously led the group because mostly my skills are planning and time management. I took responsibility, identified their strengths to work on certain areas. I could see that my maturity level is increasing ... I need to accept certain things from others, everyone is not same as me. We need to make some adjustment in our life.

(Ammar, MSc HRM)

I realised we're all sailing in the same boat ... no-one knows everything, they just pretend to be like that. So one of our group took charge, and he used to explain like a tutor, in our 'language'. Because you know the lecturer, it's like he's too fast, and we're too scared to ask. So that's how we learned – from the group leader and each other.

(Sophia, BSc Marketing)

One useful way to conceptualise the leader role could be to think of this as a responsibility for **guiding the team towards three levels of objectives:**

- **The goal for the group as a whole:** *What is the collective purpose that we all need to work towards?*
- **Individual tasks for each member of the group:** *How can each person best contribute to that shared goal?*
- **Your personal development:** *How can I grow through the experience of leadership?*

As the group leader, you certainly need to keep these aims in mind as you facilitate meetings and co-ordinate the project activities beyond those meetings. You need to ensure that everyone is involved to the best of their abilities, maximising the opportunities for overall group achievement and your personal learning.

The positive potential of group work

At the end of each academic year, students typically report that they appreciate how much they have grown through the process of interpersonal challenges. They often recognise that the most significant personal development has been achieved by being forced to go beyond previous intellectual and emotional 'comfort zones' (Leask 2010; Sedgley 2013). This can be surprising, but perhaps for that reason, also very rewarding:

In the first semester I didn't have anybody with me. I didn't feel good. Then, I realised there are many like me, but who actually take time to open up. The second semester ... I made a lot of friends through study group-work, and I started feeling good that I'm not in an unknown place. We shared, shared, shared ... so I got that emotional support ... they're ready to help me, so we didn't hide anything from each other.

(Victoria, BSc Accounting and Finance)

Chapter summary

- **A positive attitude to collaboration** goes a long way towards enabling success in group work.
- If you consciously develop that mindset before you communicate with others in a group, you will convey a more **positive appreciation** of them as individuals.
- Each person brings different, **complementary qualities** to the group work.
- So a vital key to successful team-working is your attitude towards others: Are you genuinely **curious, attentive and respectful?**
- You cannot guarantee that everyone will naturally bring that attitude, so **efficient organisation and effective communication** are also crucial to optimise success.
- However tough the experience, use group projects to **practise and develop team-working skills** that will make you stand out to future employers.

Activity Answers

Activity 10.2: Helpful objectives for a first group meeting

It is crucial to group success that you establish a clear agenda for discussion at the beginning of the meeting. Here are suggested objectives to provide that structure:

- Everyone is invited to say a little about themselves, what they think the group should set out to achieve and what they want to contribute to that process.
- Everyone commits to an agreed, common goal.
- Ensure that everyone has a clear understanding of their responsibilities by the end of the meeting. Each person agrees to specific, individual actions to be delivered by certain deadlines, reporting back to the group as necessary.
- A schedule of further group meeting dates is booked into everyone's calendars, leading to final submission of the group project by the required, final deadline.

Managing Challenges in Group Work

The previous chapter presented a range of practical ideas for effective group work. However, they are not in themselves a guarantee of success. Human nature in all its complexity intrudes into teamworking, triggering differences of opinion, personality clashes or open conflict. These are the really tricky elements of group work because they can be so entrenched in strongly held beliefs, diverse values and emotional reactivity. However, interpersonal conflicts also offer an opportunity for personal growth – one which requires real effort, maturity and open-heartedness in each person to take personal responsibility for what is going wrong, and how to change that.

This chapter therefore supports you in finding new ways of thinking and acting in group conflicts. Self-reflective techniques help you to take a step back from emotive situations, recognise your own unconscious patterns and learn how to change these for the better. These will help you immediately in group work during your time at university and for developing interpersonal employability skills longer term:

- Recognise your **'emotional positioning'** within the group to consciously support yourself in becoming more comfortable and constructive.
- Understand the **causes of group conflicts**, *including how you may be contributing to those problems.*
- Establish **what you can and cannot control** in group work situations.
- Identify the **least stressful and most productive attitude** with which you can approach challenging group situations to influence them for the better.
- **Take responsibility for your feelings, thoughts and actions** in group work by learning techniques for approaching even the most challenging situations confidently and resourcefully.

An emotional challenge

In the early stages of a degree programme, students have had little opportunity to form friendships, so it is likely that they will be allocated to groups by their tutors, perhaps on the basis of mixing gender and cultural backgrounds. Facing such a group of disparate strangers can naturally be quite daunting. Students also often find group work projects more time-consuming and stressful than working alone on individual assignments. Conflicts can easily arise, particularly under the pressure of looming assessment deadlines when it can feel difficult for you to ensure a full group commitment that reflects your own academic ambitions.

Our reactions to such conflicts can easily descend into a 'blame game'. It is quite natural for any of us to project our emotions onto other group members, holding them responsible for what is going wrong in the communication process. Yet fixing the blame on others rarely, if ever, resolves conflict.

You may well feel differently in each new group that you encounter, of course. You can experience a smooth, productive process with one group that fosters deep friendships, only to meet apparently unmanageable conflict in the next. If you do find yourself caught up in these kinds of interpersonal challenges, it can be helpful to take a step back and notice how you see yourself in relation to those around you. The figure below shows one novel way that you might like to do that:

Pause for Thought: 'Tree Blobs'

Which of the figures in the tree best represents where you instinctively feel yourself to be in your current group(s)?

(There is definitely no right or wrong answer to this question, so no need to check the Activity Answers!)

(Wilson, P and Long, I. (2018) *The Big Book of Blob Trees – Front Page* (2nd edition). Abingdon: Routledge. Reproduced by kind permission of Taylor and Francis.)

Write in your reflective journal about how it feels to be where you currently perceive yourself to be in your group.

Case study: recognising and managing intercultural conflict

The following case study explores how one student positioned herself emotionally within a group, based on her perception of how others seemed to be relating to her. This presents an opportunity to reflect on how the group could have handled personal and intercultural conflict more constructively. This is based on the real experience of a Chinese student, Li, studying at a western university.

On Li's Marketing and Enterprise module, students worked as consultants with a real-life company to develop a strategy for addressing a business problem or opportunity identified by the client. They were allocated by the tutor into groups of six students, partly based on a multicultural mix.

Li describes her experience below in her own words. Read the case study carefully, then answer the questions that follow:

The group surprised me because everyone was so confident and willing to contribute to the work. I also looked forward to contributing to the group as I knew I could finish any task because I am willing to spend time on it. Before the group work tasks were established, I did some research about the client's local competitors as I wanted to contribute something valuable in the discussion. But it turned out not to be valid because the next discussion was about the project report structure and did not go into any of the kind of details I had discovered. After that, everyone obtained a task related to the structure.

I was disappointed that my work was easy, and not related to analysis. I thought that I was not being trusted. I learned before that people should do things perfectly before they can argue for more work. So I tried my best to do things I thought valuable, and assist my team as much as I could. The team leader did assign more tasks for me in the next meeting, but not much. In this group, I saw myself as an assistant – collecting data, making tables – and I kept asking others, 'Does anybody want some help'?

At first, I felt I lost my confidence to work with local students. I believe it is hard to involve Chinese students in discussions, so forming an efficient team with such members will be more difficult. The experience in dividing the work let me feel that the team did not trust me, but on the other side, they were so confident that they would do things well. I lacked the confidence to ask them to give me some work that they were doing. I thought they would probably feel unsatisfied if my work was not better than they can do.

Those experiences have positive sides but also negative. The worst one is I lost my confidence for a long time. However, I know I am not the perfect person, and I do not need to compare myself with anyone else. What I should do is never feel shame, not be sensitive, and keep learning through plenty of mistakes. But I still doubted myself. I was afraid those people in this group may not like me, so I agreed with nearly all the opinions, and did not insist on explaining any view if anyone showed any negative response. So although I worked in this group, I did not influence the group.

However, there are some good things for me. I used to be a leader in groups in China. I liked organizing people and doing more than others. I enjoyed the feeling that others rely on me. But that is not always a positive thing. Experiences in this group let me know how to be a good follower, which is an important skill, and helps me get rid of narcissism. The group received a reasonable grade for the report, and this was awarded to all members. Also, I obtained a chance to work with students who come from a totally different background, thus I can see a miniature of international business.

This is a complex case study with no single 'right' answer to the Li's challenges. However, these questions may help you establish what the problems actually were, and what you believe caused them.

Identifying sources of group conflict

1   What does the case study suggest goes wrong in this group?

2   Is that a problem for the whole group? Why/why not?

The case study does centre on Li's perception of her own difficulties in the group. The following questions help you to consider who is responsible for these problems, and how they may have created them.

Who is responsible?

1   In what ways, if any, do you think the other members contributed to Li's unsatisfactory experience in the group?

2   In what ways, if any, do you think Li herself contributed to those problems?

As a group, you may well be able to influence members' actions in productive ways through certain collective agreements, as discussed in detail in Chapter 10. These aim to establish common ground that, in this case, may have involved Li more effectively. Sound principles for this kind of rational approach to collaborative group work are shown in Box 11.1.

Box 11.1   Some ground rules for effective group-work

- Setting clear group objectives.
- Giving time to each member to identify their relevant strengths and interests.
- Conducting self-assessments to identify personality types for team roles.
- Allocating tasks according to members' strengths and capabilities.
- Adopting a leader who takes on an extra, coordinating responsibility.
- Setting clear milestones, deadlines and a schedule of meetings.

(See Chapter 10 for more guidance.)

The purpose of this chapter, though, is to recognise that in spite of such best-laid plans, group members sometimes do not commit to those or follow them through. In this case study, we have seen that some members may have believed that they were organising the group actions quite efficiently. However, for Li at least, it is clear that a lack of communication in the early stages excluded her potentially helpful involvement. This problem could have been avoided if group members had adopted a different attitude, notably towards Li.

A more positive attitude at the early stages of group working could be characterised by any or all of the following.

Box 11.2   Constructive attitudes for effective group work

- Curiosity about each other's backgrounds.
- Expectation that each person has something important to contribute.
- Warmth/empathy.
- A recognition of the need for time to allow everyone to contribute.
- A valuing of the *process* of communication as much as the outcomes.

These kinds of positive approaches to group working may well yield real benefits. Strengthened friendships and enhanced interpersonal skills can emerge from such groups, just as tutors may hope (Elliott and Robinson 2012). The issue of personal responsibility is central to all teamwork. If you consciously own your attitude in interpersonal situations, you may be surprised not only at the difference in the quality of your own experience but also in positive changes in others' actions.

Academic results are also likely to improve through collaborative action. De Vita (2002) investigated group work on a first-year business studies programme of a UK university and found that the performance of culturally mixed groups does not depend on the individual ability of the least-able group member or the average ability of the group members. Instead, **the group work mark is more likely to reflect the performance of the most capable group member**. Assessed multicultural group work also has, on average, a positive effect on the individual average mark of all students.

However, De Vita (2005) observes that despite average group work grades being higher than for individual coursework, students are apprehensive about this form of assessment. They remain unconvinced about the value of group work, even though tutors often suggest that this emulates the teamworking dynamics of the workplace (Carroll 2005) as one student illustrates below:

> There's always at least one person who is not going to do anything. First meeting, two guys didn't show up, other two guys hadn't read the case ... I felt really stupid because I'd lost two hours. We met again and one guy didn't show up ... the other guy ... was just listening to us. So you have five people ... but just two are really working on it.

(Denis, MSc International Business Management)

Some students are frustrated with their peers, as in the above example, while others experience anxiety about their own academic abilities and disengage from the project. In a study by Storrs (2012), two students who belonged to very productive groups felt their own contributions were inadequate, much as Li did in our case study. They found it difficult to maintain enthusiasm for their group tasks amid other academic pressures and felt significant guilt as a result. This raises the question each of us needs to face when dealing with others, 'How do I really want to be in this situation?'

In Activity 11.3, you can consider how Li might answer that question.

ACTIVITY 11.3

Taking personal responsibility

1   How might Li *help herself* more in future group work?

Note your ideas below on how she could *adapt her thoughts, feelings and actions* to improve her experience in such situations.

Take a look at the Activity Answers for some further ideas on managing yourself in this kind of challenging group situation.

Empowering yourself to be an effective group member

In the last paragraph of the case study, Li showed an admirable willingness to stop projecting blame onto others for her problems with the group. Instead, she looked inward to find a way of reframing the experience as a learning opportunity for her personal development. She recognised her tendency in China to take charge of other members as a self-appointed leader. Encountering more of a 'stretch zone' in her foreign education, she learned a value to acting as a follower, rather than a leader.

Whether or not you agree with her interpretations of that self-reflection, Li clearly feels that realisation has been helpful for her. She has chosen a way of reviewing her experience to develop a deeper understanding of her personality type and how she can constructively adapt that to different situations.

Reframe your perceptions of others

It is so easy to hold others responsible for our problems. Perhaps you can change your perceptions to simply observe that *people do what they do*. And this may often be in conflict with what you would like them to do. In other words, we give ourselves stress by expecting that others should or should not do certain things and become frustrated or resentful when they do not live up to *our demands on their behaviour*.

Instead, you could use a reflective model such as the one shown in Box 11.3 to reframe your unmet expectations of group members' contributions. This is based on a framework developed by Mitchell (2002), which she simply calls *Inquiry.* Mitchell suggests there are four simple questions you can ask yourself to challenge any of your beliefs about how other people should or should not behave.

Box 11.3   Self-empowerment model for reframing interpersonal challenges

The process starts with you identifying a statement to describe another's behaviour that has upset you, **e.g. *'He should talk to me more respectfully'*.** Next, you spend some time writing reflectively around this judgement of that person from the four question prompts of Mitchell's model:

1 **Is that statement true?**
   You simply answer the question instinctively at this stage – Yes or No.

2 **Are you absolutely sure that's true?**
   Consider this question more carefully now – how realistic is it to expect everyone to fully respect you? We apply so many *'shoulds' and 'shouldn'ts'* to others' lives, as well as our own, and yet, *in reality,* all of us on some occasions do not live up to those injunctions.
   Then answer the question in the way that feels most honest – Yes or No.

3 **What happens when this is your expectation of others in group work?**
   Write expressively and at length about what you think, feel and do.

4 **How would you be if you did not have that expectation?**
   Imagine standing next to that person without your previous expectation of them. Write instinctively how you would feel if you did not have that expectation.

How might that change the way you think? How would you act differently in that situation?

This process is not necessarily suggesting that you can easily drop the stressful thought. It is simply providing another way of looking at the situation that is more likely to bring you peace of mind, clarity of intention and positive future action.

The 'turnaround'

The final step for completing that process is what Mitchell calls the *Turnaround*. You go back to your original statement and turn that around in a variety of ways, paying careful attention to which version(s) has some kind of emotional impact for you. You can then explore the implications of those to perhaps discover revealing insights for how you can approach group conflicts differently.

The self-empowerment model in practice

This is illustrated below with a relevant example commonly expressed by frustrated students in group work: *'He should have done more work for the group assessment.'*

1 **Is that statement true?**
   Yes, we all agreed to research and write up individual sections of the report. He didn't do his on time, so the rest of us had to cover that to not lose marks.

2 **Are you absolutely sure that's true?**
   Well, it still seems that he should have played his part. Although, I guess I am 'arguing with reality' because the truth is that he didn't do the work. So for me to keep insisting he should do that doesn't actually reflect what has already happened.

3 **What happens when you have that expectation of others?**
   I resent his arrogance and laziness. I feel frustrated with him and disappointed in myself that I have not been able to get him to contribute his fair share of the workload. In the last meeting, I challenged him angrily about this, reminding him that we had all agreed individual tasks to be done by a certain time, yet he hadn't submitted that to me as the leader, or come to the subsequent meetings. He just said it wasn't that important because his individual assessments carried more marks, so he was concentrating on those. I told him this was unacceptable behaviour and that we were all suffering from his lack of commitment. Now, when I see him in the corridor, we ignore each other, and it feels uncomfortable. I keep running it round my mind trying to work out how I and the other members could have made him do the work.

4 **How would you be if you did not have that expectation?**
   It seems hard to imagine, but if I didn't have that thought – that he should have done the work – and I just focussed on having achieved a good piece of work, I'd be free of the stress. In the end, we divided his task between another member and myself. It didn't take too long once we decided what to do. I could recognise that we've probably done better without his involvement, which would have been half-hearted at best. I could just relax and concentrate on my next, individual assignment, confident that I'm on track for what I want out of my degree. I wouldn't be worrying about how to handle things next time I see him. I could just acknowledge him as another student on a different learning journey.

Possible turnarounds
a) *He shouldn't do more work …*
b) *I should do more work …*
c) *I shouldn't do more work …*

Each of these is considered below:

a) *He shouldn't do more work …*
Well, that does seem to be the truth of it. He did not do the work, and the sooner you come to accept that, the better you may feel, judging by the answers to Q.4 above. You may find this makes it much easier to communicate with him more openly and respectfully, yet still frankly, in future.

b) *I should do more work …*
This may be a pragmatic realisation in university group work where project leaders do not have any authority to impose sanctions on less motivated colleagues. You cannot really control anyone else's input, only your own.

c) *I shouldn't do more work …*
Conversely, you can also choose *not to* take on the responsibilities for other group outputs, and, instead, allow others to do so. This could be challenging, just as Li discovered in the case study. Like her, you may realise that sometimes it is not a bad thing to step back and 'go with the flow'. This might force you out of your usual 'control zone', but perhaps that turns out not to be as uncomfortable as you once thought.

You can try the self-empowerment model for yourself now in Activity 11.4. Use this opportunity to discover how you can reframe a resentment you currently hold toward someone from your university experience:

ACTIVITY 11.4

Self-empowerment model practice

Write a statement that captures in just a few words your unmet expectation of someone, i.e. what you think they should or should not be doing (See Box 11.3 above if you are unsure how to start this):

Having written a statement that describes how you believe that other person should be acting differently, you can then interrogate that expectation by writing your instinctive responses to the four questions proposed in Mitchell's (2002) model:

- **Is it true that they should be acting in that way?**

- Are you sure it is true?

- What do you feel, think and do when you believe this?

- How would you be if you let go of that thought?

Then you turn around the original statement and find out how one or more of those turnarounds may free you up in some way from your stress. Write those turnarounds below (Refer to the above example if you are unsure how to do this):

Taking responsibility for your experience

Some group members do not follow even the best-laid plans for group work. *This divergence results in some kind of group conflict,* whether expressed or unspoken. In these cases, people entrench themselves into polarised positions and *project the blame for the conflict onto others.* If these members do not want to actively commit to the group's ground rules, you may not be able to overcome that non-cooperation. *You can only really change your own attitude and responses to this resistance.*

You need to recognise what is best for you in this group situation. Often enough, this will not seem ideal or 'fair'. But if you can choose to make your peace with the situation rather than insist on 'justice', then you may find that positive attitude 'ripples out' to others without the need for aggressive or defensive confrontation. *You can decide how you intend to think and act when next faced with a similar situation.* Are you going to focus on what you can control – your own thoughts and feelings?

When you recognise that the one person you can control is yourself, you can decide any of the following:

Box 11.4   The feelings you *can* control in group-work

- Your emotional state when you enter each meeting.
- The emotional qualities with which you meet others.
- The ways you think and act in the meeting.
- The tangible objectives you would like the group to achieve.
- The amount of time you are willing to invest in working towards those.
- Your strongest capabilities that you can contribute to that team effort.
- How you constructively respond to difficult situations such as group conflict.

All of this takes conscious commitment, of course. Like any other life activity, it can be easy to drift into group meetings without much forethought, especially when you are under mounting academic pressure. However, this leaves you vulnerable to acting *unconsciously*, e.g. being led too easily by others, or reacting over-defensively. Instead, you can choose to decide, **'What is most important for me in this situation?'**

Take charge of the way that you feel, think and act in meetings

You can consciously adopt a positive state when you go into group situations. As you first sit in the meeting, take a few deep breaths, bringing your attention into your body. Notice any tension and as you breathe out, soften and let go in that part of your body. You can do all of this quite unnoticeably to others.

As you settle into the meeting, remind yourself how you really want to feel while you are there. Choose a word to repeat to yourself with each breath, e.g. *calm, confident, supportive, decisive, attentive.*

Know that you can act from that positive feeling throughout the meeting. Remember that from time to time, so you **detach from the discussion**, especially during any disagreements, to come back into your body awareness and that positive emotional state. Then after a few breaths, you can re-engage in the meeting.

If it seems difficult for you to access this positive state in a meeting itself, you can 'anchor' that feeling in advance, as explained in Activity 10.1. Practise that initially every day for up to a month. Repetition is the key to the effectiveness of anchoring. When you then need the positive feeling at an anxious time in your life, such as a group meeting, apply the anchor firmly, repeating the key word in your mind, with each out-breath.

Focus on tangible objectives you would like the group to achieve

With more capability to control your own emotional state in the meeting, you have less need to expend energy on thinking or acting defensively. Instead, you can choose to stay focussed on what seems best for the group overall. Remember that this is likely to be about *the process* as much as the task. Perhaps you can suggest some of the ideas discussed in Chapter 10 to involve everyone in sharing information about themselves, and how they might best contribute to the group.

For the group task, concentrate on communicating constructively. Remember this is a two-way process – **listen carefully to others' ideas:**

- **Overtly affirm** any that you believe to be helpful.
- **Relate these to your own ideas** about what needs to be done and by when.
- **Focus on what is achievable** in the project time available.
- **Identify positive steps** towards those outcomes.

Establish a realistic personal commitment to those group objectives

Remember that you can contribute your strongest capabilities to the overall team effort. Ensure that you articulate to the group what those strengths are in terms of this particular project, e.g. existing knowledge of a relevant area; research skills; writing and editing; co-ordinating others' inputs.

You need to be clear with yourself about how much time is reasonable for you to expend on this group work in relation to your other commitments. That is a judgement that only you can make, but keep reminding yourself to stay within those limits as group work can easily take over a disproportionate amount of your time. **Important questions to ask yourself** could be:

- Do you want to take on a leadership role to develop your employability skills?
- Do you want to take charge of this project for the sake of completing the task in what you can see is a weaker group?
- Are you happy to follow someone else's lead in this particular project?
- Which task(s) would you prefer to undertake?

Chapter summary

- The employability skills that you can develop in the relatively 'safe' context of university group work will be integral to your later success in workplace team-working. Employers place great importance on this graduate attribute of effective communication and collaborative problem-solving.
- Reflective processes such as the Self-Empowerment Model can help you to step away from your emotive reactions and evaluate how you can respond more constructively and purposefully in difficult situations with others in future.
- Establish clear, positive intentions for your contribution to the group, and rehearse those beforehand.
- Understand that you are responsible for your actions but cannot control others' reactions.
- Reflect honestly after difficult interactions on what you have learned about yourself. Use this self-appraisal to adapt to future situations in the best way for you.

Activity Answers

Activity 11.1: Possible sources of group conflict

Q.1 Your answer could suggest

The case is written from Li's own perspective. So we only have one side of the story. But that is the problem in any group situation, is it not? Each of us only has a subjective view. We create our own interpretation of the rights and wrongs, especially in conflict situations such as this case.

Although this might not seem a conflict at first sight, perhaps that is only because Li does not voice her grievances about her lack of involvement. That could be termed 'hidden' or 'passive' conflict.

So the problem seems essentially to be a lack of communication. Li is frustrated by the others not asking her about the work she has done or could do for the group. She compounds that by not voicing her concerns or asserting her strengths – for the reasons noted in the case study.

Q.2 Your answer could suggest

The other members' perspectives might be that there was nothing wrong with this group. As Li did not voice her frustrations, perhaps they were genuinely unaware of her concerns. They achieved a reasonable grade through a process that they may have perceived as an efficient use of their time and a relative success.

Activity 11.2: Who is responsible for what?

Q.1 Your answer could refer to:

- *Cultural differences.*
  These affected group communication, with more members focussed on *task rather than process*, for example. Hofstede (2001) claims that low-context countries, e.g. the US, focus on completing tasks rather than building relationships in the way that high-context countries like China do.

  Perhaps the members missed some wider learning opportunities through not trying to appreciate Li's cultural background. Hofstede argues that a lack of understanding of such dimensions may lead to 'cultural myopia' which limits productive communication.

- *Lack of awareness of each other's potential strengths.*
  Another cultural dimension proposed by Hofstede is that of perceptions of time. Related to the above idea of task versus process, some countries, such as the UK, may be less willing to allow plenty of time to find out how everyone can best contribute to any group process.

  This case study may be typical of many student group work projects where most members are mainly concerned with finishing the work as soon as possible because of other individual study commitments. The pressure of multiple assignment deadlines may mean that allowing time for team-building processes seems an unaffordable luxury.

Q.2 Your answer could refer to:

- Li's lack of confidence from the earlier group encounter, and her perception that others did not trust her.
- Li's need for approval leading to her subservience.
- Li's assumptions that others' apparent self-efficacy means they are more capable than her of successfully organising the group work.

Activity 11.3: Taking personal responsibility

Q.1 Your answer could recognise:

Unless a group prioritises the benefits to be gained from team-building, and acknowledges the downside of not harnessing the knowledge and skills of each member, any problem simply remains with the individual, in this case, Li. Perhaps only she can really help herself through some of the following realisations:

- She should not expect herself to be perfect, but be willing to practise by communicating even through mistakes.
- Remind herself of her qualities and capabilities to enhance the project.
- Proactively help others understand her cultural and personal background.
- Expect that others may trust her – really meaning that she needs to trust herself.

Delivering Effective Presentations

Presenting to groups is an essential employability skill for your career in the corporate world. Like any other soft skill, becoming an effective presenter takes time and practice. This chapter enables you to accelerate that process with practical tips and proven techniques to apply in the presentation assessments on your management degree. This is divided into the two distinct stages of the presentation process:

Preparation
- Captivate your audience with engaging messages, including three verbal tactics to hook everyone's attention in the first minute.
- Create impact with strong visuals.
- Develop confidence through focussed rehearsal.

Performance
- Understand how your body language can build rapport with the audience.
- Use your voice to optimum effect with pace, emphasis and projection.
- Manage anxiety and present confidently right from the start.

ACTIVITY 12.1

Key principles of effective presentations

Think back over some different types of public presentations that you have witnessed in your life. You may have been bored by some, but others will have interested, or even fascinated you. If none come easily to mind, you could watch some TED talks on a subject of interest until you find one or more that really inspires you.

Write your thoughts below about how those impressive presenters made you 'sit up and take notice' …

See the Activity Answers for some suggested key principles of effective presentations.

This chapter provides tips and techniques to help you master these principles, which can be summarised in the four major themes below:

1 **Identifying a relevant focus and clear structure.**
2 **Creating interesting messages and visuals.**
3 **Showing enthusiasm for the subject.**
4 **Engaging actively with the audience.**

There is, however, one fundamental principle that underpins all of these.

Pause for Thought

What do you think is the most important ingredient of all that guarantees your presentation will engage, interest and convince your audience? Write your answer below:

It has been said that there are three fundamental principles to truly successful presentations – The 3Ps:

1 **Preparation**
2 **Preparation**
3 **Preparation**

The next section opens up this seemingly simplistic idea of the 3Ps to find out what fully preparing yourself and your material really entails.

Prepare for success

Establish how much information you can present

Perhaps the most common mistake made by student presenters is 'too much information, too little time'. Even experienced public speakers can fall into the trap of overwhelming an audience with too many materials and messages. This can be compounded when making group presentations. What you most want to avoid is for group members to be rushing through the presentation, trying to squeeze in too much information, and over-running each other's time slots. This simply disengages the audience. So, the first maxim of an effective presentation for everyone in your group to grasp is, 'keep it short and simple' (KISS).

An advantage of university presentations is that the tutor will set a definite time limit for each group. Once you know the timeframe, divide that equally among the number of members. You can then calculate how many slides and any other audio-visual materials each person will be able to cover. The realistic constraints of a typical student group presentation are given in Box 12.1.

Box 12.1   Planning the right balance of information and time

- It is quite common for a group to be given 10–15 minutes for a presentation.
- Assuming a typical group composition of three or four members, each student has around four minutes for their individual input.
- Let's further assume that your presentation will use a combination of PowerPoint slides and videos. The latter are optional, of course, but a short YouTube clip can help to maintain audience interest.
- A useful rule of thumb is to allow up to two minutes to present the ideas from a single slide, and perhaps a minute to show an online clip. Each presenter should only prepare two slides with one or two also perhaps using a short video.
- As a group, you may also decide that you need a brief introduction and conclusion slide. You need to allow a short time for each of those too.

You can apply the above parameters for each project you work on. One of the main aims of your first group meeting should therefore be to define the constraints of how much material each member will be creating for the presentation. **This will save you all a great deal of time in researching those topics**. The next section explores another major time-saver at this idea generation/research stage.

Identify a precise focus to your presentation

In your group assessments, the tutor may set a task to present a group report on an organisational project for a given company. In other modules, the tutor may give you more scope to generate a presentation of your own choosing. This latter case is illustrated in the example below, where your overall presentation task has been set by the tutor as follows:

> *Select a multinational enterprise (MNE) that has recently experienced a major Corporate Social Responsibility (CSR) challenge, and explain their response(s) to that in ethical terms.*

In your first group meeting, you need to allow everyone to freely contribute suggestions for the choice of company. You can then finalise that selection by considering some of the following factors:

- How easy will it be to access information online about each company?
- Which company do most members seem more interested in?

- Which of these companies has recently experienced a public challenge to its business ethics? Perhaps group members recall seeing a scandal of some kind, e.g. child labour exploitation in a foreign manufacturing plant.
- How interested will your audience be in this company's ethics? You can consider whether they may be existing consumers of that company's products, for example.

If we assume that your group has settled on Apple as your company of choice, you can now define the **topic focus**. Two possible options are suggested in Activity 12.2 for you to consider in relation to the above assignment topic:

ACTIVITY 12.2

Defining the presentation focus

Which of these two titles will be better for a 15-minute presentation?

1 *Corporate Social Responsibility and Apple Inc.*
2 *Ethical challenges with Apple employees' working conditions in Chinese manufacturing facilities*

Note the reasons for your preferred choice below:

See the Activity Answers for a critique of these two options.

Know your topic 'inside out'

Having identified your focus, the next step is to conduct rigorous research, which will enable you to produce a coherent, relevant and interesting set of materials that will engage your audience from start to finish. There is no escaping the need to familiarise yourself with the topic so thoroughly that you can **speak directly from your understanding**. By the time you present, you should only need your visual materials as simple prompts to lead your audience through the main issues of the topic.

Create strong, clear, simple presentation materials

There are two main principles to follow in creating visual material such as PowerPoint slides:

1 *Minimise the amount of text on your slides.*
   Summarise key ideas briefly, perhaps in the form of bullet points. The words should also be immediately readable, so use a large font size: 24 point is suggested as a minimum.
2 *Create attractive, intriguing graphics*
   The use of visuals, e.g. photographs, charts, line drawings, is critical to maintaining interest throughout the presentation. You need a high-impact slide in the

beginning to grab audience attention and attractive graphics regularly from then on to maintain that interest.

Activity 12.3 gives you an opportunity to judge the impact of text and graphics from students' presentations on the above topic of Apple's ethical conduct in Chinese factories:

ACTIVITY 12.3

Creating impact with presentation slides

Rank the following slides in order of most effective impact:

A.

B.

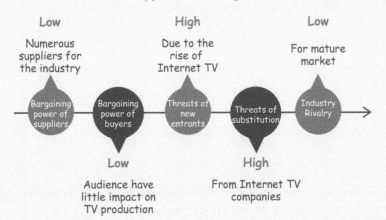

C.

The circular economy in action

Luckily for Chi-Chi, Dell's packaging is made from **100 %** renewably sourced bamboo with a **growback rate of one inch an hour**

(delltechnologies 2019)

D.

Leadership style

Advantages and disadvantages of democratic leadership:

- Solution for complex problems
- Fosters creative environments
- Strong teams are built by democratic leaders
- Can appear uncertain
- Time consuming
- It takes too long to process decisions
- It tends to become apologetic

Slide	Ranking (best impact first)
A	
B	
C	
D	

Check the Activity Answers for a suggested ranking. Then read on below for further discussion of the positives (+) and negatives (−) of each slide.

Slide A

+	• Well-researched data. • Combination of text and statistics. • Carefully formatted. • Interesting use of coloured background with white text.
−	• An overload of congested messages. • Over-ambitious slide creation: Lots of text too small to read easily. • Too many different parts to the slide. There may be useful research behind this, but the complexity will confuse some viewers.

Slide B

+	• A clear exposition of theory related to a real-life case study. • Simple graphics illustrate how Porter's five forces apply in practice. • Brief summary points are easily grasped by the audience. • Alternating colours and text sizes enable the audience to differentiate the messages easily. • Plenty of white space.
−	• The text of the five forces' balloons is too small for easy reading.

Slide C

+	• Photographs are eye-catching. • Main picture and caption will amuse or at least engage most people. • This will also intrigue the audience when used with the animation function in PowerPoint to show the picture on its own first. The presenter can then fade in the right-hand caption to relate the business message to that. • Text is large and clear, with the significant statistics highlighted for immediate impact. • Citation included for sourced data. (The photograph was taken by the author, but a citation would be needed if this had been sourced online.)
−	• There are no obvious negatives to this slide.

Slide D

+	• The first graphic gives a clear metaphor easily understood by anyone. • This is also supported by simple bullet points.
−	• The text and graphics are too small and should dominate the space more. • A bullet point list is standardised and predictable. If this is the only format used throughout your presentation, your audience will soon switch off. • The graphics are simplistic and rather uninteresting. • These are likely to have come from an online photo bank such as Google Images, and they need citations to the original sources. • The second graphic's meaning is not immediately clear.

Rehearse your knowledge of the topic

You must rehearse your presentation several times to effectively test your knowledge of the most important points to put across on the day. There are two ways you could do this:

1 Sit at your computer and run through the slides, videos or other presentation materials you will be using. Take your time, and imagine what you will say about each of the points that you have created.
2 Practise with someone who will give 'critical friend' feedback to improve aspects of the presentation they found less convincing or understandable. You could also ask them to concentrate on specific factors you are concerned about, e.g. body language. Take this opportunity to really pinpoint your key areas for improvement.

Whichever form of rehearsal you use, the purpose is to check how well prepared you are to present powerfully on the day:

Box 12.2   Practice makes (near) perfect

- As you rehearse, do take the opportunity to encourage yourself by recognising which issues you know well. This preparation is all designed to **help you feel confident** enough to deliver the topic convincingly.
- Acknowledge honestly the points where you hesitate or waffle. Practise or amend these as many times as you need. You must feel confident that you can **elaborate on each point from only a simple message or graphic**.
- Identify which visuals or messages do not have much impact. Be ruthless in eliminating or improving these. Pay particular attention to how you can **enhance visual graphics and shorten text messages.**
- As you familiarise yourself repeatedly with the content of your topic, some key themes will begin to emerge. Ensure that you become word perfect with the phrases or technical terms that capture these **crucial messages**.

Summary: preparing your presentation

- **Keep it simple:** Narrow your topic down to a realistic focus.
- **Keep it short:** Carefully calculate how many slides and video clips you can cover *unhurriedly* within the total presentation time limit.
- **Maximise visual impact:** Create graphics in a majority of slides.
- **Make it readable:** Minimal text with simple bullet points in a large font size.
- **Practise, practise, practise.**

Successful performance on the day

In employment selection opportunities such as interviews, psychologists suggest that employers make up their minds whether to give you the job in less than ten seconds (Rook 2019). First impressions are just as important in presentations. How can you ensure your audience is leaping to a favourable judgement about you?

One-minute impact

You need to make a special impact in the first minute of your presentation. Essentially, this is the time when the audience decide whether they can trust you enough to keep listening attentively – or not.

You have two main resources that determine the first impression you make on your audience:

1   Your materials, e.g. slides and possibly other resources such as videos.
2   Yourself as the presenter.

The first part of this chapter has already covered a lot of ideas about creating high-impact materials, emphasising the importance of careful, thorough preparation – 'The 3Ps'. The second half of the chapter now introduces 'The 3Vs' model for maximising your personal effectiveness on the day (Box 12.3):

Box 12.3   The 3Vs Model of Communication

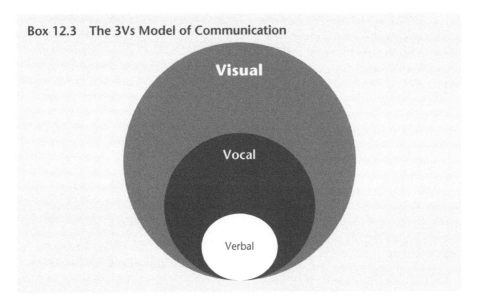

This model illustrates the relative importance of each of these interrelated facets of communication. It is immediately apparent that the major impact on the audience, especially in that first minute, is visual, followed by your vocal delivery, then last, *and also least,* your verbal messages.

The next sections consider each of these in turn so that you can maximise your effectiveness across the three aspects of the 3Vs model and combine them to best effect.

Visual

In the classroom-based presentations that students are mostly involved in, you are close to your audience and in a relatively informal space. Even if you are presenting in a lecture theatre, you will still be able to move away from a fixed delivery point such as a lectern. Your body language, i.e. movement, facial expressions, gestures, is continuously visible and makes a significant impact on your audience, even though this may be mostly at an *unconscious* level.

- *Body language*

Pause for Thought

Think back again to presentations that you have experienced before. Can you remember one presenter that you found engaging and another that did not capture your attention so much? Which aspects of their body language do you think affected your perceptions in these positive and negative ways? Add your thoughts to the suggested examples below:

Factors that engaged my attention   **Factors that distracted my attention**

E.g. Regular eye contact   E.g. Hands in pockets

This is all quite subjective, of course – what one person finds attractive in a presenter may switch off another member of the audience. However, there are some helpful general principles:

- *Body movement*

If you have some space in which to move around, then it can keep the audience 'on their own toes' if you occupy that space quite actively – moving from one side to the other at the front of the room, for example. Overall, movement is more likely to keep them watching you than if you stand still in one spot. It is not to say that is wrong, but do not be afraid to explore your own, natural style of movement as a presenter.

- *Stance*

Most people would agree that how you stand carries a strong visual impression – your audience will subconsciously recognise 'what kind of person you are' from this before you even open your mouth. There is also general agreement that this needs to be **strong but not intimidating, open but not vulnerable**. Ideally, face your audience with your feet around shoulder-width apart and arms uncrossed. It is helpful if you can lean in slightly towards your audience. This indicates **confidence and a willingness to engage**.

- *Gestures*

Some of us unconsciously move our hands around a lot when presenting, whilst others instinctively keep fairly still in the upper body. What is important here is that you allow yourself to **act naturally**. If you are comfortable in a stable stance, then the audience will see that as your congruent communication style. Conversely, if animated hand movements are a natural part of your self-expression, these can add interest to your delivery. However, you should take care to avoid nervous distractions with 'props' such as pens, glasses or coins in your pocket, for example.

- *Eye contact*

In Western cultures, making eye contact with others is perceived as an indication of assurance and credibility. This is really about showing your audience that you want to engage with them. As often as you can remember, practice **scanning the room** with your eyes as you talk, momentarily meeting as many people's gaze as possible.

This idea is easy in theory but can be quite daunting in practice. Novice presenters can tend to rely on their slides, and turn their backs to look at the screen. You can avoid this unconscious attachment to your material with a simple technique illustrated in Box 12.4.

Box 12.4   Maintaining eye contact even while referring to slides

Touch/Turn/Tell

'**Touch**' the text or graphic on the screen with a pointer in your hand closest to the screen so this *minimises your need to swivel away from the audience*. Ideally, a laser pointer on a slide remote device avoids obscuring anyone's vision and means you can control the presentation from anywhere in the room.

Turn back to the audience once you have briefly pointed out the relevant message on the screen. You can then *keep eye contact* with the group and ...

Tell them what is important for them to learn about the highlighted idea. You can elaborate on this point from your rehearsed knowledge, *without needing to turn back to the slide*.

Note that **you do not need to read out every point on the screen**. Let the audience quickly absorb the slide overall, and then focus their attention onto the one or two key points that you most want them to register.

- *Dress code*

What to wear may be a tricky question for you in the relatively informal context of classroom presentations. You might be tempted to dress as you normally do on any other university day. However, as you can see from all the above sections, you will be trying in so many other ways to make some kind of favourable first impression. So, some effort to create a smart appearance is likely to be appreciated even by an audience of your peers.

- *Watch yourself*

For ongoing refinement of your body language in front of groups, video-record your rehearsals and actual presentation. When you replay those, observe which aspect(s) of your body language you believe could be improved. Next time, you can then concentrate on consciously adapting just one particular aspect. 'Micro gains' of this kind will fit more easily with your natural style so that nothing feels or looks too awkward all at once.

Vocal

Whilst your visual appearance makes the primary impression on your audience, your voice is critical to keeping their attention throughout the presentation. Note that this is **not what you say, but how you speak.** There are three key factors to making the most of your voice – **Pace, Emphasis, Projection (PEP):**

- *Pace*

The speed of your delivery determines audience understanding. This is compromised by too much information being presented too quickly or presenters simply running their words together indistinctly. Those problems often arise as a result of nervousness, perhaps in an unconscious drive to finish as soon as possible. See the Pause for Thought box below for an important suggestion about how to moderate the speed of your delivery.

Pause for Thought

Every time you **pause** during a presentation, even for a second, you accomplish two vital requirements of successful communication:

- You **give your audience time** to register what you have just said so they can keep up with your succession of ideas.
- You give yourself time **to breathe**.

To be silent, even for a moment, can feel like the hardest thing to do when faced with an expectant audience. But do not underestimate the immense value of this simple mechanism. Short pauses create spaces between your ideas so that people can absorb each of these as **a digestible portion** of the whole presentation.

Overall, a capability to deliver your presentation as a series of discrete chunks rather than a stream of words may be the most valuable vocal skill of all. The next exercise gives you an opportunity to practise developing that.

ACTIVITY 12.4

Pausing for effect

Here is an extract of text from an essay:

> *Massive streams of data are generated from smartphones, computers and other mobile devices. Online advertisers actively collect and harness the benefits of such valuable data assets. Big Data technologies enable companies to translate those countless data into insightful patterns about consumers. Couldry and Turow (2014) observe that these Big Data technologies will drive the advertising industry to a profound form of personalised product promotions.*

Now look at the same text as a presentation script. This has been separated into sections so that the end of each line represents a brief pause in delivery.

> *Massive streams of data are generated from smartphones,*
> *computers,*
> *and other mobile devices.*
> *Online advertisers actively collect,*
> *and harness,*
> *the benefits of such valuable data assets.*
> *Big Data technologies enable companies to translate those countless data*
> *into insightful patterns about consumers.*
> *Couldry and Turow (2014)*
> *observe that these Big Data technologies will drive the advertising industry*
> *to a profound form of personalised promotion.*

You could try reading that out loud to hear how the pausing creates a stronger delivery to a group of listeners. Additionally, you can listen to two versions of the text – with and without the indicated pauses – on the online companion to this book.

You may have heard that the pauses produced a more compelling version of the script. However, there is a further way that you can strengthen the impact of pausing:

- *Emphasis*

Certain words are more important than others. The purpose of emphasis is to help your listeners recognise these key words.

Try the following exercise to practise effective use of word emphasis:

ACTIVITY 12.5

Stressing for effect

This exercise looks at the same extract from Activity 12.4, but with certain words now highlighted in bold. These are stressed more emphatically. Again, you could try reading this out aloud or listen to it on the companion website:

> *Massive streams of **data** are generated from **smartphones**,*
> ***computers**,*
> *and other **mobile devices**.*
> ***Online advertisers** actively **collect**,*
> *and **harness**,*
> *the benefits of such **valuable** data assets.*
> ***Big Data technologies** enable companies to **translate** those countless data*
> *into **insightful patterns** about **consumers**.*
> ***Couldry and Turow** (2014)*
> *observe that these Big Data technologies will **drive** the **advertising industry***
> *to a **profound** form of **personalised promotion**.*

You can see from this exercise that the stressed words are almost always nouns, e.g. *smartphones* and verbs, e.g. *drive*. These convey the important new information in each sentence. Occasionally, certain adjectives are stressed to indicate the extra strength of a certain noun, e.g. *valuable, profound.* Minor words like *the, and, to, with* ... are not stressed.

You can practise the skills of pausing and stressing in Activity 12.6:

ACTIVITY 12.6

Speaking slowly, clearly and emphatically
  a) Break the following paragraph down into separate lines so that you recognise each point at which to pause.
  b) Emphasise the important words as illustrated in Activity 12.5.
  c) Read this aloud to hear how well your version works and suits your natural and preferred way of speaking.

If possible, record yourself and then compare your delivery with the online version.

Policy makers, on the other hand, are passing legislation to regulate information collection practices. These often mandate an overt style of data collection with a clear consent from the public to opt into that. Striking the balance between serving relevant, personalised adverts and the consumer perception of vulnerability seems to be a major challenge for online advertisers.

See the Activity Answers for a suggested version of pausing and stressing for this text.

● *Projection*

This is about ensuring that your voice carries clearly to all parts of the room. You can do this is by opening your body posture so that your head is naturally lifted to face the back wall of the room rather than the front row of the audience. From the beginning of the presentation, you can then consciously project your voice toward a level on that wall above the heads of the people sitting right at the back.

Once you have established this way of speaking to the back of the room, your voice will tend to unconsciously stay at that level. But if you want to make really sure of that in a larger venue such as a lecture theatre, why not ask someone in that back row straightaway to confirm whether they can hear you.

It is possible that the room acoustics might need you to use a microphone. That may feel artificial at first, but you will then achieve the right volume for everyone to distinctly hear everything you say without needing to shout or strain your voice.

Verbal

There are a number of ways you can tailor your verbal messages to hook your listeners' attention in the critical opening stage of your presentation:

● *Establish common ground*

A major aim of your opening remarks is to gain rapport with your audience. As we have noted earlier, they quickly decide whether they like you and can trust your ideas. This means you need to frame your introduction in terms that speak to them directly and empathically.

This can include using the second person in your opening remarks, as illustrated by the examples in Box 12.5.

Box 12.5   Relating empathically by using the *second person*

Examples:

You *all know what a dominant position Amazon holds in the online marketplace, but* **you** *may be less aware of the ethical controversies that have confronted the company in recent times.*

This presentation will expose some of the more damaging media revelations about the treatment of workers so that **you** *better understand the current challenges these have raised for Amazon's public and employee relations.*

- **Hook the audience's attention**

Create clear and concise messages that make people sit up and pay attention. Here are some options you could choose from for your opening statements.

Box 12.6   Opening gambits

1   Pose a question

Black Friday is one of Amazon's busiest shopping days. Yet in 2017, the company's Italian workers went on strike that day. Why do you think that was …?

(Pause for audience consideration. This is a rhetorical question – used only for thought-provoking effect, not direct response.)

… Well, Amazon's choice of products and fast deliveries had been damaging local business and disrupting the flow of local economies. This is one example of how Amazon's global impact has become an ethical issue. Over the next fifteen minutes, we'll explore whether this US company's meteoric rise signals a new era of individual consumer choice or big business control.

2   Facts and figures

We all know Amazon is big, but perhaps you didn't realise just how big … last year, Amazon accounted for 43 per cent of US online retail sales.

This presentation will first explain the major factors in the company's spectacular financial performance of the last ten years. But then we will consider the imminent business impact of ethical challenges now posed by Amazon's controversial employee relations practices in its warehousing facilities across the world.

3   A personal reflection

I've been an enthusiastic Amazon customer for several years now, undoubtedly like many of you in the audience here today. I can rather guiltily admit that around half the entries on my bank statement each month are Amazon orders.

But if you looked at my last statement, you would see no such entries. Since I began doing the research for this presentation, I've been shocked to discover how the company treats its employees. I'd like to explain to you today the reasons for this significant change in my consumer behaviour.

You can see that the opening delivery of a business presentation tells the audience what to expect. That key message then needs to be recapitulated at the final stage, usually in a conclusion slide. In other words:

1 *Tell them what you're going to tell them* [Introduction].
2 *Tell them about that in detail* [Body].
3 *Tell them what you've just told them* [Conclusion].

Be calm

Whilst there are a number of ideas suggested in this chapter about how to best present yourself, the most important takeaway from all of this is to be *as relaxed as possible*. When trying any of these new ideas, remember the golden rule of presentations – you still have to be yourself and sound authentic.

Here are some proven tips for staying centred in yourself even in this challenging situation:

- *Breathing*

  Most important of all, remember to breathe. This is more easily said than done when you are delivering your presentation. So, **before you start**, you can help yourself by breathing *consciously* while you are waiting to go on:

  Concentrate first on your out-breath. Many people assume they need to take a deeper in-breath first, but actually you have to create the space in your lungs for that with a longer out-breath. Breathe out through your mouth and soften down the front of your body. Allow your posture to sink a little inwards and downwards to help gently expel the breath from your lower abdomen. You can then breathe in quite fully but easily through your nose. Repeat that a few times. Notice how your mind settles in harmony with your body. This simple mechanism is entirely within your control, whenever you choose to remember it, and quite invisible to others.

  You can practise this technique with the online companion recording.

- *Make informal connections with your audience*

  You can establish some rapport even **before you begin** your formal delivery by chatting to one or more members of the audience while everyone is arriving and settling into their seats. Greeting them informally in a welcoming, friendly way is not only about their engagement but also your own confidence. Mixing informally and talking conversationally settles anxiety that can otherwise arise if you wait to start your presentation from an isolated position at the front.

- *Concentrate on your strengths*

  Remember the anchoring exercise in Activity 10.1. Practise this confidence-building technique as **part of your preparation** for potentially daunting situations. You can apply your anchor to re-establish a positive emotional state before or during the presentation itself.

Summary: performance on the day (the 3Vs)

Visual

- Dress in a way that makes you feel confident.
- Engage directly with the audience – be interested in them.
- Start with a solid stance – feet shoulder-width apart.

Vocal

- Keep a steady pace – learn to enjoy regular pauses.
- Emphasise key points strongly and clearly.
- Project your voice to the back of the room.

Verbal

- Hook audience attention with a thought-provoking opening.
- Explain only the most important point(s) on each slide.
- Speak from your knowledge – practise, practise, practise.

Activity Answers

Activity 12.1: Key principles of effective presentations

Perhaps some of the following principles characterised the enjoyable presentations that you reflected on in this Activity:

- The main theme was identified from the beginning.
- The structure showed a logical connection between each stage of the presentation.
- It was relevant to your interests as a member of that particular audience.
- The key messages were clear and succinct.
- The topic was delivered in a way that provoked audience questions, which may have developed into deeper discussions.
- The presenter spoke enthusiastically, revealing a genuine passion for the subject.
- They engaged with different members of the audience using direct eye contact, friendly facial expressions and open body language.

Activity 12.2: Defining the presentation focus

X *Corporate Social Responsibility and Apple Inc.*

This title is too broad – it could be covering environmental issues, employee relations, financial governance … the audience will be unclear what to expect. Equally importantly, the group members will not know what to concentrate on when conducting their research. If the research topic is not defined more precisely right from the start of that process, they will easily waste a lot of time exploring different facets of the complex world of Apple's global business. The resulting structure across the whole presentation may then be quite incoherent.

✓ *Ethical challenges with Apple employees' working conditions in Chinese manufacturing facilities.*

The intended coverage has been made much more precise by concentrating on one ethical issue – working conditions – and then narrowing that down to a geographical area of operations too. Whilst students may at first be apprehensive about taking such a focussed approach, this is always the best way with research projects of any kind. It is a win–win tactic from both sides of the academic relationship:

1 From the perspective of tutors' expectations, they value precision in students' work. Clear identification of specific issues gains higher grades in all types of academic assignments.
2 As student researchers, a narrow focus from the beginning means less time and energy spent on finding the right information. Your search is automatically pinpointed to certain keywords and sections of text in relevant academic sources.

Activity 12.3: Creating impact with presentation slides

Evaluating these slides is, of course, a matter of subjective judgement. Here is one way that they could be ranked in descending order with the most engaging first:

Ranking	Slide
1	C
2	B
3	A
4	D

See the explanations following this activity within the chapter for the rationale of the above ranking.

Activity 12.6: Speaking slowly, clearly and emphatically

Policy makers,
*on the **other** hand,*
*are passing **legislation***
*to **regulate** information collection practices.*
*These often mandate an **overt** style of **data collection***
*with a **clear consent** required from the **public***
*to **opt** into that.*
*Striking the **balance** between serving relevant, **personalised ads***
*and the consumer perception of **vulnerability***
*seems to be a **major challenge** for **online advertisers.***

Personal Development Planning

Make the Most of Your Learning Journey

This book has explored the academic and personal challenges that students can experience on a management degree programme. Each chapter has offered proven strategies for how to overcome those barriers to success. The question that remains is: What will that success really mean for you?

This chapter captures three common threads of personal development planning. These enable you to explicitly formulate what you really want to experience from your university learning journey and systematically work towards the achievement of those goals:

Box 13.1   Three key principles for congruent self-development

Decide what you really want	Plan backwards from your goal
• The primary question that drives your life	• Rehearsing your ideal outcomes
• Finding your mission	• Identifying the milestones
• Creating well-formed outcomes	• Allocating realistic time scales

Be yourself

Your personal SWOT analysis:
• Strengths – You are already enough
• Worries – You'll see it when you believe it
• Opportunities – Step-by-step progression
• Tendencies – Changing what does not work

Each of these steps to personal success is discussed in detail below with activities for you to apply in daily life.

What do you really want to experience?

Your primary question

Entrepreneur and life coach, Tony Robbins, proposes that each person's life is driven at an unconscious level by a primary question (Robbins Research International 2018). This question originates from your early life when you naturally had limited control over your circumstances. Formed to protect you at that time, this question often restricts your current adult life, which now offers far greater opportunities.

Robbins challenges his clients to become conscious of the primary question that has guided their lives until now, recognising how this generates negative thoughts and actions. He asserts that this self-awareness will enable you to interrupt those unhelpful patterns and replace them with more successful behaviour.

The first step is to realise what that primary question has been:

ACTIVITY 13.1

Identifying your primary question

Step 1: The question that has been driving your life so far

Settle yourself comfortably in a seated position. Take some time to become calm and centred. If you need a relaxation induction to help you do that, you could use the 'Four Points of Contact' as described below, and which you can listen to on the companion website:

1 As you breathe out, take your awareness right down to your feet, feeling the floor beneath them.

2 On the next out-breath, breathe down into your upper legs to feel the seat beneath you, and sink a little more comfortably into that.

3 As you breathe out again, take that down through your arms into your hands so that you feel the warmth of them in your lap.

4 On a further out-breath, soften your back, letting your shoulders drop a little, so that you feel your weight resting more comfortably against the seat support behind you.

As you continue to relax more and more comfortably, bring the intention into your mind to discover the primary question that has been driving your daily life experience. After two more breaths, this awareness can arise from within you so that you clearly understand the question that has been trying to help you so far in your life.

Take those two breaths calmly and easily now, and allow that realisation to form in your mind. Once you have it, open your eyes and write that down exactly as it has come to you.

My primary question has been:

This primary question may be surprising for you. Yet you may well recognise how that has somehow been limiting you from experiencing more fully what life can offer you.

Step 2: The question that could guide your life from now on

So what could be a more expansive, fulfilling question for you to live by? Go back into your relaxed state now through a few deeper breaths, and allow the realisation to come into your awareness during the next few breaths. Then write that down:

My new primary question can be:

Articulating your mission

Your new primary question could form the basis for your personal mission. Covey et al. (2003: 107) assert that your mission involves 'connecting with your own unique purpose and the profound satisfaction that comes from fulfilling it'. Creating a personal mission is first and foremost about *becoming who you really want to be.*

Using your new primary question as the starting point, you can develop that into a simple, short statement that encapsulates a compelling vision of your future. For example, let's assume that your new primary question is, 'How can I experience fulfilment today?' You could create a mission statement from that for your university learning journey as, 'To be a curious student focussed each day on learning what is most important for me.'

Most of all, remember that your mission is *your unique purpose.* Do not consider for one moment what anyone else might think about that. Your old primary question is likely to have been set by your perception of what others expected of you – how to gain their approval, how to protect yourself from their disapproval – whereas your new primary question and mission are *only about what is best for you.*

Well-formed outcomes

The achievement of objectives is highly dependent on how well-defined they are (NACADA 2007). The SMART goals theoretical framework is one common example of this idea which you are likely to already be familiar with from your studies. Another way of specifying your objectives is considered in this chapter. This refers to the concept of *well-formed outcomes* (Bandler 2010; Harris 2016). The key characteristics of how to establish these congruent, motivational goals are shown below.

Box 13.2   Well-formed outcomes

When you create your personal objectives, ensure that they meet these criteria:

1 **Positive**

   Your statements of intent need to be expressed in positive terms, i.e. *what you want to experience*, not what you want to avoid.

2 **Personal**

   These must be set and sustained *by you*. Because these outcomes are about what you want, you define them in terms that are so meaningful they *compel you* to reach them.

3 **Ecological**

   This refers to your *personal* ecology. Imagine what it will mean for you to achieve this outcome, and ensure that there are no negative consequences to that.

4 **Sensory**

   They are expressed in terms that mean you will know you have reached the outcome because you had already defined what you will *see, hear* and, most importantly, *feel* when you get there.

To help you better understand what a well-formed outcome might look like, here is an example from the university context of working collaboratively with other students:

I will listen carefully to others' views in group meetings so that I can relate my own views to theirs, and agree on shared objectives that motivate us to work together supportively.

You can set these personal objectives for all areas of your life, not just your studies:

ACTIVITY 13.2

Your holistic set of immediate, personal objectives

Write one well-formed outcome that you want to experience *within the next three months* under each of these headings:

Academic	Career
Social	Health
Family	Spiritual

Re-read your objectives carefully to check that each one meets *all four criteria* of well-formed outcomes in Box 13.2.

Keep this statement of your well-formed outcomes prominently visible so that you see them regularly, reminding you of the activities that you want to engage in each day to fulfil yourself as a *proactive* person.

You can update these at appropriate times and use the process to establish longer-term objectives, producing a set of well-formed outcomes for each academic year and a further set for your full university journey.

Plan backwards from your goal

Once you have articulated a well-formed outcome in a certain aspect of your life, you can then map out how you will reach that. As experts from different fields of self-management have observed, the steps to achieving objectives need to be planned backwards from that outcome (Rugg et al. 2008; Bandler 2010; New England College 2018). You can follow the planning sequence identified in Box 13.3.

Box 13.3   Developing an action plan to achieve your goal

1 Start from the experience that you want

First, create your sensory experience: Imagine the day that you achieve this goal. Take yourself deeply into that by *seeing, hearing and feeling* what you experience as you move through those 24 hours. Intensify that further by brightening the images, enriching the sounds and strengthening the feelings.

2 Identify the ultimate step

What will you need to do immediately before that day to make it happen in the ways you have just imagined? Write down your answer as soon as you realise what that last step will be.

3 Identify your penultimate step

What must you do immediately before the above step, to enable that to then happen? Write down this preceding step now.

4 Plan right back to your starting point now

Continue the process of working your way backwards until you know *what you need to do today.* This first step starts the whole process in motion that will lead you to the fulfilment of your desired outcome.

5 Create a timeframe

Estimate dates to each of the identified steps so that you can keep track of *when you must begin and end each task* (see Box 3.1).

Your plans for different goals will naturally overlap one another. So make sure to observe the third feature of well-formed outcomes in Box 13.2 – Personal Ecology. Keep track of the various outcomes that you aim to experience in different aspects of your life from Activity 13.2. Ensure that no single plan will interfere with your progress towards other goals. You are aiming for a harmonious work–life balance. This is where the weekly planning tools suggested in Chapter 3 can ensure that you allow time for all the important experiences in your life (see Box 3.3).

Recognise all that you are

The next section introduces a personal evaluation framework. This is based on the organisational audit tool known as 'SWOT' analysis: *Strengths; Weaknesses; Opportunities; Threats.* That concept has been around for over 50 years now, being widely applied in most contexts of business life as a practical way for organisations to holistically assess all the factors affecting business decisions. You are likely to be asked to conduct SWOT analyses on companies for various modules on your business and management degree.

In view of the proven reliability of the SWOT model, it seems reasonable to consider this type of framework for a more personal evaluation of how to make the best decisions along your own learning journey as a university student. It is certainly helpful to remind yourself of all your positive attributes (**Strengths**) and great prospects for academic and personal development as a university student (**Opportunities**).

As regards *Threats* and *Weaknesses,* it may make sense in the competitive context of an organisational SWOT analysis to consider these factors that have to be pre-empted or mitigated for continuing business success. However, in this individual SWOT analysis, those two factors are replaced by others that do not propose personal deficiencies but instead recognise **aspects of your mindset that you can change in constructive ways**. These are partly shaped by *how you perceive* the academic and social pressures facing you at university (**Worries**), and *your habitual ways of reacting* to those stressors (**Tendencies**).

All four elements of the **personal SWOT analysis** are explained in more detail below:

Strengths

A central theme of this book has been *self-efficacy* – believing in your capability to succeed by focussing primarily on your positive attributes. So the SWOT analysis naturally begins with cataloguing your strengths.

Think about what you are most proud of in yourself that has been instrumental in reaching university. **Affirm the capabilities** that you know will continue to support your progress as a successful student here. Think of the positive ways that your family and friends would describe you. This is not a time for false modesty. Take plenty of time to gather together as many strengths as possible under this especially important banner of the SWOT analysis. You can collate those in the framework in Activity 13.3 below.

Worries

Collins Dictionary (2018) defines pressure as:

'A force that compels. A series of urgent claims or demands.'

Academically, university students have a continuous series of urgent claims on their time – chiefly in the form of group projects, individual coursework and exams. It is these external assessments that can be especially stressful aspects of the learning journey with their demands for extensive reading and writing in the deepening shadow of looming deadlines. They will naturally provoke anxiety in any student, and the challenge is to **keep those worries in perspective**. This part of your analysis is therefore about *rationally* identifying the pressures of academic requirements and other personal challenges in the coming semester.

Opportunities

You have already created a great opportunity in your life by reaching university in the first place. Now, a whole range of new experiences awaits you, to be determined by the choices you make in the time ahead.

Referring back to Activity 13.2, take some time to recognise the opportunities in the near future that will **move you towards the achievement of your well-formed outcomes**. These opportunities could include your module classes, skills workshops, internships, union societies, social events: you have a wealth of possibilities available to you at university.

Tendencies

The personal SWOT analysis framework proposes that rather than looking for your 'weaknesses' (a process likely, in itself, to weaken self-efficacy), you can choose to recognise that everyone has a set of *habitual behaviours* that limit or even sabotage their potential achievements.

> '*Habit – A tendency or disposition to act in a particular way. A learned behavioural response that has become associated with a particular situation.*'
>
> (Collins 2018)

The first step in **unlearning these responses** is to honestly acknowledge what your counter-productive tendencies are.

Compile the four elements of your individualised SWOT analysis now in Activity 13.3.

ACTIVITY 13.3

Your personal SWOT analysis

A simple SWOT matrix template is presented below. You can complete this here, on the companion website or create your own version as you prefer. You could even create this in a larger scale on a poster for your wall. Gather your ideas for each quadrant by using the clustering process first shown in Chapter 2 (Box 2.1) or simply as a list in each box if you prefer:

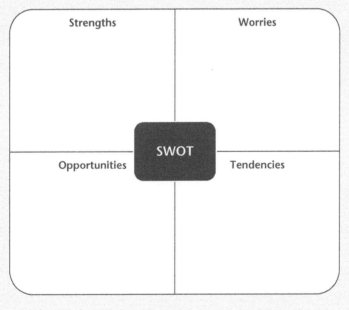

Apply your personal SWOT analysis to fulfilling your purpose

You can now 'join the dots' of this final chapter – to recognise how your personal audit from the *SWOT analysis* can enable you to achieve each of the *well-formed outcomes* that make up the holistic *mission* of your university learning journey:

You are already enough (strengths)

If you have clustered your strengths fully, honestly and fairly in the first part of the SWOT analysis, you will see that you have an amazing set of personal resources available at any moment. You already have what you need to become a successful student. You can consistently reinforce your self-efficacy by deliberately recalling these capabilities every day.

Create a 'mantra' that encapsulates one or more of these strengths. Make it present, personal and positive, e.g.

My kindness helps me find the best in others.

I am calm and comfortable in this situation.

I always find the understanding that I need.

Repeat your chosen mantra regularly. You can synchronise this with your steps when walking, running or simply with your breathing when sitting. Adopt new mantras for different times and situations – create one now in Activity 13.4.

ACTIVITY 13.4

Accentuate your strengths with positive affirmations

Acknowledge a situation that feels difficult for you at the moment. That could be anything – confusing assignment research, personality clash, dental treatment … Look back at your clustered strengths from the SWOT analysis. Which leap out at you as most useful for dealing with this current challenge?

Create a simple mantra from each strength that you recognise in yourself, and capture that in a single sentence:

My affirmation for this situation is:

Sit quietly, and repeat this to yourself as you concentrate on breathing calmly and smoothly. Let the feeling of that strength build in you with each successive breath.

Practise this whenever you remember – it is so easy to do and invisible to others, even in social situations. Put that into practice before you go into the challenging situation, and repeat it to yourself while you are there.

Step-by-step progression (opportunities)

Each one of the action planning steps illustrated in Box 13.3 is an opportunity. Make sure to schedule all of these into your semester and weekly planning tools referred to in Chapter 3. This requires you to be proactive in recognising those opportunities in the first place and to take full advantage of them as they come along.

Try the backwards planning process in Activity 13.5 below for one of your current well-formed outcomes.

ACTIVITY 13.5

Planning to capitalise on every opportunity

1 Take yourself forward to the completion day of a well-formed outcome. Write that outcome into the heading box below, along with the deadline. Take some time to imagine what you will see, hear and feel when you have achieved that.

2 Identify the last action that you need to take to reach that goal, and make a brief note of that in the first row.

3 Identify the action needed before that, writing a note of that in next row below.

4 Continue the process until you have *brought yourself back to now* and the first opportunity you can take to start moving toward the successful achievement of that goal.

5 Allocate essential start dates for each action.

A sample planning chart is illustrated below. You can download this from the companion website or create your own version to map out the series of steps as fully as you like.

My well-formed outcome is:	Completion date:
Action needed	Start date

You'll see it when you believe it (worries)

What if much of the apparent pressure that you identified in this section of your SWOT analysis is actually self-imposed?

> *'The psychological condition of fear is divorced from any concrete and true immediate danger. This ... is always of something that might happen, not of something that is happening now. You can always cope with the present moment, but you cannot cope with something that is only a mind projection.'*
>
> (Tolle 2001: 43)

Chapter 3 explored how procrastination often occurs as a consequence of trying to avoid the things we are afraid of by keeping them 'off in the future'. Thoughts of failure or not doing well enough stop us from starting on a project here and now. Yet, actually, that is the only place and time that we can act.

Take one of the major, external factors you identified in the *Worries* section of the SWOT analysis. Apply the cognitive-behavioural reframing process outlined below in Activity 13.6 to transform the anxiety you had been feeling about that into a more constructive perspective.

ACTIVITY 13.6

Changing the way that you perceive pressures

You can use the spaces below to record your responses, or you could start using the reframing process in your journal.

1 **Identify the trigger**
   Write a short statement to describe the external source of stress:

2 **Recognise your emotional reaction**
   Capture your main emotions about that situation in just a few words. What are the first feelings that you have when you start to re-experience that?

3 **Express your thoughts**
   Write out fully and uncensored what your mind tells you about this situation. Do not analyse, simply vent all the worries that this stressful situation evokes in you. Use prompts such as, 'This means that ...', ' ... because ...', '... and so I ...' to delve deeper into the 'story' your mind creates around this situation.

4 Verify the thoughts

Once you have exhausted your chain of thoughts, go back through each separate statement, rationally examining whether this is actually true or not. You verify the statements as either False (F), True (T) or Don't know (DK). Strive to be as objective as you can be. Question whether this reflects the factual reality that someone else would observe in this situation (T) or whether this is created from your perceptions (F).

Go back through each of your thoughts in Step 3 above now, using the F / T / DK verification system.

5 Reframe your self-criticism

Identify up to three of the false statements that seem to have a strong emotional charge for you. Reframe these below as positive affirmations, i.e. transform the opposite of each statement into a constructive call to action. For example, if one of your false concepts is, *'I can't complete this project in time'*, you can reframe this as, *'I progress each day to meet the deadline successfully'*.

Remember the abiding principle of affirmations – personal, present, positive – and write your reframed statements below:

6 Create a new reality

Now imagine yourself in each of the positive scenarios represented by those affirmations. **See, hear and feel** the experience of overcoming what had only been a mental projection.

Change what does not work (tendencies)

We can all recognise that some habits are not helpful. We enact these negative tendencies quite unconsciously, i.e. without thinking much about their effect on our lives. We will have learned this behaviour when we were younger, probably as a reaction to circumstances beyond our control. We then (irrationally) keep repeating this out of habit, even though it is no longer useful. However, this also means that **we can choose to replace or at least modify unhelpful tendencies** with a more effective behaviour at this different stage of life.

You may not need to eradicate that tendency altogether. Taking the common example of displacement activities (distractions from productive endeavours) such as social media, you can make a commitment to limit the frequency and duration of these. You need a sufficient motivation, of course, to convince yourself of the need to concentrate on an important study project instead, for example. But you can then promise yourself the reward of a short period of downtime on social media.

Sometimes, though, you might realise the need to break a particularly unhelpful tendency more radically. Only you can choose to change your habits. This might seem hard at first, but if you motivate yourself to interrupt the pattern for a set period, ideally every day for a month, you might be surprised to find that it no longer has a hold on you.

Take one habitual tendency that you know impedes your progress. Work out how you would like to change or stop that in Activity 13.7 below.

ACTIVITY 13.7

Replace an unproductive tendency with useful behaviour

The habit I would like to change is:

Because it is undermining me by ...

Eliminating or reducing this habit will help me to ...

I can enact this change by doing the following ...

I will maintain this change each day for _____ days.

Chapter summary

- Choose **a primary question** that guides you to make the most of your university learning journey.
- Develop that into **a long-term mission** statement with a series of short-term milestones as **well-formed outcomes** that are positive, personal, ecological and sensory-based.
- **Plan backwards** from these objectives.
- Conduct your **individual SWOT analysis** based on these principles:
  - You are already enough.
  - You create your own opportunities by proactive planning.
  - You can reframe worries into positive affirmations.
  - You can change what does not work.

References

Association of American Colleges and Universities (2016) *Critical thinking VALUE rubric.* https://www.aacu.org/value/rubrics/critical-thinking Accessed 22 November 2017.

Bandler, R. (2010) *Guide to trance-formation: Make your life great.* London: HarperCollins.

Bandura, A. (1997) *Self-efficacy: The exercise of control.* New York: Freeman.

Bassot, B. (2016) *The reflective journal* (2nd edition). London: Red Globe Press.

Birkbeck, University of London (2019) *Full-time and part-time study explained.* http://www.bbk.ac.uk/prospective/full-time-and-part-time-study-explained Accessed 21 September 2019.

Bolton, G. and Delderfield, R. (2018) *Reflective practice: Writing and professional development* (5th edition). London: Sage.

CPD Certification Service (2019) *CPD explained.* https://cpduk.co.uk/explained Accessed 7 July 2019.

Cameron, J. (1995) *The artists way.* London: Pan Macmillan.

Carroll, J. (2005) Strategies for becoming more explicit. In Carroll, J. and Ryan, J. (editors) *Teaching international students: Improving learning for all.* Abingdon: Routledge. 26–34.

Collins (2018) *English dictionary* (13th edition). Glasgow: HarperCollins.

Cotton Incorporated (2019) *Cotton lifestyle monitor.* https://www.cottoninc.com/about-cotton/cotton-websites/lifestyle-monitor/ Accessed 22 September 2019.

Cottrell, S. (2017) *Critical thinking skills: Developing effective analysis and argument* (3rd edition). London: Red Globe Press.

Covey, S.R., Merrill, A.R. and Merrill, S.R. (2003) *First things first.* New York: Fireside.

De Vita, G. (2002) Does assessed multicultural group work really pull UK students' average down? *Assessment & Evaluation in Higher Education* 27(2) 153–161.

De Vita, G. (2005) Fostering intercultural learning through multicultural group work. In Carroll, J. and Ryan, J. (editors) *Teaching international students: Improving learning for all.* Abingdon: Routledge. 75–83.

Dweck, C. (2006) *Mindset: The new psychology of success.* New York: Random House.

Elbow, P. (1998) *Writing with power: Techniques for mastering the writing process* (2nd edition). New York: Oxford University Press.

Elliott, C. and Robinson, S. (2012) MBA imaginaries: Projections of internationalization. *Management Learning* 43(2) 157–181.

Gibbs, G. (1988) *Learning by doing: A guide to teaching and learning methods.* Oxford: Further Education Unit, Oxford Polytechnic.

Grinder, J. and Bandler, R. (1981) *Trance-formations.* Moab: Real People Press.

Harris J. (2016) *Ultimate well formed outcomes technique.* http://julia-harris.com/wp-content/uploads/2016/04/Ultimate-Well-Formed-Outcomes-Cheatsheetonline.pdf Accessed 1 March 2019.

Hicks, E. and Hicks, J. (2004) *Ask and it is given: Learning to manifest your desires.* London: Hay House.

High Speed Training (2016) *One week time management plan: Three famous techniques.* https://www.highspeedtraining.co.uk/hub/time-management-plan/ Accessed 15 December 2018.

Hofstede, G. (2001) *Culture's consequences: Comparing values, behaviors, institutions and organizations across nations* (2nd edition). Thousand Oaks, CA: Sage.

Kimmel, K. and Volet, S. (2012) University students' perceptions of and attitudes towards culturally diverse group work: Does context matter? *Journal of Studies in International Education* 16(2) 157–181.

McLean, P. and Ransom, L. (2005) Building intercultural competencies: Implications for academic skills development. In Carroll, J. and Ryan, J. (editors). *Teaching international students: Improving learning for all.* Abingdon: Routledge. 45–62.

Learnhigher (2019) *Time management.* http://www.learnhigher.ac.uk/learning-at-university/time-management/ Accessed 22 September 2019.

Leask, B. (2010) 'Beside me is an empty chair': The student experience of internationalisation. In Jones, E. (editor) *Internationalisation and the student voice: Higher education perspectives.* Abingdon: Routledge. 3–17.

Mindtools (2018) *Effective scheduling: Planning to make the best use of your time.* https://www.mindtools.com/pages/article/newHTE_07.htm Accessed 15 December 2018.

Mitchell, B.K. (2002) *Loving what is: Four questions that can change your life.* London: Rider.

Moon, J. (2006) *Learning journals: A handbook for reflective practice and professional development* (2nd edition). London: Routledge.

NACADA (2007) *Goal setting for study abroad learning outcomes.* https://www.nacada.ksu.edu/Resources/Academic-Advising-Today/View-Articles/Goal-Setting-for-Study-Abroad-Learning-Outcomes.aspx Accessed 18 March 2019.

Neville, C. (2006) *Effective learning series booklet: Group work.* Bradford: Bradford University School of Management.

Neville, C. (2007) *Effective learning series booklet: Time management.* Bradford: Bradford University School of Management.

Neville, C. (2016) *The complete guide to referencing and avoiding plagiarism* (3rd edition). London: Open University Press.

New England College (2018). *Backwards planning: A process for goal setting.* https://www.newenglandcollegeonline.com/resources/educational/backwards-planning-a-process-for-goal-setting/ Accessed 5 March 2019.

Oxford Brookes University (2017) *Study skills: Gibbs reflective cycle* https://www.brookes.ac.uk/students/upgrade/study-skills/reflective-writing-gibbs/ Accessed 10 November 2017.

Pearson (2015) *The status of critical thinking in the workplace.* https://www.pearsoned.com/blog-archive/higher-education/ Accessed 5 January 2019.

Reid, S. (2009) *The learning process in intercultural collaboration evidence from the eChina–UK programme.* Warwick: The Centre for Applied Linguistics. University of Warwick.

Rico, G. (2000) *Writing the natural way* (2nd edition). Los Angeles: Tarcher.

Robbins Research International (2018) *Are you living your primary question?* https://www.tonyrobbins.com/living-primary-question/ Accessed 28 February 2019.

Robbins Research International (2019) *Secrets for effective goal-setting.* https://www.tonyrobbins.com/news/secrets-for-effective-goal-setting/ Accessed 25 February 2019.

Rook, S. (2019) *The graduate career guidebook* (2nd edition). London: Macmillan.

Rugg, G., Gerrard, S. and Hooper, S. (2008) *The stress-free guide to studying at university.* London: Sage.

Ryan, J. (2010) Teaching international students. *HEA Academy Exchange* 9 14–16.

Sedgley, M.T. (2013) *Learning journeys with international Masters students in UK higher education.* PhD thesis, University of Bradford.

Storrs, D. (2012) 'Keeping it real' with an emotional curriculum. *Teaching in Higher Education* 17(1) 1–12.

Strauss, P. and Mooney, S. (2011) Painting the bigger picture: Academic literacy in postgraduate vocational education. *Journal of Vocational Education and Training* 63(4) 539–550.

Targetjobs (2018) *Teamwork: It's high on the graduate recruiters' wishlist.* https://target-jobs.co.uk/careers-advice/skills-and-competencies/300764-teamwork-its-high-on-the-graduate-recruiters-wishlist Accessed 5 February 2019.

Tolle, E. (2001) *The power of now.* London: Hodder and Stoughton.

UKCES: UK Commission for Employment and Skills (2016) *Employer skills survey 2015: Skills in the labour market.* https://www.gov.uk/government/uploads/system/uploads/attachment_data/file/525449/UKC004_Summary_Report__May_.pdf Accessed 4 December 2016.

UNC: University of North Carolina at Chapel Hill (2019) *Studying 101: Study smarter not harder.* https://learningcenter.unc.edu/tips-and-tools/studying-101-study-smarter-not-harder/ Accessed 10 August 2019.

University of Bradford (2017) *MBA Programme Specification 2017/18.* https://www.bradford.ac.uk/T4/programme-specifications/MBA-Exec-DL-17-18v0.2.pdf Accessed 21 September 2019.

University of Bradford Career and Employability Services (2018) *Application forms.* https://www.brad.ac.uk/careers/applications/application-forms/ Accessed 8 February 2018.

University of Kent (2018) *Assignment survival kit: ASK.* https://www.kent.ac.uk/ai/ask/ Accessed 15 December 2018.

Wilson, P. (2004) *The blob tree – All you need to know.* www.pipwilson.com/2004/11/blob-tree_110181146915869209.html Accessed 31 March 2019.

Index

www.ingramcontent.com/pod-product-compliance
Ingram Content Group UK Ltd.
Pitfield, Milton Keynes, MK11 3LW, UK
UKHW051936280225
455697UK00004B/93